SOCIAL PSYCHOLOGY OF POLITICAL POLARIZATION

The 21st-century political landscape has been defined by deep ideological polarization and, as a result, scientific inquiry into the psychological mechanisms underlying this divide has taken on increased relevance.

The topic is by no means new to social psychology. Classic literature on intergroup conflict shows how pervasive and intractable these group conflicts can be, how readily they can emerge from even minimal group identities, and the hedonic rewards reaped from adopting an "us vs. them" perspective. Indeed, this literature paints a bleak picture for the efficacy of any interventions geared toward reducing intergroup discord. But advances in the psychology of moral judgments and behavior, in particular greater understanding of how moral concerns might inform the creation and stability of political identities, offer new ways forward in understanding partisan divides.

This volume brings together leading researchers in moral and political psychology, offering new perspectives on the moral roots of political ideology, and exciting new opportunities for the development of more effective applied interventions.

Piercarlo Valdesolo is Assistant Professor at Claremont McKenna College, California. Using methodology from social and cognitive psychology, his research focuses on how our emotional states—such as compassion, awe, and gratitude—affect our decisions and behaviors with regard to trust, cooperation, blame, and punishment.

Jesse Graham is Assistant Professor of Psychology at the University of Southern California. His research is centered on morality and ethics, ideology, values, political psychology, implicit attitudes, religion, culture, and social justice.

SOCIAL PSYCHOLOGY OF POLITICAL POLARIZATION

Edited by Piercarlo Valdesolo and Jesse Graham

NEW YORK AND LONDON

First published 2016
by Routledge
711 Third Avenue, New York, NY 10017

and by Routledge
2 Park Square, Milton Park, Abingdon, Oxon OX14 4RN

Routledge is an imprint of the Taylor & Francis Group, an informa business

© 2016 Taylor & Francis

The right of the editors to be identified as the authors of the editorial material, and of the authors for their individual chapters, has been asserted in accordance with sections 77 and 78 of the Copyright, Designs and Patents Act 1988.

All rights reserved. No part of this book may be reprinted or reproduced or utilized in any form or by any electronic, mechanical, or other means, now known or hereafter invented, including photocopying and recording, or in any information storage or retrieval system, without permission in writing from the publishers.

Trademark notice: Product or corporate names may be trademarks or registered trademarks, and are used only for identification and explanation without intent to infringe.

Library of Congress Cataloging in Publication Data
Psychology of political polarization / edited by Piercarlo Valdesolo and Jesse Graham.
pages cm
Includes bibliographical references and index.
ISBN 978-1-138-81063-1 (hb : alk. paper) -- ISBN 978-1-138-81064-8 (pb : alk. paper) -- ISBN 978-1-315-64438-7 (alk. paper) 1. Divided government--United States. 2. Political parties--United States. 3. Political culture--United States. 4. Political psychology. 5. Social psychology. 6. United States--Politics and government. I. Valdesolo, Piercarlo.
JK2261.P8 2016
324.01'9--dc23
2015029999

ISBN: 978-1-138-81063-1 (hbk)
ISBN: 978-1-138-81064-8 (pbk)
ISBN: 978-1-315-64438-7 (ebk)

Typeset in Bembo
by Saxon Graphics Ltd, Derby

Printed and bound in the United States of America by
Edwards Brothers Malloy on sustainably sourced paper

CONTENTS

List of Illustrations	*vii*
Contributors	*ix*

Introduction: Ideological Divides, in Society and in
Social Psychology   1
Piercarlo Valdesolo and Jesse Graham

SECTION I
Ideological Divides in Society   5

1   Liberals and Conservatives are (Geographically) Dividing   7
    Matt Motyl

2   The Left–Right Landscape Over Time: The View from a
    Western European Multi-Party Democracy   38
    Hulda Thórisdóttir

SECTION II
Psychological Mechanisms of Ideological Divides   59

3   Ideological Differences in the Expanse of Empathy   61
    Adam Waytz, Ravi Iyer, Liane Young, and Jesse Graham

vi Contents

4   Are Conservatives from Mars and Liberals from Venus?   78
Maybe Not So Much
Linda J. Skitka and Anthony N. Washburn

5   Moral Coherence and Political Conflict   102
Peter H. Ditto and Brittany S. Liu

6   Restraining Self-Interest or Enabling Altruism:
Morality and Politics   123
Nate C. Carnes and Ronnie Janoff-Bulman

7   From Silos to Synergies: The Effects of Construal Level
on Political Polarization   143
Jaime L. Napier and Jamie B. Luguri

SECTION III
Ideological Divides in Social Psychology   **163**

8   The Politics of Social Psychological Science: Distortions in
the Social Psychology of Intergroup Relations   165
*Lee Jussim, Jarret T. Crawford, Sean T. Stevens, and
Stephanie M. Anglin*

9   Political Diversity in Social Psychology: Problems and
Solutions   197
Yoel Inbar and Joris Lammers

Index   *211*

ILLUSTRATIONS

Figures

1.1	Ideological Enclavement Theory conceptual model.	8
2.1	The distribution of left–right self-placement in Iceland from 1987–2013.	43
2.2	Left–right self-placement from 1987–2013 for voters for the main political parties. The numbers in parentheses indicate the range of percentage of votes each party has received in general elections from 1987–2013.	45
2.3	Perceptions of the People's Alliance/Left–Greens on the left–right scale by voters of each of the other parties. The solid black line graphs self-placement of People's Alliance/Left–Green voters. The graph shows that voters of the People's Alliance/Left–Greens place themselves closer to the middle than voters of any other party perceive them.	48
2.4	Perceptions of the Social Democratic Alliance on the left–right scale by voters of each of the other parties. The solid black line graphs self-placement of SDA voters.	48
2.5	Perceptions of the Progressive Party on the left–right scale by voters of each of the other parties. The solid black line graphs self-placement of Progressive Party voters.	49
2.6	Perceptions of the Independence Party on the left–right scale by voters of each of the other parties. The solid black line graphs self-placement of Independence Party voters.	49

viii illustrations

2.7a–f Attitudes towards six political issues across time. The grey bars show averages, the blac line Pearson's correlation with left–right self-placement.

2.7a Environmental issues should be prioritized over economic growth. 52

2.7b Taxes should be reduced. 52

2.7c Decrease progress in capital area to increase prosperity in rural areas. 53

2.7d Attempts to ensure gender equality have gone too far. 53

2.7e EU application is desirable. 54

2.7f Ease restrictions on agricultural imports. 54

4.1 A motivated correction model of ideological reasoning. 82

4.2 Attributional patterns as a function of political orientation. 88

6.1 Model of moral motives. 126

7.1 Feelings of warmth toward "non-normative groups" (gay men, lesbians, Muslims, and atheists) as a function of political ideology and baseline construal level (Luguri, Napier, & Dovidio, 2012; Study 1). 147

7.2 Feelings of warmth toward "non-normative groups" (gay men, lesbians, Muslims, and atheists) as a function of political ideology and construal condition (Luguri, Napier, & Dovidio, 2012; Study 2). 148

7.3 Endorsement of individualizing and binding values as a function of construal condition and political orientation (conservative or liberal, graphed one standard deviation above and below and mean, respectively; Napier & Luguri, 2013). 152

7.4 Mean endorsement of political policies (higher numbers indicate more endorsement of the liberal position) as a function of construal condition (abstract vs. concrete), identity condition (national vs. partisan), and political orientation (conservative or liberal, graphed one standard deviation above and below and mean, respectively; Luguri & Napier, 2013). 154

Tables

2.1 Left–right self-placement from 1987–2013, 0 = left and 10 = right. 41

2.2 Bivariate correlation (Pearson's r) between left–right self-placement and demographic variables. 46

4.1 Study results that were consistent with the dispositional, ideological script, and motivated reasoning hypotheses. 92

8.1 Comparison of three studies of stereotypes and person perception. 183

CONTRIBUTORS

Stephanie M. Anglin, Rutgers University

Nate C. Carnes, University of Massachusetts at Amherst

Jarret T. Crawford, The College of New Jersey

Peter H. Ditto, University of California at Irvine

Jesse Graham, University of Southern California

Yoel Inbar, University of Toronto Scarborough

Ravi Iyer, University of Southern California

Ronnie Janoff-Bulman, University of Massachusetts at Amherst

Lee Jussim, Rutgers University and Stanford University

Joris Lammers, Cologne University

Brittany S. Liu, Kalamazoo College

Jamie B. Luguri, Yale University

Matt Motyl, University of Illinois at Chicago

x Contributors

Jaime L. Napier, Yale University

Linda J. Skitka, University of Illinois at Chicago

Sean T. Stevens, Rutgers University

Hulda Thórisdóttir, University of Iceland

Piercarlo Valdesolo, Claremont McKenna College

Anthony N. Washburn, University of Illinois at Chicago

Adam Waytz, Northwestern University

Liane Young, Boston College

INTRODUCTION

Ideological Divides, in Society and in Social Psychology

Piercarlo Valdesolo and Jesse Graham

This volume brings together leading researchers in moral and political psychology, offering new perspectives on the deep ideological polarization that has defined the recent political landscape. Though social psychologists have long studied processes relevant to political ideology such as social identity and intergroup conflict, the contributors to this volume all seek to understand, in one way or another, the moral roots of political ideology. This emerging theoretical approach affords exciting new opportunities for both basic empirical research as well as the development of more effective applied interventions geared toward reducing intergroup discord.

Section I: Ideological Divides in Society

The first two chapters by Motyl and Thórisdóttir point to the scope of the problem, showing both the stability of ideological divisions across time and cultures (Thórisdóttir) as well as new ways in which our political populace is dividing (Motyl). Motyl proposes the Ideological Enclavement Theory, which argues that people's preference for different communities depends on their gut-level intuitions about the match between their own political ideology and the community's ideology. Furthermore, the theory proposes that people migrate to ideologically matching areas, creating politically homogeneous enclaves defined not only by increased well-being, cooperation, and trust, but also by conflict, demonization, hostility, prejudice, and violence toward ideological outgroups. Thórisdóttir uses data from the Icelandic National Election Studies from 1987–2013 to demonstrate the enduring nature of left–right distinctions over time, and tests whether polarization has *in fact* increased in proportion to public perception. In addition to drawing an important distinction between perceived and actual

2 Piercarlo Valdesolo and Jesse Graham

polarization, this work suggests how such datasets can be used to compare the relationship between ideological divisions and different political structures across cultures.

Section II: Psychological Mechanisms of Ideological Divides

The next five chapters focus on particular psychological mechanisms underlying ideological differences. Waytz and colleagues reconceptualize the popular notion of liberals as more empathetic than conservatives (i.e. the "empathy gap") as a difference not in the degree to which individuals experience the emotional state, but in the targets of their concern. Liberals and conservatives preferentially empathize toward different subsets of their "moral circles," with conservatives inclined to prioritize smaller moral circles over larger ones (family over friends, nation over world, humans over non-humans), and liberals inclined toward the opposite. Appreciating this distinction would not only change rhetoric surrounding the perceived empathic deficiency of conservatives, but inform the ways in which political issues might be framed to better trigger liberal and conservative empathic responses.

Skitka and Washburn identify a consistent difference in attributional style across ideology, known as the *ideo-attribution effect*. While liberals tend to focus on the causal power of situational or institutional forces when explaining important societal issues (e.g. poverty, crime, gay rights, foreign aggression), conservatives tend to focus on the causal role of the individual, and these attributional styles significantly predict varying levels of support for social programs. But despite the difference in conclusions liberals and conservatives tend to draw from their causal attributions, the authors emphasize that their respective policy preferences are developed through very similar psychological processes, and that interventions might best be geared toward channeling these processes toward similar endpoints.

Ditto and Liu describe two lines of research identifying a bias in the degree to which both liberals and conservatives "factualize" their moral intuitions. Though moral judgments are better predicted by affective reactions than deliberation, people are motivated to believe that their values are grounded in principle. As a result, moral intuitions trigger the creation of coherent moral narratives which in turn distort relevant factual beliefs. This tendency helps explain the many differences in factual beliefs across ideologies, and suggests that polarization might be attenuated by targeting the distortion of what *is* by what we believe *ought to be*.

Carnes and Janoff-Bulman draw from work on self-regulation theory to offer a new model of differences in moral motivations across ideologies. They argue that differences in policy positions and preferences are rooted in distinct attentional, physiological, and learning response profiles. These individual differences predict moral concerns, which in turn predict attitudes about a variety of political issues. The authors offer a causal explanation for these motivational orientations, locating the crucial distinction in the degree to which liberals and conservatives emphasize group-based moral concerns, and address the antecedents, consequences, and possibilities for bridging the ideological gap.

Finally, Napier and Luguri show that political attitudes can change depending on whether individuals consider issues from a big-picture (abstract) approach compared to a more focused (concrete) approach. Using insights from construal level theory, their research finds that thinking abstractly vs. concretely can influence prejudice toward outgroups (e.g. homosexuals, atheists, Muslims) and the degree to which liberals and conservatives value "individualizing" moral foundations (care and fairness) compared to "binding" moral foundations (ingroup loyalty, purity, and deference to authority). These shifts in construal level have consequences for polarization: abstract thinking reduces polarization when national identities are made salient, but has the opposite effect when partisan identities are made salient.

Section III: Ideological Divides in Social Psychology

The final two chapters of the volume consider the consequences of political partisanship in social psychology itself, demonstrating the political homogeneity of the field, the causes of such homogeneity, and the potential consequences such an environment has on the validity of our science.

Jussim and colleagues argue that there is a systemic bias in social psychology favoring a liberal worldview. They point to research ranging from seminal work on expectancies to modern evidence for implicit bias as examples of how small effects become exaggerated in ways consistent with liberal positions, while other effects that challenge such worldviews (e.g. stereotype accuracy) are marginalized or ignored. They advocate for a non-partisan approach to scientific inquiry which does not prioritize evidence consistent with one political ideology over the other.

Finally, Inbar and Lammers present research demonstrating that social psychologists are overwhelmingly politically liberal. They offer several possible reasons for this pattern, including self-selection, norms among social scientists, and unintended or overt discrimination. They consider some of the consequences of homogeneity for the validity of scientific research and the public's perception of the field's credibility, and suggest several simple ways forward to make social psychology a welcoming field regardless of political ideology.

Taken together, this volume's chapters add a much-needed psychological depth to our understanding of ideological divisions both in society and in academia. They demonstrate the many levels at which we can understand the problem—socio-ecological, interpersonal, individual—and the many theoretical lenses helpful for explaining its origins and suggesting ways to bridge the divides. While all of the chapters offer insights into potential solutions to partisanship and political deadlock, it is nevertheless clear that our science is much further along in diagnosing the problem than in establishing ways to fix it. It is our hope that this volume can serve as a call to action for scholars—especially at junior levels—seeking to apply the theories and methods of social psychology to the pernicious and ever-growing social problem of ideological divides.

SECTION I
Ideological Divides in Society

1

LIBERALS AND CONSERVATIVES ARE (GEOGRAPHICALLY) DIVIDING

Matt Motyl

Conservatives may not be from Mars and liberals may not be from Venus, but they are dividing into red and blue worlds. And this has become increasingly so in recent decades. Despite the fact that most national elections are relatively close, where the winner prevails by a couple of percentage points, the United States of America is becoming increasingly the (not so) United Red and Blue States of America. This is most pronounced in smaller, more localized geographic units like neighborhoods and census tracts, where one party wins elections in a landslide and residents rarely communicate with people who hold differing political values (Bishop, 2009; Mutz, 2006). Blue communities are home to disproportionately many Democrats and red communities are home to disproportionately many Republicans, and both these communities and the residents of these communities differ in many ways beyond simple partisan identification. For example, residents of blue communities are more likely to identify as "spiritual, but not religious," while residents of red communities are much more likely to identify as religious (Abramowitz, 2012). Similarly, 50% of residents in Red America own guns, but only 19% of residents in Blue America own guns. Moreover, recent survey data suggests that lesbian, gay, bisexual, and transgender (LGBT) individuals report feeling stigmatized and they do not belong in red states where the majority of the population has supported banning same-sex marriage and forbidding non-heterosexuals from teaching in public schools (Lick, Tornello, Riskind, Schmidt, & Patterson, 2012). This sense of not belonging triggers selective migration to places where people feel that they are accepted and that they do belong (Motyl, 2014; Motyl et al., 2014). Some evidence even suggests that LGBT individuals may be fleeing red communities and heading for greener (or, more rainbow-patterned) pastures (Lewis, N. M., 2012; Smart & Klein, 2013). With LGBT individuals emigrating from red communities, there are fewer opportunities for people in red communities to befriend LGBT individuals. These are just a few instances of a broader phenomenon of ideological migration that has resulted in the growing segregation of Red America and Blue America.

In this chapter, I propose Ideological Enclavement Theory to explain how Red and Blue America emerged and what the consequences of living in these ideologically-segregated enclaves are. This theory identifies two primary antecedent causes. First, people have gut-level intuitions about the ideology of different enclaves, and when the ideology of a community matches people's personal ideology, people infer that they would fit in that community. Second, when people have the opportunity to do so, they will selectively migrate into enclaves that share their ideology. This ideological migration process operates to satisfy basic psychological needs, like the need to belong and a sense of physical security, and to pursue higher-level psychological goals, like self-transcendence. The consequences of satisfying these personal psychological needs fall into three main categories. First, at the individual level, people in fitting enclaves should experience greater well-being, less uncertainty about their understanding of the world, and better physical health. Second, at the within-community level, the enclaves with a relatively more homogeneous ideology should exhibit higher levels of cooperation, social capital, social support, and trust. Third, at the between-community level, intergroup relations between these opposed ideological camps should be characterized by conflict, demonization, hostility, prejudice, and violence (see Figure 1.1). I review each of these hypotheses in detail next.

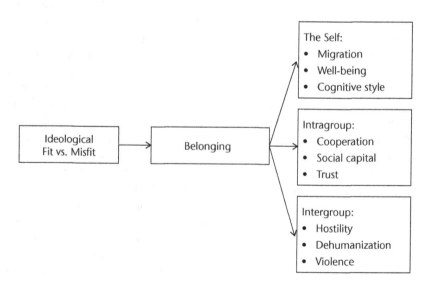

FIGURE 1.1 Ideological Enclavement Theory conceptual model.

Homophily and Enclavement

People surround themselves with people similar to them. Generally, the more similar our neighbors are to us, the better. This tendency toward homophily (love of the same) is pervasive and reliable, yet little is known about why homophily happens (for a review, see McPherson, Smith-Lovin, & Cook, 2001). Whites tend to live in communities with more whites; blacks tend to live in communities with more blacks (Dixon & Durrheim, 2003). While racial and ethnic homophily have been the most extensively studied, it appears along numerous other lines, too. For example, Sunni Muslims tend to live in communities with more Sunni Muslims; Shi'a Muslims tend to live in communities with more Shi'a Muslims (French, Purwono, & Triwahyuni, 2011). Jews create social networks with forty times as many Jews as would be expected given the percentage of the total population that they comprise (Fischer, 1977). These social groups are relatively fixed and have a long history, so they may not be optimal cases for learning much beyond the apparent fact that we like to be similar to those around us.

By looking at the behavior of more fluid groups with shorter histories, we can get a closer look at how homophily emerges. In extreme cases, groups are told that they do not belong and they relocate en masse to promote their survival. For example, the Church of Latter Day Saints spent its first 50 years of existence as a highly mobile group, being told that they did not belong and being subjected to violent attacks from residents of their temporary homes until finally settling in the largely uninhabited mountains of Utah (Bushman, 2005). Similarly, since emigrating from World War II-era Europe in favor of the newly established Israel, Jews have been entrenched in a particularly intractable conflict with Palestinians over who belongs on what territory in the region (Bar-Tal, 1998). This migration occurs in less extreme cases, too. In this chapter, I review evidence demonstrating how people with more orthodox, traditional, and conservative moral ideologies cluster into communities where most other residents are conservative while people with more modern, progressive, and liberal ideologies tend to cluster into communities where most other residents are liberal (Bishop, 2009; Huckfeldt, Johnson & Sprague, 2002; McDonald, 2011; Motyl & Iyer, 2014; Motyl & Iyer, 2015b). Importantly, this clustering does not seem to be simply a result of social influence, but rather that people may be inspired to emigrate from places where they perceive that they do not fit and migrate to places where they perceive that they fit better.

People Have an Intuitive Understanding of the Moral Values of Enclaves

> People don't need to check voting records to know the political flavor of a community. They can smell it.
>
> Bill Bishop, 2008, p. 23

At face value, people do not seem to have accurate, explicit knowledge of the ideological values endorsed in a given community. Rather, people tend to assume that others share their beliefs, and this in turn leads them to inaccurately perceive the attitudes and values of others (Hoch, 1987; Ross, Greene, & House, 1977). Some scholars even challenge people's knowledge of their own attitudes and preferences, suggesting that people may not even have the ability to describe their own positions (e.g., Nisbett & Wilson, 1977). This inability to introspect on one's own attitudes and to accurately assess others' attitudes makes the often-demonstrated attitudinal inconsistency and poor political knowledge among Americans unsurprising (Campbell, Converse, Miller, & Stokes, 1960; Carpini & Keeter, 1996). While this work on self-knowledge of one's attitudes paints a bleak picture for the prospect of selective migration into morally- and ideologically-fitting communities, some social psychological theories propose that people have intuitions, or gut-level pre-conscious emotional perceptions, that guide later thinking (Haidt, 2001, 2007). The Ideological Enclavement Theory hypothesizes that people have an intuitive understanding of the moral values of small socio-ecological areas (e.g., neighborhoods), particularly by way of various cues in the social and physical environment.

Ambient Belonging Cues

One of the fundamental human motives is to belong and to be a valued member of social groups (Baumeister & Leary, 1995). This may be due to the benefits that belonging grants to those who have it. For example, belonging to supportive coalitions increases the likelihood of mating relationships and surviving despite existential threats (Kesebir & Pyszczynski, 2011; Tooby & Cosmides, 1996). This evolutionary tale provides one explanation for why people readily form social groups, even in the most minimal of circumstances (e.g., randomly on the basis of eye color or dot-overestimation; Tajfel, Billig, Bundy, & Flament, 1971). When there are numerous groups to which people may join, they will choose the groups that seem to bolster their relational value, provide them with better social exchange partners who may help them to best achieve their goals, and reinforce their self-concept and important values (McGregor, Nail, Marigold, & Kang, 2005; Neuberg & Cottrell, 2008; Pyszczynski, Greenberg, Solomon, & Maxfield, 2006).

To determine which groups may best confer these benefits, people evaluate characteristics ranging from explicitly social cues to more subtle environmental cues. Explicit social cues communicate belonging for majority group members and a lack of belonging for minority group members. For example, women participating in math, science, and engineering class video conferences reported feeling that they did not feel like they belonged in those fields when the cameras focused on a disproportionate number of men than women. Yet, when cameras depicted a more balanced ratio of women to men, these women perceived a greater sense of belonging (Murphy, Steele, & Gross, 2007). Similarly, black students in majority white student schools reported that they felt like they did not belong at that school (see Lewis, V. A., 2012; Oyserman, Brickman, Bybee, & Celious, 2006; and, Walton & Cohen, 2011, for similar evidence in higher education). Thus, communities comprised of group members who physically resemble us may be especially alluring.

This similarity attraction effect robustly predicts who gets selected as social interaction partners (Byrne, 1971). Similarity in physical features may be such an important factor in who we choose to interact with because it may signal that the prospective interaction partners who look like us share similar genetics, may feel and think like us, and share our important values. And, surrounding ourselves with partners who share in our experiences, perceptions of reality, and possibly even a greater proportion of our genes is comforting (Buss, 1987; Byrne & Clore, 1970; Hardin & Higgins, 1996; Motyl et al., 2011; Swann, 1987). The fact that people are capable of predicting others' attitudes above chance from simply viewing a short video clip of them lends suggestive support for the idea that physical similarity conveys attitude similarity (see Ambady, Bernieri, & Richeson, 2000). In a direct test of this hypothesis, MacKinnon, Jordan, and Wilson (2011) found that participants viewed physically similar others as being attitudinally similar, too, even in the absence of attitudinal information. Furthermore, perceived attitude similarity mediated the effect of physical similarity on liking for that partner, and expectations that that partner would like and accept the participant. Additionally, recent surveys from Pew Research indicate that liberal and conservative Americans are drawn to very different types of communities ("Political Polarization in the American Public," Pew Research, 2014). Predictably, 77% of liberal adults reported wanting to live in urban centers with high population density, compact homes (e.g., condominiums), walkable neighborhoods with extensive public transportation, cultural institutions like museums and theaters, and greater ethnic diversity. In contrast, conservative Americans wanted to live in more suburban or rural communities with low population density, larger single-family homes, good parking for their personally-owned vehicles, many religious institutions, and less ethnic diversity. Emily Badger, journalist at the *Washington Post*, concluded that "[this] is an enduring stereotype—conservatives prefer McMansions while liberals like urban enclaves—but one that is grounded in reality" ("Conservatives are from McMansions, liberals are from the city," Badger, 2014). These data are correlational, limiting the strength of the conclusions that can be drawn from them, but the convergence of data from multiple samples using multiple methods suggests that there are differences in the physical spaces within Blue America and Red America.

Ideological similarity, though, is typically more difficult to determine than physical similarity. Thus, people need to use cues other than visible characteristics of potential interaction partners. It may be that attitudes, identities, ideologies, moral worldviews, and personalities are represented through ambient cues in the environment. If environments inhabited by people with different identities and personalities *look* different, observers may be capable of inferring the identities and personalities of the inhabitants (Gosling, Ko, Mannarelli, & Morris, 2002). In an initial test of this hypothesis, Gosling and colleagues (2002) recruited participants to complete popular measures of personality characteristics and then sent a team of observers to assess the home and office environments of these participants. They found that not only did observers of these environments agree in their judgments about what different cues in these environments suggested about the inhabitants' personalities, but also that observers were remarkably accurate in predicting the participating inhabitants' personalities (especially in terms of extraversion, conscientiousness, and openness to experience). This perceptive capability permits people to determine where they would be more likely to find similar others who share their ideological values, who they seem to be seeking to satisfy their need to belong (Baumeister & Leary, 1995). Specifically, the presence of cues in an environment that may be incongruent with people's identities may lead people to feel that they do not belong in that environment. In a series of experiments testing this possibility, Cheryan, Plaut, Davies, and Steele (2009) found that computer science classrooms with identity cues of the computer science students, like the presence of *Star Trek* posters, video games, comic books, and soda cans, led women to feel that they did not belong in those classes and actually decreased women's interest in choosing to spend time in that environment. The presence of identity-incongruent cues, like the stereotypically-masculine computer science cues in this study, was more important in determining women's sense of belonging than was the number of other women in the classroom.

Perhaps, as suggested by Erving Goffman (1963), people's concerns about their identity are intricately linked with elements in the physical spaces they occupy. Some subtle environmental cues may convey more direct ideological and moral content. Companies signal their acceptance (or rejection) of minority group members through presence (or absence) of brochures and posters identifying "safe spaces" for members of diverse social groups. Communities signal their acceptance (or rejection) of adherents of different moral and religious worldviews through displays endorsing particular moral and religious codes. Regions signal their acceptance of different attitudes and values through their voting support for differing policy proposals affirming or condemning attitude objects and social behaviors. Indeed, black professionals felt that they did not belong and experienced heightened threat in companies that promoted a colorblind ideology through their diversity training programs (Purdie-Vaughns, Steele, Davies, Ditlmann, & Crosby, 2008). Similarly, non-Christians reported a reduced sense of belonging when in the presence of Christmas decorations (i.e. signals of a welcoming environment for Christians; Schmitt, Davies, Hung, & Wright, 2010). And, lesbian, gay, bisexual, transgender, and queer people felt like they belonged less in states with legislation banning same-sex marriage and in states with legislation that did not include sexual orientation among protected groups in hate crimes legislation (Lick, Tornello, Riskind, Schmidt, & Patterson, 2012). Taken together, various ideological cues in the physical environment play a significant role in whether inhabitants of those environments feel like they belong.

Ideology and Ambient Cues

On its surface, ideology may seem to be a difficult characteristic on which to cluster, as ideologies are diverse and may not be on display very often (e.g., highly partisan elections occur only every 2 to 4 years, most religious holidays occur once a year, and other moral or ideological events occur even less frequently). Historically, this may have been true. However, throughout the late 20th century and into the first decade of the 21st century, the nature of mass politics has changed a great deal. In *The American Voter*, Campbell, Converse, Stokes, and Miller (1960) demonstrated that, according to nationally-representative National Election Study (NES) data from the previous decade, people were ideologically "innocent" and held views that did not consistently adhere to a particular ideology. One public opinion scholar joked that "public opinion appeared to be like butter on a grill – it just moves all over the place!" (personal communication, N. Winter). This volatility of public opinion seems to be shifting and people appear to be more ideological now than in United States history. Some debate this view by pointing to the decreasing membership in both major political parties and an increased tendency for people to describe themselves as "moderate" and identify as "political independents" (see Avlon, 2010). To some extent, people may be dis-identifying with parties because they want to view themselves as independent and objective decision-makers (Hawkins & Nosek, 2012), but this bears little relation to their partisan behavior. People may appear less partisan, but further examination suggests that these independents display the same political preferences as partisans on either side of the political aisle. Specifically, in two studies, Hawkins and Nosek (2012) demonstrate that people who implicitly identify with Democrats or Republicans or who admit to generally "leaning" toward preferring Democrats or "leaning" toward preferring Republicans are largely indistinguishable from traditional partisans in the original 7-point NES political identification question. In support of this, Bafumi and Shapiro (2009) argue that partisanship has returned and is more ideological than at any point in the last 30 years. Examining NES data over this time shows that, when accounting for people who say they are independent but "lean" toward one party or another, the number of pure independent voters is at its lowest level since the 1950s. In their analysis of General Social Survey data, they find that Democrats and Republicans have diverged on most political issues. The sharpest divergences are on racial issues and tolerance of differences in moral issues such as abortion, same-sex marriage, and school prayer. Furthermore, Bafumi and Shapiro (2009) show that not only are partisans polarizing on these issues, positions on these issues are becoming increasingly related to religious, moral, and family values.

Today, the liberal vs. conservative "culture wars" imply that core values span most of a person's moral worldview, and that there are important differences between people who adhere to one worldview or another. Much in the same way that race is discussed, there are cultural and lifestyle differences between liberals and conservatives. Hunter (1992) argues that conservatives and Republicans prefer an "orthodox" lifestyle that is rooted in respect for authority and a tendency toward tradition. He argues that liberals and Democrats, on the other hand, prefer a "progressive" lifestyle that tends more toward challenging authority in pursuit of promoting human flourishing for all citizens equally. Hetherington and Weiler (2009) examined this hypothesis by looking at how traditional, non-political behaviors in one's life space predict their political behaviors in the broader social context. They found a very strong correlation between parents' belief in spanking their children as a necessary form of discipline and their support for President George W. Bush in the 2004 presidential election (Pearson's rs ranged from .79 to .83 across two analyses). Numerous other scholars demonstrate a considerable correlation between moral and political identities (e.g., Abramowitz, 2012; Graham, Haidt, & Nosek, 2009; Haidt & Graham, 2007; Koleva et al., 2012). Thus, ideology has expanded far beyond networks of political attitudes.

As ideological identities have expanded, now including attitudes toward affirmative action, taxes, war, and same-sex marriage, personality traits (e.g., openness to experience), church attendance, and parenting styles, they may be more visible in society. Indeed, people with liberal moral worldviews were significantly more likely to have varied books and music, art supplies, many books, international maps, movie tickets, and international cultural memorabilia in their bedrooms and office spaces than were people with more conservative moral worldviews (Carney, Jost, Gosling, & Potter, 2008). People with conservative moral worldviews were significantly more likely to have sports-related décor, postage stamps, alcohol bottles, ironing boards, laundry baskets, and American flags in their bedrooms and office spaces than were people with more liberal moral worldviews. Organization and style of these spaces also differed between moral worldviews. Specifically, liberals tended to have darker, messier, more cluttered spaces whereas conservatives tended have cleaner, more brightly-lit, and less cluttered spaces (Carney et al., 2008). Thus, ideology may be considered a fundamental individual difference that bears a number of visible cues, making it easier for people to determine whether particular environments support particular moral worldviews and whether the inhabitants of those environments are morally similar.

Furthermore, communities with different moral worldviews also seem to lure different types of businesses and companies (Chinni & Gimpel, 2011). Communities that tended to vote for Republican candidates had more than twice as many gun stores as bookstores. In contrast, communities that tended to vote for Democratic candidates had more than twice as many bookstores as gun stores. Upon delving further into these data, Gimpel and Karnes found that conservative communities had disproportionately more *Wal-Marts* and liberal communities had disproportionately more *Whole Foods* and *Starbucks*. Conservative communities preferred conservative talk radio to National Public Radio (NPR), and were populated with Evangelical and Mainline Protestant Churches. Liberal communities preferred NPR, and even Air America when available, to conservative talk radio and had a relative paucity of churches. Taken together, these findings lead to the stereotypic caricature painted by syndicated columnist Dave Barry (2008):

> As Americans, we must ask ourselves: Are we really so different? Must we stereotype those who disagree with us? Do we truly believe that ALL red-state residents are ignorant racist fascist knuckle-dragging NASCAR-obsessed cousin-marrying road-kill-eating tobacco-juice-dribbling gun-fondling religious fanatic rednecks; or that ALL blue-state residents are godless unpatriotic pierced-nose Volvo-driving France-loving left-wing Communist latte-sucking tofu-chomping holistic-wacko neurotic vegan weenie perverts?

Of course, the answer is that Americans are not all of these things (or at least the vast majority of Americans, regardless of their political ilk, are not). However, the data reviewed above shed some light as to where these stereotypes emerge. Inhabitants of Red American communities do tend to like NASCAR and do tend to be religious. Inhabitants of Blue American communities do tend to like swanky coffee shops that serve lattes and do tend to prefer grocery stores that cater to vegan dietary preferences. These are the so-called grains of truth to the liberal and conservative stereotypes, but they are just that—grains of truth that vastly oversimplify to categories of people that describe most Americans.

In an initial examination of this hypothesis, Motyl and Iyer (2015b) sought to determine whether individuals holding differing ideologies had preferences for distinct types of activities, characteristics, and stores. They found that liberals preferred communities with more bicycle paths, hybrid cars, universities, used bookstores, coffee shops, art walks, and organic markets. In contrast, conservatives

16 Matt Motyl

preferred communities with more sport-utility vehicles, military bases, gun stores, professional football teams, and protestant churches. In follow-up studies, liberals and conservatives read descriptions of communities that included these subtle cues or more explicit cues of moral worldview (specifically, the percentage of people who are liberal or conservative). As predicted, participants did not differ in how they evaluated communities described with the subtle or explicit cues. Regardless of whether the ideological cues were explicit or subtle, participants reported that they preferred communities congruent with their own ideological values and that this tendency was linked to participants' perceptions that they would feel a greater sense of belonging in ideologically-similar communities. This work provides further support for the Ideological Enclavement hypothesis that people are capable of inferring the ideological leanings of communities through the ambient cues of moral values present in the communities. Furthermore, the capability of inferring communities' values allows people to determine whether their personal moral values fit with the communities' moral values, and thereby, people may intuit where they could best satisfy their need to belong.

Intuitions Steer Selective Migration into Ideological Enclaves

Human groups have long migrated as they have sought to satisfy their basic human needs. Early humans emigrated from Africa seeking access to food and water, protection from the extreme climatic elements, safety from competing, hostile groups of other humans, and in search of social connections (Richerson & Boyd, 2005; Kenrick, Griskevicius, Neuberg, & Schaller, 2010). Modern humans migrate for these reasons, but for many others, too. People consider the activities different residences would permit, the proximity to (or distance from) family members, the availability of desirable occupations, and whether they would feel a sense of belonging in those communities (Motyl, 2014; Motyl, Iyer, Oishi, Trawalter, & Nosek, 2014). It is this pursuit of belonging that may lead to the emergence of increasingly ideologically- and morally-homogeneous enclaves.

Migration and Mobility

Roughly half of the American population changed their residence between 1995 and 2000 (Schmitt, 2001), and an estimated 40–50 million Americans move each year (Florida, 2008). Understanding how people make these residential migration decisions is complex (Oishi, 2010). Employment, family, finances, personality, and temperament all influence migration (Jokela, 2009; Jokela, Kivimäki, Elovainio, & Keltikangas-Järvinen, 2009; Winstanley, Thorns, & Perkins, 2002). People likely make these decisions in ways that help them pursue their goals. For example, experts in particular occupations tend to move to communities seeking such specialists (Florida, 2004), and extroverts may move to communities with more socially-stimulating environments (Furnham, 1981). In these cases, the migrants may be assuming that the residents living in their destination communities are similar. Indeed, actual residential mobility and even contemplating migrating increases people's familiarity-seeking behavior (Oishi, Miao, Koo, Kisling, & Ratliff, 2012). As discussed above, ideological and moral similarity appears to be more appealing than mere surface-level similarity (see also Haidt, Rosenberg, & Hom, 2003). So, an influence on migration may be seeking environments populated by ideologically-similar others (Byrne, Clore, & Smeaton, 1986; Karylowski, 1976; Werner & Parmelee, 1979).

A complementary possibility is that people migrate away from communities based on feeling repulsed by the preponderance of dissimilar others (Rosenbaum, 1986). People may migrate when they feel they do not belong in their current community. In some cases, people may find the moral values of their current community disgusting, or threatening to their worldview, eliciting unpleasant existential anxiety (Haidt & Graham, 2007; Motyl, Vail, & Pyszczynski, 2011; Schimel, Hayes, Williams, & Jahrig, 2007). This identity-related, threat-induced migration seems to play a role in the segregation of ideological and religious groups around the world, including Serbians, Croatians, Muslims, Jews, Albanians, Hindus, Sikhs, Buddhists, and Christians (Lim, Metzler, & Bar-Yam, 2007). It stands to reason that this could also play a role in the ideological segregation of Red America and Blue America. When evaluating residential options, people may be especially likely to move away from communities with values that are ideologically incongruent.

The Ideological Migration Hypothesis

Regardless of whether people are generally being attracted to or repulsed from different communities, it is clear that people desire communities where they share ideological values with their neighbors and are connected to each other in their ideological identity. Cultures lacking sufficient social integration displayed higher suicide rates than those with sufficient social integration (Durkheim, 1893). More recently, cross-cultural sociological research demonstrates that in 68 different countries greater social integration predicted reduced suicide rates (Lenzi, Colucci, & Minas, 2012). In the United States, the suicide rate for liberals living in conservative communities that preferred Senator John McCain, and for conservatives living in liberal communities that supported President Barack Obama, were both higher than the rate for liberals living in communities that supported President Obama and conservatives living in communities that supported Senator McCain in the months after the 2008 Presidential election (Classen & Dunn, 2010). In other words, people with ideologies incongruent with the ideology of the communities in which they lived exhibited heightened suicide rates relative to the people with ideologies that were more congruent

18 Matt Motyl

with the ideologies of the communities in which they lived. Luckily, though, there are less drastic solutions to resolve a lack of ideological fit between person and community; people can pack up and move.

Herein lies the Ideological Enclavement Theory's ideological migration hypothesis. When people perceive that their ideological values do not fit in their current community, they perceive that they do not belong and are increasingly likely to migrate to a new, more ideologically-fitting community. Community-level, sociological data provide support for this hypothesis, suggesting that people are migrating away from ideologically-misfitting communities and toward ideologically-fitting ones (Bishop, 2009). These aggregate-level data, though, do not clarify the psychological processes contributing to migration. The correlational, aggregate community data do not, for example, address the possibility that the ideology of the majority group in a given community are gradually adopted by the minority group through social influence (Asch, 1956; Cialdini & Goldstein, 2004; Festinger, 1964; Harton, & Bullock, 2007; Latané, 1981; Sinclair, Lowery, Hardin, & Colangelo, 2005).

In an individual-level test of this hypothesis, Motyl and colleagues (2014) found that people do indeed seek communities with ideological values that fit with their own. In Study 1, we found correlational evidence in a large, national sample suggesting that people who lived in communities where their ideologies were misfit were more likely to have migrated in the past, and when those people migrated, they selected communities more congruent with their own personal ideologies. In Study 2, we found more correlational evidence in a different national sample showing that participants were able to accurately identify the ideological values of communities (possibly by intuiting fit vs. misfit via a community's ambient cues of ideology). Perceiving the ideologies of the communities in which they resided as misfit with their own ideologies decreased their sense of belonging and engendered an increased desire to migrate to a different community. Importantly, sense of belonging fully mediated the relationship between ideological fit and migration desire, suggesting that the mediating psychological mechanism may, in fact, be sense of belonging. In Study 3, we experimentally manipulated participants' perceptions of community ideologies and found that when participants thought that their community was becoming more ideologically incongruent, participants expressed a decreased sense of belonging and an increased desire to migrate to a new community. Similarly, Americans who voted for Governor Romney in his bid for the U.S. Presidency expressed a greater willingness to emigrate from the United States on the day following Governor Romney's electoral loss to President Obama, as they perceived the nation to be growing increasingly liberal and at odds with their conservative moral values (Motyl, 2014). These findings lend support for Ideological Enclavement Theory's ideological migration hypothesis, suggesting that ideological fit affects migration tendencies, and that the relationship is driven by people's desire to

Liberals and Conservatives are (Geographically) Dividing **19**

satisfy their belonging needs. Furthermore, ideological migration leads to the emergence of ideological enclaves with ever-increasing homogeneity in their ideologies.

Living in ideologically-homogeneous communities has numerous consequences for individuals, their interactions with other individuals, intragroup functioning, and intergroup relations. I turn now to a detailed discussion of these consequences.

Ideological Enclaves Promote Intrapersonal, Interpersonal, and Intragroup Thriving

This tendency to migrate into increasingly ideologically-homogeneous communities may have a number of positive consequences. Individuals migrate to homogeneous enclaves to increase their sense of belonging with their communities. Having a strong sense of belonging has many positive psychological consequences such as improved academic performance, reduced mental and physical health problems, and subjective well-being (Haslam, Jetten, Postmes, & Haslam, 2008; Leary, 2009; Major & O'Brien, 2005; Sheldon & Bettencourt, 2010; Walton & Cohen, 2011). Further, ideological homogeneity may reduce daily interpersonal conflict with dissimilar others. Indeed, among types of diversity, ideological moral diversity is very unpopular (Haidt, Rosenberg, & Hom, 2003). Without fear of reprisal for expressing one's values, one may be able to more easily form strong interpersonal bonds and accumulate social capital (see Coleman, 1988; Putnam, 2000).

With better social bonds and increased social capital, people may more easily flourish. When people feel like their values match their environment, they experience greater subjective well-being and increased self-esteem (Fulmer et al., 2010). In turn, heightened subjective well-being promotes longevity, reduces bad cholesterol and blood pressure, and expedites recovery from negative emotional experiences (Danner, Snowdon, & Friesen, 2001; Fredrickson, 2000; Fredrickson & Joiner, 2002; Fredrickson & Levenson, 1998). People may even be reducing the suicide rate by migrating into these enclaves where they are buffered from moral despair and "social disintegration" (Classen & Dunn, 2010; Durkheim, 1893).

Within-group functioning may also be enhanced by ideologically-homogeneous communities. For example, increasing a sense of belonging among marginalized groups can increase academic achievement (Schmitt, Oswald, Friede, Imus, & Merritt, 2008; Walton & Cohen, 2011). Similarly, work teams composed of employees with similar values outperformed works teams composed of employees with diverse values (Baugh & Graen, 1997; Ely & Thomas, 2001; Guillaume, Brodbeck, & Riketta, 2012; Hartel & Fujimoto, 1999). And, employees prefer working in teams comprised of individuals with similar values, more so than teams comprised of individuals with similar

20 Matt Motyl

demographic characteristics (Hobman, Bordia, & Gallois, 2003; Jehn, Chadwick, & Thatcher, 1997; Pelled, 1996).

Political scientists have demonstrated that ideological diversity in people's social networks can lead to disengagement from politics. For example, Huckfeldt, Mendez, and Osborn (2004) suggest that ideological heterogeneity within one's social network decreases voter turnout. Similarly, McClurg (2006) suggests that the partisan composition of one's neighborhood context determines mobilization. Specifically, conversations with people who disagree with a citizen have unique effects contingent upon whether that person is in the minority or majority in that neighborhood. If that citizen is in the majority, experiencing disagreement within the social context will have no discernible effect on their tendency to vote. However, if that citizen is in the minority, experiencing disagreement within the social context will reduce their person's tendency to vote. In other words, liberals living in Red America and conservatives living in Blue America may participate in the political process less. This reduced participation may further accentuate the perception of communities being more liberal or more conservative than they actually are. Thus, ideologically-homogeneous communities may be positive for their ideologically-fit citizens (although, negative for the ideologically-misfit citizens).

Ideological Enclaves Foster Intergroup Despising

The emergence of ideological enclaves leads to the segregation of liberals and conservatives into Blue and Red America, respectively. Voluminous past research demonstrates that a lack of positive contact between members of different groups leads to increased intergroup conflict (for a review, see Pettigrew & Tropp, 2006).

Bias

This environmental segregation has profound psychological effects, which operate to further environmental segregation and catalyze political change. In classic social psychological research, researchers invited a group of kids to attend a summer camp (Sherif et al., 1961). These kids were selected based on how psychologically "normal" they were. After being selected, the researchers randomly assigned them to one of two groups who would reside in two separate camps that were segregated from one another in Robber's Cave National Park in Oklahoma. When these two arbitrarily-determined groups became aware of each other's existence, conflict ensued. When these two groups participated in competitive games of baseball or tug-of-war, they became viciously hostile toward one another. On several occasions camp counselors had to break up fights occurring between members of each of these groups. More recent social psychological research has shown that people demonstrate in- and outgroup bias even when they are arbitrarily assigned to groups based on their purported performance on a mundane visual perception task (even though their feedback was determined before they participated to ensure true random assignment to groups; see Tajfel, 1970). Tajfel showed that the mere categorization of people into groups, even without any real distinctions between the groups can foster group bias. When groups are more meaningful and are of great importance to their members, group bias becomes even more extreme (Motyl & Pyszczynski, 2010; Pyszczynski, Motyl, & Abdollahi, 2009). Liberals and conservatives do not simply show a positive bias toward their own groups, but also an intense hatred for the other side (Crawford, Modri, & Motyl, 2013).

Polarization and Extremitization

Real groups that correspond with a set of values and principles can foster much more intense group polarization and engender hostility against outgroup members. Generally, groups tend to become increasingly extreme in their attitudes the more they communicate with likeminded others and avoid encountering alternative viewpoints. For example, Sunstein (2009) reports a set of studies in which he examined groups of people he expected to be impartial and objective—Federal Judges. He categorized judges based on whether they were Democratic- or Republican-appointed. These judges sat on panels consisting of three members that had four possible combinations, all Democratic-appointed, all Republican-appointed, two-Republican-appointed and one-Democratic-appointed, or two-Democratic-appointed and one-Republican-appointed. Therefore, this polarization hypothesis could be tested by comparing the tendency of homogeneous groups of judges on their rulings on social issues cases to each other and to the heterogeneous groups of judges. Sunstein found that on gay rights cases, all Republican-appointed judges voted in favor of gay rights 16% of the time whereas Democratic-appointed judges voted in favor of gay rights 57% of the time. However, when Republican-appointed judges sat on homogeneous panels they voted in favor of the gay rights' plaintiff 14% of the time whereas when the Democratic-appointed judges sat on homogeneous panels they voted in favor of gay rights 100% of the time. This basic pattern of effects held across a series of other issues ranging from support for affirmative action to redressing sex discrimination. These findings suggest that when people are in a homogeneous group where they are surrounded by others who corroborate their beliefs, they tend to become more radical in their beliefs. In some extreme cases, this cycle of increasing animosity may precipitate political violence (Motyl & Pyszczynski, 2010; Motyl, Rothschild, & Pyszczynski, 2009; Motyl, Vail, & Pyszczynski, 2011; Pyszczynski, Motyl, & Abdollahi, 2009; Pyszczynski, Vail, & Motyl, 2009). Thus, as these ideological enclaves emerge and the inhabitants have less contact with people holding different values, the

22 Matt Motyl

inhabitants will be increasingly likely to polarize and become more extreme in their beliefs.

Naïve Realism

People tend to think that they view the world objectively and that everyone else makes judgments based on this same "objective" reality (Keltner & Robinson, 1996). Every person, based on myriad factors, perceives the world in different ways. There are differences in people's auditory, olfactory, and visual sensory abilities. There are differences in the experiences people accumulate over time. In cases where people live in geographically distinct locations and are given specific biased information about the world, this discrepancy in their own perceived objectivity and their perception that others see the world as they do is problematic. Keltner and Robinson (1996) argue that people tend to assume that when others disagree on a matter of "objective" truth, they are doing so out of ideological bias which prevents them from seeing the objective truth. Inherent in this notion of naïve realism is that the perceivers, no matter how biased they may actually be, perceive themselves to be objective and more moderate than those who disagree with them.

Motivated Reasoning and Extremist Attitudes

This process requires some degree of mental gymnastics, but the human mind is gifted with the incredible powers of motivated reasoning. This motivated reasoning allows people to seek out confirmation of whatever they want to believe and disconfirmation of that which they do not want to believe (Kunda, 1990). In cases where people encounter information that fits with their understanding of the world, they ask, "Can I believe this?" The answer is almost always "yes." Alternately, where people encounter information that challenges their understanding of the world, they ask, "Must I believe this?" The answer is almost always "no." Consider, for example, the suggestion that President Barack Obama is the anti-Christ. If you believe that he is, you will likely cite passages from religious texts and possibly mention the end times. If you do not believe that he is, you will likely assume that people who make such claims should report to their nearest mental hospital. There is, however, an important disjoint here that seems to characterize much of modern-day American politics. People have a belief that skirts any hope of deliberation and makes the quick assumption that anyone who disagrees with you must be mentally imbalanced (Kosloff, Greenberg, Schmader, Dechesne, & Weise, 2010; Pyszczynski, Henthorn, Motyl, & Gerow, 2010). Consider, for another example, the view of conservative political talk radio show host Michael Savage (2005) who argues that liberalism is a mental disorder. His view is that one must be mentally ill to support liberal immigration, national security, and economic policies. However, liberals often characterize him (and many of his conservative pundit brethren) as "moonbats" or "wingnuts" (Avlon, 2010; Franken, 2004). These motivated conclusions do not facilitate political conversations or deliberations moving a people ever closer to political solutions. Rather, these processes escalate conflict between groups who live in very different red- and blue-colored worlds.

Implicit Misunderstanding

These distinct understandings of the world create "mind-blindness" and "moral empathy gaps" where people "just can't get" others who hold views discrepant from their own (Ditto & Koleva, 2011). This mental block preventing people from understanding the merit of others' beliefs and how others can be good, moral beings even if they do not share the same ideological worldview enhances political conflict. This recognition of others' moral intuitions is difficult because intuitions are often ineffable. In this respect, moral intuitions are similar to implicit cognitions. Implicit political cognition and moral intuitions represent hard-to-describe (if at all possible) gut-level reactions to one's world. These gut-level reactions emerge from a confluence of forces ranging from genetics, socialization, and one's present environment (Alford, Funk, & Hibbing, 2005; Huckfeldt, Johnson, & Sprague, 2002; Sears, 1975). These implicit cognitions sometimes diverge from what people explicitly say they believe and implicit cognitions appear to be slower to change, perhaps because they are more resistant to socially-desirable responding and more likely to represent one's automatic evaluation of a party, person, or policy based on their past and current experiences. Recent research suggests that these implicit cognitions and intuitions may be better predictors of subsequent political behaviors, including voting choice, than explicit self-reported attitudes are (Arcuri, Castelli, Galdi, Zogmaister, & Amadori, 2008). While the field of implicit political cognition is still in its toddlerhood (Stone, Johnson, Beall, Meindl, Smith, & Graham, 2014), it should be considered in any comprehensive analysis of intergroup relations, and interventions should be considered that reduce implicit biases, in addition to explicit biases.

Comparing and Contrasting Theories

Social psychological research has long emphasized the importance of the situation on the individual (e.g., Bronf enbrenner, 1977; Cohen & Leung, 2010; Lewin, 1951). Examples of social influence effects in the laboratory and in everyday life are numerous. In laboratory studies, participants adopt the public attitude of those around them on non-moral issues, such as the movement of a dot or the length of a line (Asch, 1951; Sherif, 1936). In other settings, descriptive and injunctive norms may lead participants to behave in ways consistent with what others in those settings are doing. For example, people recycle more when the social norm is to recycle (Cialdini, Kallgren, & Reno, 1991). In some cases, people will socially "tune" their attitudes to be more amenable to the expected attitudes held by future interaction partners (Lowery, Hardin, & Sinclair, 2001). Broader theories (e.g., Dynamic Social Impact Theory—DSIT, hereafter) argue that culture is created in a bottom-up fashion and that attitudes within a given culture emerge through communication with others in that culture (Harton & Bullock, 2007; Nowak, Szamrej, & Latané, 1990). Together, this tradition of research has been informative, showing how malleable attitudes and behaviors are.

Much of this thinking, though, stems from a time when societies were less residentially mobile. As societies have become more mobile, people have greater flexibility to choose different environments (Oishi, 2010). People seem to choose communities, in part, based on how similar they perceive the values of those communities to be to their own personal moral values (Bishop, 2009; McDonald, 2011; Motyl, 2014; Motyl et al., 2014). This is not to say that people's attitudes are resistant to change once they select a community to inhabit, but it does add a top-down component to the dynamic social impact perspective. DSIT claims, "if everyone around you loves sweet tea and keeps offering it to you, you may come to try it and like it yourself" (Harton & Bullock, 2007, p. 523). This claim is very plausible. However, it seems that even if everyone around you loves intelligent design in biology classrooms and they keep offering to include it in your local public school's curriculum, you are probably not likely to change your pre-existing conviction that intelligent design has no place in a biology classroom. Indeed, when it comes to sacred values and moral convictions, people are less likely to change their position on these issues (see Bauman & Skitka, 2009; Haidt & Hersh, 2001; Skitka, Bauman, & Sargis, 2005; Taber & Lodge, 2006; Tetlock, Kristel, Elson, Lerner, & Green, 2000). Rather, people respond to counter-attitudinal arguments in these contexts with a more critical eye, seeking all the reasons why the counterargument to their own position is incorrect (Ditto & Lopez, 1992; Kunda, 1990). In some cases, information that counters one's own ideological values elicits anxiety and strong emotional reactions which affects later behavior and judgments of others (Haidt, 2001; Schimel et al., 2007). These affective and motivated cognitive reactions are not likely to result in attitude change (Petty & Krosnick, 1995). Rather, people may resist social influence and polarize as they become more entrenched in their pre-existing attitudinal positions (Lord, Ross, & Lepper, 1979; Munro & Ditto, 1997). Thus, Ideological Enclavement Theory proposes that one way people respond to disagreement in their community is by disengaging and potentially migrating to a different community where there is more agreement on ideological issues.

Future Directions

Ideological Enclavement Theory, which seeks to understand the cleavages between ideological groups, is supported by voluminous past research, but requires more direct tests of its specific claims. This theoretical approach claims that people intuit belonging from subtle ideological cues in their environments. Indirect evidence (e.g., Cheryan et al., 2009) and preliminary research (e.g., Motyl & Iyer, 2015b) support this idea, but more direct tests are necessary. Specifically, the theory predicts that people would be able to infer the values of different locations in communities as a result of the cues in those locations. This work has yet to be conducted.

Ideological Enclavement Theory incorporates research from diverse communities within the social sciences demonstrating the consequences of belonging, having person–organization match, or culture-person congruence on individuals, the groups individuals belong to, and the relationships between different groups (e.g., Hobman, Bordia, & Gallois, 2003). For the most part, ideological fit has relatively more positive consequences for individuals and the groups they belong to and relatively more negative consequences for intergroup relations. This trade-off is worrisome. Future research should examine ways to capture the positive effects of moral fit for the individual without the negative effects of moral fit for intergroup relations.

Thriving, but Not Despising?

Ingroup love and outgroup hate are distinct constructs (Brewer, 1999; Halevy, Bornstein, & Sagiv, 2008; Waytz, Young, & Ginges, 2014). The separateness provides the encouraging possibility that interventions promoting one do not necessarily harm the other. Rather, it *may* be possible to promote ingroup love without also promoting intergroup hatred. Past research provides some possible ways to promote individual, within-group thriving, *and* between-group thriving.

Shared Humanity and Shared Values

In intergroup conflicts, particularly when the groups hold differing moral worldviews, members of each group tend to view each other as qualitatively different in essence, and often as evil, ignorant, incompetent, and insane (Kruglanski & Fishman, 2006; Motyl et al., 2009; Motyl & Ditto, in prep.; Pyszczynski, Motyl, & Abdollahi, 2009). Thus, promoting a sense that outgroup members share basic human characteristics and desires may lead to improved intergroup relations, without any negative consequences for the individual. In a series of studies, Motyl, Hart, and colleagues (2011) demonstrated that eliciting a sense of shared humanity through depicting basic human activities (like eating dinner with one's family) or asking people to reflect on positive or negative childhood experiences led to reduced implicit hostility against Arabs, reduced support for war, and increased support for using peaceful diplomatic means in resolving international disputes. Furthermore, these effects were mediated by the sense that members of outgroups had shared experiences and were similar to ingroup members in simple, human ways. These findings are encouraging, although they rely on making salient to individuals ways in which outgroup members may be similar to them and this intervention may be particularly short-lived.

Superordinate Identities and Threats

Shared goals promote intergroup cooperation and intergroup relations more generally (Sherif, 1958; Sherif et al., 1961). While goals of people holding different moral worldviews may often differ, there are some threats that face all people in a particular country or everywhere around the world. For example, in the wake of the terrorist attacks of September 11, 2001, liberals and conservatives in the United States set aside their hostility toward one another and identified more strongly with the more inclusive, superordinate group of being "Americans" (see Pyszczynski, Solomon, & Greenberg, 2003). This temporary rise in the endorsement of the American identity resulted in increased church attendance, support for their president, and dramatic increases in pro-social behaviors like donating blood and volunteering for food kitchens. These activities appear to be especially important predictors of social integration and the suicide rate (Lenzi et al., 2012). While these effects were short-lived, countries mired in intractable conflicts show similar effects. Israel provides one instance of prolonged cooperation between their left-wing and right-wing coalitions and broader societal integration, possibly as a result of continued superordinate threat from attack (Castano, 2004). In each of these examples, another social group poses the threat that fosters a more superordinate identity within country and one could argue that this is not promoting improved intergroup relations (at a higher level of analysis, between country as opposed to within country). However, people face numerous threats from non-human groups. Global climate change, for example, could have profound implications for people regardless of their national identity. Pyszczynski, Motyl, Vail III, Hirschberger, Arndt, and Kesebir (2012) demonstrated that prompting people to consider the potential negative consequences of global warming led to improved intergroup relations in terms of support for using extreme military tactics, support for war, support for peace-making and diplomacy, and support for the use of terrorist attacks. Importantly, this effect was not limited to American college students. Rather, this effect was shown for liberals and conservatives in the United States and replicated in Israel and Palestine on non-student populations during the 2009 bombings, and in Iran among fundamentalist Muslims. These studies provide support for the gloomy prospect of promoting individual, within-group, and between-group thriving without exacerbating human relations at a different level of analysis. Moreover, given the intensity of the conflict between the groups examined in the aforementioned studies, it seems more likely that emphasizing superordinate identities and superordinate threats will be effective in relatively less intense conflicts, like that seen in the American culture wars.

Cross-group Contact and Friendships

Under certain conditions, members of different groups may view each other more positively if they have more contact with one another (Allport, 1954; Pettigrew & Tropp, 2006). This approach has been adopted by various groups around the world in attempts to improve intergroup relations. For example, organizations like *Children of Abraham* in Israel foster summer camps where Israeli and Palestinian children come together and get to know one another in a non-threatening environment and may lay the groundwork for cross-nationality friendships. Similarly, groups like *To The Village Square* sponsor regular dinners and events bringing together American liberals and conservatives to promote more civil dialogue between them. The actual effectiveness of these interventions has not yet been demonstrated, but conceptually they should improve intergroup relations without any negative consequences for individuals or within-group functioning.

Intergroup friendships are not especially common. In the United States, people's own political ideology is an excellent predictor of their friends' political ideology (Poteat, Mereish, Liu, & Nam, 2011). Most people had some ideological heterogeneity within their social network, but substantial ideological segregation existed. Research on Australian participants suggests that selecting ideologically-similar social interaction partners is driven by a fear of rejection from people with discrepant ideological values (Barlow, Louis, & Hewstone, 2009). Analogously, people tend to overestimate the likelihood that they would not get along with members of other groups and that this may lead to more stressful interactions and reduce the desirability of having these intergroup interactions (Mallett, Wilson, & Gilbert, 2008; Trawalter, Richeson, & Shelton, 2009). Importantly though, among participants who do have positive contact with outgroup members, attitudes toward that outgroup were more positive (Mallett et al., 2008; Poteat et al., 2011). Given the anticipated discomfort, fostering these positive contact situations may be difficult. Some educators propose that classes on dialogue at universities may serve as a good platform, as students with diverse backgrounds could be required to participate. In one qualitative study of this type of course at the University of Illinois, it appears that these courses seem to have some positive effects for intergroup relations—particularly in helping people with divergent ideologies come to understand each other's beliefs (Hess, Rynczak, Minarik, & Landrum-Brown, 2010). In more rigorous quantitative work, people who are randomly assigned to make friends who belong to different racial and ethnic groups display decreases in stress, as indexed by cortisol reactivity in intergroup interactions (Page-Gould, Mendoza-Denton, & Tropp, 2008). Given that stress associated with intergroup interactions is linked with fear of rejection (Barlow et al., 2009), buffering people's sense of self-integrity may also reduce the anxiety-induced intergroup interaction discomfort. Indeed, partisans who affirmed their self-concept in the days before the 2008 US Presidential election were less partisan in their evaluation of the other party's candidate's debate performance,

28 Matt Motyl

were more positive toward the opposition candidate, and more willing to consider alternative perspectives (Binning, Sherman, Cohen, & Heitland, 2010). Thus, affirming people's self-concepts and buffering them from their fear of rejection may increase the likelihood of people from different groups choosing to interact with each other, and to interact in ways that have positive, longer-lasting consequences.

This list of prospective interventions is not exhaustive, but includes three broad categories of techniques that are relevant to identity and belonging concerns embedded in Ideological Enclavement Theory. Humanization of outgroup members, recategorization of group boundaries to be more inclusive, and the formation of positive relationships with members of other groups all improve intergroup relations, and none of them seem to do so at the expense of the individual.

Conclusion

It is well-documented that people are drawn toward similar others and that they tend to cluster with people similar to them. Most research on this subject has focused on racial homophily and racial segregation, with little attention given to important identity-related concerns, to potential psychological mechanisms driving this tendency, and the potential consequences of this process that leads to the emergence of homogeneous and segregated communities. The Ideological Enclavement hypothesis described in this chapter provides a theoretical framework to better understand how this process works and what the different consequences may be. Specifically, this approach proposes that people intuit a sense of belonging in different physical spaces. In the absence of explicit knowledge of the values held by people in different physical spaces, people may use subtle cues to determine whether they would belong there or not. Sometimes these cues may be surface-level, demographic characteristics, which provides some understanding of the emergence of racially segregated communities. Other times, these cues may be deeper-level cues that are implicitly linked with moral values, like the proportion of hybrid cars to sport-utility vehicles in a community, which provides further understanding of the emergence of ideologically-segregated communities. Then, Ideological Enclavement Theory proposes that people are incited to migrate when they intuit that they do not belong in their community, and when they migrate, they migrate to communities where they intuit a greater sense of belonging. This theory then proposes three categories of consequences. First, living in ideologically-fitting communities promotes individual happiness, health, and well-being. Second, living in ideologically-homogeneous enclaves promotes social capital, social integration, and within-group cooperation. Third, the ideologically-segregated enclaves give way to increasingly hostile interactions between groups living in other ideological and moral enclaves with discrepant ideological and moral values. This theoretical approach brings to life and gives broader meaning to Frazier's claim that the "spatial pattern of the community is the basis of a moral order" (1962, p. 613).

References

Abramowitz, A. I. (2012). *The Polarized Public*. Boston, MA: Pearson Higher Ed.

Alford, J. R., Funk, C. L., & Hibbing, J. R. (2005). Are political orientations genetically transmitted? *American Political Science Review, 99*(02), 153–167.

Allport, G. W. (1954/1979). *The Nature of Prejudice*. Reading, MA: Addison-Wesley.

Ambady, N., Bernieri, F. J., & Richeson, J. A. (2000). Toward a histology of social behavior: Judgmental accuracy from thin slices of the behavioral stream. In M. P. Zanna (Ed.), *Advances in Experimental Social Psychology* (Vol. 32, pp. 201–271). San Diego, CA: Academic Press.

Arcuri, L., Castelli, L., Galdi, S., Zogmaister, C., & Amadori, A. (2008). Predicting the vote: Implicit attitudes as predictors of the future behavior of decided and undecided voters. *Political Psychology, 29*(3), 369–387.

Asch, S. E. (1951). Effects of group pressure upon the modification and distortion of judgments. In H. Guetzkow (Ed.), *Groups, Leadership, and Men* (pp. 222–236). Pittsburgh: Carnegie Press.

Asch, S. E. (1956). Studies of independence and conformity: I. A minority of one against a unanimous majority. *Psychological Monographs: General and Applied, 70*(9), 1.

Avlon, J. (2010). *Wingnuts: How the Lunatic Fringe is Hijacking America*. New York, NY: Beast Books.

Badger, E. (2014, June 12). Conservatives are from McMansions, liberals are from the city. *Washington Post*. Retrieved 9/1/2014 from http://www.washingtonpost.com/blogs/wonkblog/wp/2014/06/12/your-house-says-an-awful-lot-about-your-politics/?tid=sm_fb

Bafumi, J., & Shapiro, R. Y. (2009). A new partisan voter. *The Journal of Politics, 71*(01), 1–24.

Bar-Tal, D. (1998). Societal beliefs in times of intractable conflict: The Israeli case. *International Journal of Conflict Management, 9*(1), 22–50.

Barlow, F. K., Louis, W. R., & Hewstone, M. (2009). Rejected! Cognitions of rejection and intergroup anxiety as mediators of the impact of cross-group friendship on prejudice. *British Journal of Social Psychology, 48,* 389–405.

Barry, D. (2008). ThinkExist quotations. Retrieved July 1, 2014 from http://thinkexist.com/quotation/and-as-americans-we-must-ask-ourselves-are-we/1329345.html

Baugh, S. G., & Graen, G. B. (1997). Effects of team gender and racial composition on perceptions of team performance in cross-functional teams. *Group & Organization Management, 22,* 366–383.

Bauman, C. W., & Skitka, L. J. (2009). In the mind of the perceiver: Psychological implications of moral conviction. In D. Bartels, C. W. Bauman, L. J. Skitka, & D. Medin (Eds.) *Moral Judgment and Decision Making: Psychology of Learning and Motivation* (pp. 341–364). San Diego, CA: Academic Press.

Baumeister, R. F., & Leary, M. R. (1995). The need to belong: Desire for interpersonal attachments as a fundamental human motivation. *Psychological Bulletin, 117,* 497–529.

Binning, K. R., Sherman, D. K., Cohen, G. L., & Heitland, K. (2010). Seeing the other side: Reducing political partisanship via self-affirmation in the 2008 presidential election. *Analyses of Social Issues and Public Policy, 10,* 276–292.

30 Matt Motyl

Bishop, B. (2009). *The Big Sort: Why the Clustering of Like-Minded America is Tearing us Apart*. Boston, MA: Houghton-Mifflin Harcourt.

Brewer, M. B. (1999). The psychology of prejudice: Ingroup love or outgroup hate? *Journal of Social Issues, 55*, 429–444.

Bronfenbrenner, U. (1977). Toward an experimental ecology of human development. *American Psychologist, 32*(7), 513.

Bushman, R. L. (2005). *Joseph Smith: Rough Stone Rolling*. New York, NY: Alfred A. Knopf.

Buss, D. M. (1987). Selection, evocation, and manipulation. *Journal of Personality and Social Psychology, 53*(6), 1214.

Byrne, D. E. (1971). *The Attraction Paradigm* (Vol. 11). New York: Academic Press.

Byrne, D., & Clore, G. L. (1970). A reinforcement model of evaluative responses. *Personality: An International Journal 1*, 103–128.

Byrne, D., Clore, G. L., & Smeaton, G. (1986). The attraction hypothesis: Do similar attitudes affect anything? *Journal of Personality and Social Psychology, 51*, 1167–1170. DOI: 10.1037/0022-3514.51.6.1167

Campbell, A., Converse, P., Stokes, D. E., & Miller, W. E. (1960). *The American Voter*. New York: John Wiley & Sons, Inc.

Carney, D. R., Jost, J. T., Gosling, S. D., & Potter, J. (2008). The secret lives of liberals and conservatives: Personality profiles, interaction styles, and the things they leave behind. *Political Psychology, 29*, 807–840.

Carpini, M. X. D., & Keeter, S. (1996). *What Americans Know about Politics and Why It Matters*. Stamford, CT: Yale University Press.

Castano, E. (2004). European Identity: A social-psychological perspective. In: R. K. Herrmann, T. Risse and M. B. Brewer (Eds.) *Transnational Identities. Becoming European in the EU* (pp. 40–58). Lanham, MD: Rowman & Littlefield.

Cheryan, S., Plaut, V. C., Davies, P. G., & Steele, C. M. (2009). Ambient belonging: How stereotypical cues impact gender participation in computer science. *Journal of Personality and Social Psychology, 97*, 1045–1060.

Chinni, D., & Gimpel, J. (2011). *Our Patchwork Nation: The Surprising Truth about the "Real" America*. New York: Penguin.

Cialdini, R. B., & Goldstein, N. J. (2004). Social influence: Compliance and conformity. *Annual Review of Psychology, 55*, 591–621.

Cialdini, R. B., Kallgren, C. A., & Reno, R. R. (1991). A focus theory of normative conduct: A theoretical refinement and reevaluation of the role of norms in human behavior. *Advances in Experimental Social Psychology, 24*(20), 1–243.

Classen, T. J., & Dunn, R. A. (2010). The politics of hope and despair: The effect of presidential election outcomes on suicide rates. *Social Science Quarterly, 91*, 593–612. DOI: 10.1111/j.1540-6237.2010.00709.x

Cohen, D., & Leung, A. K. Y. (2010). A CuPS (Culture X Person X Situation) perspective on violence and character. *Human Aggression and Violence: Causes, Manifestations, and Consequences*. Washington, DC: American Psychological Association.

Coleman, J. S. (1988). Social capital in the creation of human capital. *American Journal of Sociology*, S95–S120.

Crawford, J. T., Modri, S., & Motyl, M. (2013). Bleeding-heart liberals and hard-hearted conservatives: Subtle political dehumanization through differential attributions of human nature and human uniqueness traits. *Journal of Social and Political Psychology, 1*(1), 86–104, DOI:10.5964/jspp.v1i1.184

Danner, D. D., Snowdon, D. A., & Friesen, W. V. (2001). Positive emotions in early life and longevity: Findings from the nun study. *Journal of Personality and Social Psychology, 80*(5), 804.

Ditto, P. H., & Koleva, S. P. (2011). Moral empathy gaps and the American culture war. *Emotion Review, 3,* 331–332. DOI: 10.1177/1754073911402393

Ditto, P. H., & Lopez, D. F. (1992). Motivated skepticism: Use of differential decision criteria for preferred and nonpreferred conclusions. *Journal of Personality and Social Psychology, 63,* 568–584.

Dixon, J., & Durrheim, K. (2003). Contact and the ecology of racial division: Some varieties of informal segregation. *British Journal of Social Psychology, 42*(1), 1–23.

Durkheim, E. (1893). 1984. *The Division of Labor in Society.* New York: The Free Press.

Ely, R. J., & Thomas, D. A. (2001). Cultural diversity at work: The effects of diversity perspectives on work group processes and outcomes. *Administration Science Quarterly, 46,* 229–273.

Festinger, L. (1964). Behavioral support for opinion change. *Public Opinion Quarterly,* 404–417.

Fischer, C. S. (1977). *Networks and Places: Social Relations in the Urban Setting.* New York: Free Press.

Florida, R. (2004). *The Rise of the Creative Class and How it's Transforming Work, Leisure, Community and Everyday Life* (Paperback Ed.). New York: Basic Books.

Florida, R. (2008). *Who's Your City? How the Creative Economy Is Making Where to Live the Most Important Decision of Your Life.* New York, NY: Basic Books

Franken, A. (2004). *Lies and the Lying Liars Who Tell Them.* New York: Penguin.

Frazier, E. F. (1962). Desegregation as an object of sociological study. In A. M. Rose (ed.), *Human Behavior and Social Processes* (pp. 608–624). London, UK: Routledge.

Fredrickson, B. L. (2000). Extracting meaning from past affective experiences: The importance of peaks, ends, and specific emotions. *Cognition & Emotion, 14*(4), 577–606.

Fredrickson, B. L., & Joiner, T. (2002). Positive emotions trigger upward spirals toward emotional well-being. *Psychological Science, 13*(2), 172–175.

Fredrickson, B. L., & Levenson, R. W. (1998). Positive emotions speed recovery from the cardiovascular sequelae of negative emotions. *Cognition & Emotion, 12*(2), 191–220.

French, D. C., Purwono, U., & Triwahyuni, A. (2011). Friendship and the religiosity of Indonesian Muslim adolescents. *Journal of Youth and Adolescence, 40*(12), 1623–1633.

Fulmer, C. A., Gelfand, M. J., Kruglanski, A. W., Kim-Prieto, C., Diener, E., Pierro, A., & Higgins, E. T. (2010). On "feeling right" in cultural contexts: How person-culture match affects self-esteem and subjective well-being. *Psychological Science, 21*(11), 1563–156.

Furnham, A. (1981). Personality and activity preference. *British Journal of Social Psychology, 20*(1), 57–68.

Goffman, E. (1963). *Behavior in Public Places: Notes on the Social Organization of Gatherings.* New York: Free Press of Glencoe.

Gosling, S. D., Ko, S. J., Mannarelli, T., & Morris, M. E. (2002). A room with a cue: Personality judgments based on offices and bedrooms. *Journal of Personality and Social Psychology, 82,* 379–398.

Graham, J., Haidt, J., & Nosek, B. (2009). Liberals and conservatives use different sets of moral foundations. *Journal of Personality and Social Psychology, 96,* 1029–1046.

Guillaume, Y. R. F., Brodbeck, F. C., & Riketta, M. (2012). Surface- and deep-level dissimilarity effects on social integration and individual effectiveness related outcomes in work groups: A meta-analytic integration. *Journal of Occupational and Organizational Psychology, 85,* 80–115.

Haidt, J. (2001). The emotional dog and its rational tail: A social intuitionist approach to moral judgment. *Psychological Review, 108,* 814–834.

Haidt, J. (2007). The new synthesis in moral psychology. *Science, 316,* 998–1002.

Haidt, J., & Graham, J. (2007). When morality opposes justice: Conservatives have moral intuitions that liberals may not recognize. *Social Justice Research, 20*(1), 98–116.

Haidt, J., & Hersh, M. A. (2001). Sexual morality: The cultures and emotions of conservatives and liberals. *Journal of Applied Social Psychology, 31*(1), 191–221.

Haidt, J., Rosenberg, E., & Hom, H. (2003). Differentiating diversities: Moral diversity is not like other kinds. *Journal of Applied Social Psychology, 33,* 1–36.

Halevy, N., Bornstein, G., & Sagiv, L. (2008). "In-group love" and "Out-group hate" as motives for individual participation in intergroup conflict: A new game paradigm. *Psychological Science, 19*(4), 405–411.

Hardin, C. D., & Higgins, E. T. (1996). Shared reality: How social verification makes the subjective objective. In R. M. Sorrentino & E. T. Higgins (Eds.), *Handbook of Motivation and Cognition, Vol. 3: The Interpersonal Context* (pp. 28–84). New York, NY: The Guilford Press.

Hartel, C. E. J., & Fujimoto, Y. (1999). Explaining why diversity sometimes has positive effects in organizations and sometimes has negative effects in organizations: The perceived dissimilarity openness moderator model. *Academy of Management Best Papers Proceedings,* August.

Harton, H. C., & Bullock, M. (2007). Dynamic social impact: A theory of the origins and evolution of culture. *Social and Personality Psychology Compass, 1,* 521–540. DOI: 10.1111/j.1751–9004.2007.00022.x.

Haslam, S. A., Jetten, J., Postmes, T., & Haslam, C. (2008). Social identity, health and well-being: An emerging agenda for applied psychology. *Applied Psychology, 58,* 1–23.

Hawkins, C. B., & Nosek, B. A. (2012). Motivated independence? Implicit party identity predicts political judgments among self-proclaimed independents. *Personality and Social Psychology Bulletin, 38*(11), 1437–1452.

Hess, J. Z., Rynczak, D., Minarik, J. D., & Landrum-Brown, J. (2010). Alternative settings for liberal–conservative exchange: Examining an undergraduate dialogue course. *Journal of Community & Applied Social Psychology, 20,* 156–166.

Hetherington, M. J., & Weiler, J. D. (2009). *Authoritarianism and Polarization in American Politics.* New York, NY: Cambridge University Press.

Hobman, E. V., Bordia, P., & Gallois, C. (2003). Consequences of feeling dissimilar from others in a work team. *Journal of Business and Psychology, 17,* 301–325.

Hoch, S. J. (1987). Perceived consensus and predictive accuracy: The pros and cons of projection. *Journal of Personality and Social Psychology, 53*(2), 221.

Huckfeldt, R., Johnson, P. E., & Sprague, J. (2002). Political environments, political dynamics, and the survival of disagreement. *The Journal of Politics, 64*(01), 1–21.

Huckfeldt, R., Mendez, J. M., & Osborn, T. (2004). Disagreement, ambivalence, and engagement: The political consequences of heterogeneous networks. *Political Psychology, 25,* 65–95.

Hunter, J. D. (1992). *Culture Wars: The Struggle to Control the Family, Art, Education, Law, and Politics in America.* New York: Basic Books.

Jehn, K. A., Chadwick, C., & Thatcher, S. M. B. (1997). To agree or not to agree: The effects of value congruence, individual demographic dissimilarity, and conflict on workgroup outcomes. *International Journal of Conflict Management, 8,* 287–305.

Jokela, M. (2009). Personality predicts migration within and between US states. *Journal of Research in Personality, 43,* 79–83.

Jokela, M., Kivimäki, M., Elovainio, M., & Keltikangas-Järvinen, L. (2009). Personality and having children: A two-way relationship. *Journal of Personality and Social Psychology, 96*(1), 218.

Karylowski, J. (1976). Self-esteem, similarity, liking and helping. *Personality and Social Psychology Bulletin, 2,* 71–74.

Keltner, D., & Robinson, R. J. (1996). Extremism, power, and the imagined basis of social conflict. *Current Directions in Psychological Science,* 101–105.

Kenrick, D. T., Griskevicius, V., Neuberg, S. L., & Schaller, M. (2010). Renovating the pyramid of needs: Contemporary extensions built upon ancient foundations. *Perspectives on Psychological Science, 5,* 292–314.

Kesebir, P., & Pyszczynski, T. (2011). A moral-existential account of the psychological factors fostering intergroup conflict. *Social and Personality Psychology Compass, 5*(11), 878–890.

Koleva, S. P., Graham, J., Iyer, R., Ditto, P. H., & Haidt, J. (2012). Tracing the threads: How five moral concerns (especially Purity) help explain culture war attitudes. *Journal of Research in Personality, 46*(2), 184–194.

Kosloff, S., Greenberg, J., Schmader, T., Dechesne, M., & Weise, D. (2010). Smearing the opposition: Implicit and explicit stigmatization of the 2008 US Presidential candidates and the current US President. *Journal of Experimental Psychology: General, 139*(3), 383.

Kruglanski, A. W., & Fishman, S. (2006). The psychology of terrorism: "Syndrome" versus "tool" perspectives. *Terrorism and Political Violence, 18,* 193–215.

Kunda, Z. (1990). The case for motivated reasoning. *Psychological Bulletin,* 108, 480–498.

Latané, B. (1981). The psychology of social impact. *American Psychologist, 36*(4), 343.

Leary, M. R. (2009). Affiliation, acceptance, and belonging: The pursuit of interpersonal connection. In S. Fiske, D. Gilbert, & G. Lindzey (Eds.), *Handbook of Social Psychology* (5th ed., Vol. 2, pp. 864–897). Hoboken, NJ: Wiley.

Lenzi, M., Colucci, E., & Minas, H. (2012). Suicide, culture, and society from a cross-national perspective. *Cross-Cultural Research, 46,* 50–71.

Lewin, K. (1951). *Field Theory in Social Science: Selected Theoretical Papers* (Edited by Dorwin Cartwright.). New York: Harper.

Lewis, N. M. (2012). Remapping disclosure: Gay men's segmented journeys of moving out and coming out. *Social & Cultural Geography, 13,* 211–231.

Lewis, V. A. (2012). Social energy and racial segregation in the university context. *Social Science Quarterly, 93,* 270–290.

Lick, D. J., Tornello, S. L., Riskind, R. G., Schmidt, K. M., & Patterson, C. J. (2012). Social climate for sexual minorities predicts well-being among heterosexual offspring of lesbian and gay parents. *Sexuality Research and Social Policy, 9,* 99–112.

Lim, M., Metzler, R., & Bar-Yam, Y. (2007). Global pattern formation and ethnic/cultural violence. *Science, 317,* 1540–1544.

Lord, C. G., Ross, L., & Lepper, M. R. (1979). Biased assimilation and attitude polarization: The effects of prior theories on subsequently considered evidence. *Journal of Personality and Social Psychology, 37*(11), 2098.

34 Matt Motyl

Lowery, B. S., Hardin, C. D., & Sinclair, S. (2001). Social influence effects on automatic racial prejudice. *Journal of Personality and Social Psychology, 81*(5), 842.

MacKinnon, S. P., Jordan, C. H., & Wilson, A. E. (2011). Birds of a feather sit together: Physical similarity predicts seating choice. *Personality and Social Psychology Bulletin, 37,* 879–892.

Major, B., & O'Brien, L. T. (2005). The social psychology of stigma. *Annual Review of Psychology, 56,* 393–421.

Mallett, R. K., Wilson, T. D., & Gilbert, D. T. (2008). Expect the unexpected: Failure to anticipate similarities leads to an intergroup forecasting error. *Journal of Personality and Social Psychology, 94*(2), 265.

McClurg, S. D. (2006). Political disagreement in context: The conditional effect of neighborhood context, disagreement and political talk on electoral participation. *Political Behavior, 28,* 349–366.

McDonald, I. (2011). Migration and sorting in the American electorate: Evidence from the 2006 Cooperative Congressional Election Study. *American Politics Research, 39*(3), 512–533.

McGregor, I., Nail, P. R., Marigold, D. C., & Kang, S. J. (2005). Defensive pride and consensus: Strength in imaginary numbers. *Journal of Personality and Social Psychology, 89*(6), 978.

McPherson, M., Smith-Lovin, L., & Cook, J. M. (2001). Birds of a feather: Homophily in social networks. *Annual Review of Sociology, 27,* 415–444.

Motyl, M. (2014). "If he wins, I'm moving to Canada": Ideological migration threats following the 2012 US Presidential Election. *Analyses of Social Issues and Public Policy, 14*(1), 123–136.

Motyl, M., & Iyer, R. (2014). Will the real fundamental difference underlying ideology please stand up? *Behavioral and Brain Sciences, 37*(03), 322–323.

Motyl, M., & Iyer, R. (2015a). Diverse crowds using diverse methods improves the scientific dialectic. *Behavioral and Brain Sciences.* Manuscript in preparation.

Motyl, M., & Iyer, R. (2015b). The ecology of ideology. Manuscript in preparation.

Motyl, M., & Pyszczynski, T. (2010). The existential underpinnings of the cycle of terrorist and counterterrorist violence and pathways to peaceful resolutions. *International Review of Social Psychology, 3,* 267–291.

Motyl, M., Hart, J., Pyszczynski, T., Weise, D., Cox, C., Maxfield, M., & Siedel, A. (2011). Subtle priming of shared human experiences eliminates threat-induced negativity toward Arabs, immigrants, and peace-making. *Journal of Experimental Social Psychology, 47,* 1179–1184.

Motyl, M., Iyer, R., Oishi, S., Trawalter, S., & Nosek, B. A. (2014). How ideological migration geographically segregates groups. *Journal of Experimental Social Psychology, 51,* 1–14.

Motyl, M., Rothschild, Z., & Pyszczynski, T. (2009). The cycle of violence and pathways to peace. *Organisational Transformation and Social Change, 6,* 153–170.

Motyl, M., Vail, K., & Pyszczynski, T. (2011). Waging terror: Psychological motivation in cultural violence and peacemaking. *The Day That Changed Everything: The Impact of 9–11* (pp. 23–36).

Munro, G. D., & Ditto, P. H. (1997). Biased assimilation, attitude polarization, and affect in reactions to stereotype-relevant scientific information. *Personality and Social Psychology Bulletin, 23*(6), 636–653.

Murphy, M. C., Steele, C. M., & Gross, J. G. (2007). Signaling threat: How situational cues affect women in math, science, and engineering settings. *Psychological Science, 18,* 879–885.

Mutz, D. C. (2006). *Hearing the Other Side: Deliberative Versus Participatory Democracy.* New York, NY: Cambridge University Press.

Neuberg, S. L., & Cottrell, C. A. (2008). Managing the threats and opportunities afforded by human sociality. *Group Dynamics: Theory, Research, and Practice, 12*(1), 63.

Nisbett, R. E., & Wilson, T. D. (1977). Telling more than we can know: Verbal reports on mental processes. *Psychological Review, 84*(3), 231.

Nowak, A., Szamrej, J., & Latané, B. (1990). From private attitude to public opinion: A dynamic theory of social impact. *Psychological Review, 97*(3), 362.

Oishi, S. (2010). The psychology of residential mobility: Implications for the self, social relationships, and well-being. *Perspectives on Psychological Science, 5,* 5–21.

Oishi, S., Miao, F. F., Koo, M., Kisling, J., & Ratliff, K. A. (2012). Residential mobility breeds familiarity-seeking. *Journal of Personality and Social Psychology, 102*(1), 149.

Oyserman, D., Brickman, D., Bybee, D., & Celious, A. (2006). Fitting in matters: Markers of in-group belonging and academic outcomes. *Psychological Science, 17,* 854–861.

Page-Gould, E., Mendoza-Denton, R., & Tropp, L. R. (2008). With a little help from my cross-group friend: Reducing anxiety in intergroup contexts through cross-group friendships. *Journal of Personality and Social Psychology, 95,* 1080–1094.

Pelled, L. H. (1996). Demographic diversity, conflict, and work group outcomes: An intervening process theory. *Organization Science, 7,* 615–631.

Pettigrew, T. F., & Tropp, L. R. (2006). A meta-analytic test of intergroup contact theory. *Journal of Personality and Social Psychology, 90,* 751–783.

Petty, R. E., & Krosnick, J. A. (1995). Attitude strength: An overview. In R. E. Petty & J. A. Krosnick (Eds.), *Attitude Strength: Antecedents and Consequences* (pp. 1–24). Mahwah, NJ: Lawrence Erlbaum.

Pew Research (2014, June 12). *Political Polarization in the American Public.* Pew Research Center. Retrieved January 15, 2015 from http://www.people-press.org/2014/06/12/political-polarization-in-the-american-public/

Poteat, V. P., Mereish, E. H., Liu, M. L., & Nam, J. S. (2011). Can friendships be bipartisan? The effects of political ideology on peer relationships. *Group Processes & Intergroup Relations, 14,* 819–834.

Purdie-Vaughns, V., Steele, C. M., Davies, P. G., Ditlmann, R., & Crosby, J. R. (2008). Social identity contingencies: How diversity cues signal threat or safety for African Americans in mainstream institutions. *Journal of Personality and Social Psychology, 94*(4), 615.

Putnam, R. D. (2000). *Bowling Alone: The Collapse and Revival of American Community.* New York: Simon & Schuster.

Pyszczynski, T., Greenberg, J., Solomon, S., & Maxfield, M. (2006). On the Unique Psychological Import of the Human Awareness of Mortality: Theme and Variations. *Psychological Inquiry, 17*(4), 328–356. 10.1080/10478400701369542

Pyszczynski, T., Henthorn, C., Motyl, M., Gerow, K. (2010). Is Obama the Anti-Christ? Racial priming, extreme criticisms of Barack Obama, and attitudes toward the 2008 US presidential candidates. *Journal of Experimental Social Psychology, 46,* 863–866.

Pyszczynski, T., Motyl, M., & Abdollahi, A. (2009). Righteous violence: Killing for god, country, freedom, and justice. *Behavioral Sciences of Terrorism and Political Aggression, 1,* 12–39.

Pyszczynski, T., Motyl, M., Vail III, K. E., Hirschberger, G., Arndt, J., & Kesebir, P. (2012). Drawing attention to global climate change decreases support for war. *Peace and Conflict: Journal of Peace Psychology, 18*(4), 354.

Pyszczynski, T., Solomon, S., & Greenberg, J. (2003). *In the Wake of 9/11: Rising above the Terror.* Washington, DC: American Psychological Association.

Pyszczynski, T., Vail III, K. E., & Motyl, M. S. (2009). The cycle of righteous killing: Psychological forces in its prevention and the promotion of peace. *Home-grown Terrorism: Understanding and Addressing the Root Causes of Radicalisation among Groups with an Immigrant Heritage in Europe, 60,* 227.

Richerson, P. J., & Boyd, R. (2005). *Not by Genes Alone: How Culture Transformed Human Evolution.* Chicago, IL: University of Chicago Press.

Rosenbaum, M. E. (1986). The repulsion hypothesis: On the nondevelopment of relationships. *Journal of Personality and Social Psychology, 51*(6), 1156.

Ross, L., Greene, D., & House, P. (1977). The "false consensus effect": An egocentric bias in social perception and attribution processes. *Journal of Experimental Social Psychology, 13*(3), 279–301.

Savage, M. (2005). *Liberalism is a Mental Disorder: Savage Solutions.* New York, NY: Thomas Nelson Publishing.

Schimel, J., Hayes, J., Williams, T., & Jahrig, J. (2007). Is death really the worm at the core? Converging evidence that worldview threat increases death-thought accessibility. *Journal of Personality and Social Psychology, 92*(5), 789.

Schmitt, E. (2001, August 6). Census data show a sharp increase in living standard. *New York Times.* Retrieved from www.nytimes.com/2001/08/06/national/06CENS.html

Schmitt, M. T., Davies, K., Hung, M., & Wright, S. C. (2010). Identity moderates the effects of Christmas displays on mood, self-esteem, and inclusion. *Journal of Experimental Social Psychology, 46,* 1017–1022.

Schmitt, N., Oswald, F. L., Friede, A., Imus, A., & Merritt, S. (2008). Perceived fit with an academic environment: Attitudinal and behavioral outcomes. *Journal of Vocational Behavior, 72*(3), 317–335.

Sears, D. O. (1975). Political socialization. In F. I. Greenstein and N. W. Polsby. (Eds.), *Handbook of Political Science* (Vol. 2, pp. 93–153). Reading, MA: Addison-Wesley.

Sheldon, K. M., & Bettencourt, B. A. (2010). Psychological need-satisfaction and subjective well-being within social groups. *British Journal of Social Psychology, 41,* 25–38. DOI: 10.1348/014466602165036

Sherif, M. (1936). *The Psychology of Social Norms.* New York: Harper.

Sherif, M. (1958). Superordinate goals in the reduction of intergroup conflict. *The American Journal of Sociology, LXIII,* 349–356.

Sherif, M., Harvey, O. J., White, B. J., Hood, W. R., & Sherif, C. W. (1961). *Intergroup Cooperation and Conflict: The Robber's Cave Experiment.* Norman, OK: University of Oklahoma Book Exchange.

Sinclair, S., Lowery, B. S., Hardin, C. D., & Colangelo, A. (2005). Social tuning of automatic racial attitudes: The role of affiliative motivation. *Journal of Personality and Social Psychology, 89*(4), 583.

Skitka, L. J., Bauman, C. W., & Sargis, E. G. (2005). Moral conviction: Another contributor to attitude strength or something more? *Journal of Personality and Social Psychology, 88*(6), 895.

Smart, M. J., & Klein, N. J. (2013). Neighborhoods of affinity: Social forces and travel in gay and lesbian neighborhoods. *Journal of the American Planning Association, 79,* 110–124.

Stone, S., Johnson, K. M., Beall, E., Meindl, P., Smith, B., & Graham, J. (2014). Political psychology. *Wiley Interdisciplinary Reviews: Cognitive Science, 5*(4), 373–385.

Sunstein, C. R. (2009). *Radicals in Robes*. New York: Basic Books.

Swann, W. B. (1987). Identity negotiation: Where two roads meet. *Journal of Personality and Social Psychology, 53*(6), 1038.

Taber, C. S., & Lodge, M. (2006). Motivated skepticism in the evaluation of political beliefs. *American Journal of Political Science, 50*(3), 755–769.

Tajfel, H. (1970). Experiments in intergroup discrimination. *Scientific American, 223*(5), 96–102.

Tajfel, H., Billig, M. G., Bundy, R. P., & Flament, C. (1971). Social categorization and intergroup behaviour. *European Journal of Social Psychology, 1*(2), 149–178.

Tetlock, P. E., Kristel, O. V., Elson, B., Lerner, J. S., & Green, M. C. (2000). The psychology of the unthinkable: Taboo trade-offs, forbidden base rates, and heretical counterfactuals. *Journal of Personality and Social Psychology, 78,* 853–870.

Tooby, J., & Cosmides, L. (1996). *Friendship and the Banker's Paradox: Other Pathways to the Evolution of Adaptations for Altruism*. New York: Oxford University Press.

Trawalter, S., Richeson, J. A., & Shelton, J. N. (2009). Predicting behavior during interracial interactions: A stress and coping approach. *Personality and Social Psychology Review, 13,* 243–268.

Walton, G. M., & Cohen, G. L. (2011). A brief social-belonging intervention improves academic and health outcomes of minority students. *Science, 331,* 1447–1451.

Waytz, A., Young, L. L., & Ginges, J. (2014). Motive attribution asymmetry for love vs. hate drives intractable conflict. *Proceedings of the National Academy of Sciences, 111,* 15687–15692.

Werner, C., & Parmelee, P. (1979). Similarity of activity preferences among friends: Those who play together stay together. *Social Psychology Quarterly,* 62–66.

Winstanley, A., Thorns, D. C., & Perkins, H. C. (2002). Moving house, creating home: Exploring residential mobility. *Housing Studies, 17*(6), 813–832.

2

THE LEFT–RIGHT LANDSCAPE OVER TIME

The View from a Western European Multi-Party Democracy

Hulda Thórisdóttir

Anyone who studies, observes, or participates in politics in the West is bound to acknowledge the existence and importance of the left–right political dimension. In this chapter I examine how voters have used the left–right scale over time in Iceland, a stable, multi-party, democratic state. The data comes from the Icelandic National Election Studies from the years 1987 to 2013. After a brief definition of terms and a succinct description of left–right in the Icelandic context, I will seek to address several well-known critiques and debates pertaining to the left–right dimension: the potential irrelevance of the left–right dimension, perceived and actual polarization, and political sorting based on demographics or party allegiance.

Generally, those on the right tend to believe that social changes should happen slowly and that current social order is in place for a good reason. The right is also associated with stronger belief in the importance of authorities (Jost et al., 2003a, 2003b; Kirk, 1982; Muller, 2001; Wilson, 1973).

As capitalism with its inevitable economic inequality slowly became the dominant social order in the West after the Industrial Revolution, those on the right tended to support and defend it. The right-wing support for capitalism and the free market was, however, not universal, as some felt it represented a radically changed social order and continued to support more traditional societal arrangements. This friction within the right-wing camp has continued to this day with the current separation into economic and social conservatism (Lipset, 1981; Muller, 1997) causing some uneasy alliances within the same political party. This has also led to the common critique of the left–right dimension that it lumps together opinions that do not have a logical connection (Conover & Feldman, 1981; Kerlinger, 1984) and as a result creates artificial opinion barriers between people and parties (Brittan, 2012).

The left, however, is associated with redistribution of wealth and more active involvement of the state to guarantee the welfare of its citizens. For most of the 20th century, the left–right labels were primarily linked to social class and the workers' struggle, but that changed in the 1960s when young and educated people in the West started to reject traditionalism and call for societal changes, primarily in the form of increased economic and social equality for all (Adams, 2001; Noël & Thérien, 2008).

The Icelandic Left and Right

Iceland is a representative democracy and a parliamentary republic with a multi-party system in which the parties line up clearly on the left–right dimension. Governments are always formed by a coalition of two or more parties as no single party has ever received the majority of votes. In Icelandic politics the terms left, right, and center are frequently used by both political elites and the general public to describe the political stance of parties, politicians, and policies. Studies in Iceland have shown that the left–right dimension in Icelandic politics is primarily determined by attitudes toward capitalism and economic redistribution (Bengtsson, Hansen, Hardarson, Narud & Oscarsson, 2013; Grendstad, 2003). Social issues, on the other hand, play a negligent role in determining the left–right stance.

The political scene has been dominated by more or less the same four large political parties since the 1930s. Although there have been some mergers and separations during this time, with the occasional new party, the number of parties has never been higher than eight and a four-party pattern has continued to re-emerge (Kristinsson, 2007). The left–right stance of these parties is generally undisputed. The right wing has been mostly united in the Independence Party since its foundation in 1929. The left has been more fractioned, with parties coming and going. Today, however, the Left–Green Movement furthest to the left, and the pro-EU Social Democratic Alliance closer to the middle, in most ways echo their older counterparts with different names (the People's Alliance and the Social Democratic Party, respectively). The Progressive Party, a former farmers' party, is a relatively small center party, albeit with substantial political clout due to its ability to form coalition governments with both left- and right-wing parties. Typically, the Independence Party is the largest, receiving around 35% of the national vote, followed by the Social Democratic Alliance with around 25–30%, with the Left–Greens and the Progressive Party each receiving 10–20% (Statistics Iceland, n.d.a).

The Icelandic National Election Study (ICENES) has been conducted following every parliamentary election since 1983 (Hardarson, e.d.). As a rule, parliamentary elections are held every four years. In 2009 elections were held two years prematurely due to political turmoil following the economic crisis in the fall of 2008 and the subsequent downfall of the government. ICENES is a

40 Hulda Thórisdóttir

wide-ranging phone survey conducted by nationally recognized survey companies using a nationally representative sample drawn from the Icelandic national registry.[1]

Has the Left–Right Scale Lost Meaning to Voters over Time?— Issue 1

One of the main arguments made during the "end of ideology" debate initiated by members of the Michigan school (Bell, 1960; Converse, 1964; Giddens, 1994, Lipset, 1960) was that the left–right label used to have meaning but that it had lost it in the wake of World War II and the Cold War. Another argument was that modern-day politics, at least in the West, had assimilated left and right ideas into current combinations of capitalism and state-run safety-nets and services. Advocates of the left–right dimension have said despite its simplicity, the left–right continues to be the most parsimonious and powerful measure of political ideology we have (Feldman, 2003; Fuchs and Klingemann, 1990; Jost, 2006; Knight, 1999; Noël & Thérien, 2008). This is reflected not only in the fact that the left–right language is ubiquitous in all political discourse (e.g., Jennings, 1992; McCarty, Poole & Rosenthal, 2007) but also in people's willingness to place themselves on the left–right scale when prompted. Noël and Thérien (2008) reported a summary from the World Values Survey (WVS), a large international survey project covering close to 80 societies. They found that only 22.4% of people worldwide refused to place themselves on the scale, the residents of former communist countries in Eastern Europe being among the most likely to refuse.

In Noël and Thérien's summary of the WVS from 1999–2001, only 9.5% of Icelanders said they did not know, or refused to answer, when asked to place themselves on the left–right scale. Although this number indicates that the left–right scale has a meaning in the minds of Icelanders, we do not know if it has been increasing or decreasing over time. The first issue to address is therefore:

Question 1a: Has the number of Icelandic voters willing to place themselves on the left–right scale changed over time?

A sure sign of the left–right scale having lost its meaning over time would be a decline in the number of people who placed themselves on the scale. A summary of overall self-placement scores from 1987 until 2013 can be seen in Table 2.1. This does not indicate that the scale has become meaningless over time. The percentage of respondents willing to place themselves on the left–right scale went up from a low of 75% in 1987 to a high of 91% in 1999, although with a noticeable downward trend toward 83.10% in the two post-economic crisis elections in 2009 and 2013. It remains to be seen whether the low response rate in 2013 can be attributed mostly to the political upheaval following the economic collapse or whether this is a new trend that is here to stay.

The Left–Right Landscape over Time **41**

TABLE 2.1 Left–right self-placement from 1987–2013, 0 = left and 10 = right.

Year	N	% placement	% picking 5*	Mean	St.dev
1987	1745	78.20	28.5	5.40	2.40
1991	1491	75.00	27.8	5.37	2.36
1995	1721	79.70	30.8	5.51	2.13
1999	1631	91.00	31.0	5.56	2.32
2003	1446	90.00	28.5	5.41	2.20
2007	1595	87.30	26.2	5.50	2.13
2009	1385	84.80	28.1	5.15	2.10
2013	1484	83.10	21.8	5.41	2.10

*Out of people who placed themselves on the scale.

People's willingness to use the left–right scale could mask another way in which the scale has lost meaning. As was discussed above, several studies have maintained that the extremities of left and right belong to the past and that politics has met in the middle. If this is true, we would expect to see a change in the way Icelanders use the left–right scale. Specifically, the number of people placing themselves in the middle could be expected to have risen. If, on the other hand, the left–right dimension represents an enduring political cleavage, such clustering around the mean would not take place. The second issue addressed is therefore:

Question 1b: Has the number of participants selecting the middle option remained stable or increased over time?
Average left–right self-placement remained remarkably stable from 1987 until 2007, ranging from 5.37 to 5.56 on the eleven-point 0–10 scale. This indicates that on average, Icelanders consider themselves to be slightly right of center. In 2009, six months after the economic collapse, there was a noticeable shift to the left, as the mean dropped to 5.15. An independent-samples t-test comparing 2007 and 2009 confirms this to be a significant drop (t (2566) = 4.18, $p < 0.01$).

It is possible, however, that the left–right distinction has lost meaning in another sense. People may feel that the extremities of the left and right belong to the past, and that ideas and policies have reached a happy middle-ground position. In that case, although people can use the left–right scale, and will do so when asked by survey companies, we would expect a noticeably increased tendency to use the middle of the scale, or 5. As can be seen from Table 2.1, this is not the case, as the percentage of people choosing 5 has not increased over time—in fact, there is quite a dramatic drop in use of this middle point in 2013. In sum, there is little sign of the left–right dimension having lost its meaning to voters over time as evidenced by two observations: First, the percentage of respondents willing to place themselves on the scale has waxed and waned over time with no clear sign of a permanent downward trend. Second, the number of people opting for the middle of the scale (neither left nor right) has not increased over time, if anything

42 Hulda Thórisdóttir

a sharp decrease was seen following the political upheaval that began after the economic crisis in 2009.

Have Voters Become Truly Polarized?—Issue 2

The idea of political polarization has primarily been discussed in the United States, less so in Europe. In the US most seem to agree that polarization has taken place at the political elite level such as in Congress and in the media (Fiorina & Abrams, 2008). A lively discussion, however, has taken place among scholars on whether there truly has been a polarization among the general electorate. One reason for the liveliness of the polarization discussion is due to lack of conceptual clarity. Different scholars, and different areas of study, mean different things by "polarization."

Abramowitz and colleagues (Abramowitz & Saunders, 2005; Abramowitz & Saunders, 2008) have analyzed the National Election Studies over time and find evidence for an electorate becoming more consistently liberal or conservative on issues, and concluded that this tendency is more pronounced for people with a high level of knowledge and interest in politics. According to these authors, partisan polarization has also increased, as is evident from a rising correlation between left–right self-placement and identification with either the Democratic or Republican Party. In addition, geographical and religious polarization has also been on the rise, as seen by states in the United States becoming solidly either so-called red states or blue states, and by the strong alignment between religiosity and conservatism (Abramowitz & Saunders, 2008).

No research exists on whether polarization has been on the rise among the Icelandic public. The media paints a picture of the Parliament as increasingly divided: while in the good old days parliamentarians used to share both lunches and issue stances across parties, this is not so any more (Hjörvar, 2012; Pressan.is, 2012; Stephensen, 2012). In general, however, it is probably safe to say that there is no general impression that Icelanders have become more ideologically divided over the last 25 years or so. The issue will at first be examined by looking at the left–right dimension only:

Question 2a: Has the distribution of left–right placement increased over time, thus indicating increased real polarization on the left–right dimension within the Icelandic electorate?
In the light of the highly stable mean left–right placement over time discussed above, an increased standard deviation would reflect an increased spread in political opinions, and probably be indicative of polarization, whereas a reduction in standard deviation would reflect more clustering around the middle. Increased standard deviation is thus a necessary condition for polarization to have occurred on the left–right scale, but not a sufficient one. As can be seen in the last column of Table 2.1, the standard deviation has remained stable across time, ranging from 2.10 to 2.40. Thus, overall, there is no sign of real polarization in Icelanders' left–right self-placement. The consistency in the distribution becomes even more apparent when

graphed. Figure 2.1 shows bar graphs of the distribution for left–right self-placement for all eight surveys. As is immediately apparent, all distributions are highly similar, with perhaps the exception of 2013. Around 22–31% pick the number 5 and a very low percentage of respondents place themselves at the two most extreme categories on the left (zero on the scale) or right (ten on the scale).

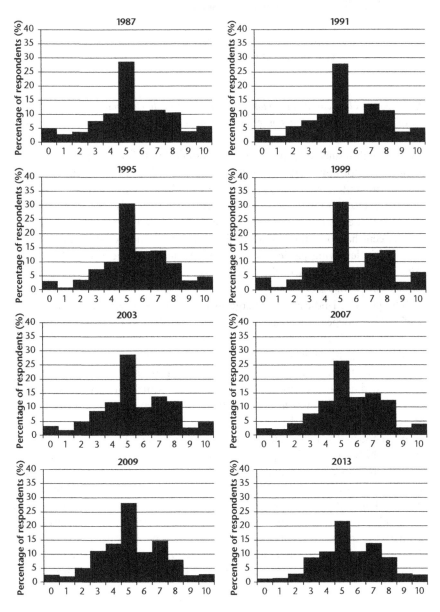

FIGURE 2.1 The distribution of left–right self-placement in Iceland from 1987–2013.

Fiorina and Abrams (2008) disagree with the conclusions of Abramowitz and Saunders, and point out the necessity of distinguishing between polarization and sorting. Polarization means a genuine increase in the distribution of opinions in which fewer people share a middle ground. Sorting, on the other hand, refers to subgroups within the larger distribution (based on partisanship, geography, religion, etc.) aligning themselves closer with ideological or partisan labels. Fiorina argues that research unequivocally points to sorting but that real polarization on political opinions has not been taking place among the American public (Fiorina & Abrams, 2008). This requires the following issue to be explored:

Question 2b: Has political sorting taken place in the Icelandic electorate, such that subgroups based on political party affiliation or demographic variables have aligned themselves more closely with either the left or the right over time?

Even though results so far do not indicate political polarization, it is possible that while voters for some parties are moving toward the left, others are moving more toward the center, etc. Figure 2.2 graphs left–right self-placement across time for voters for all main political parties. We see that the self-placement of voters for the Independence Party, the Progressive Party, the Women's Alliance, and the Left-Greens have remained quite stable across time. The two shifts in the graph are both in left-wing parties, the People's Alliance and the Social Democratic Alliance, shifting further to the right across time by little less than one point on this eleven-point scale.

The political landscape to emerge in Figure 2.2 is as expected (Kristinsson, 2007). The Independence Party is consistently furthest to the right, followed by the Progressive Party, then the Social Democratic Alliance (SDA), with the Left–Greens being the leftmost party. The rightward shift of the SDA could be explained by the most left-leaning voters for the party in 1999 and 2003 having moved to the Left–Greens in later years. At the same time, business oriented right-wing-leaning voters from the Independence Party may have moved to the SDA, mostly because of the latter party's pro–European Union stance.

At first glance it may seem surprising that, for example, in 2009 the overall average shifted leftward despite voters of no party having moved to the left. This can be explained by taking into account that the number of voters behind each party varies between surveys. In the year 2009, for example, the Independence Party was widely blamed for playing a crucial role in the economic collapse and therefore it took a dramatic hit in the elections, going from 36.6% to 23.7%. That year, the Left–Greens went from 14.3% to 21.7%. Thus, although the self-placement of voters who remain loyal to their party has not changed, those who leave may assimilate their views slightly to that of their new party.

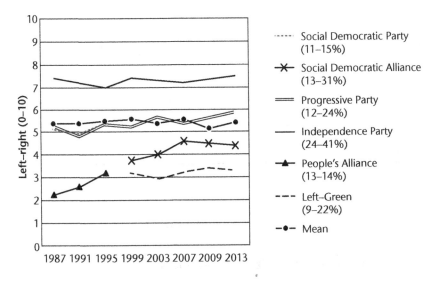

FIGURE 2.2 Left–right self-placement from 1987–2013 for voters for the main political parties. The numbers in parentheses indicate the range of percentage of votes each party has received in general elections from 1987–2013.

Another possible take on polarization is subgroup sorting on left–right self-placement by demographic variables. An increased correlation over time between left–right placement and a particular demographic variable would be a sign of such sorting. Sorting can be the result of parties to the left or right specifically targeting certain demographic groups in their policy position. An example would be a right-wing party emphasizing the importance of religious and traditional values, or a left-wing party emphasizing accessible childcare, maternity leave and other issues typically important to women. Table 2.2 graphs the bivariate correlation between left–right placement and gender, family income, education, and religiosity. Only gender and family income show a consistent significant correlation with left–right. Men are more likely to be further to the right than women, and higher family income is related to more right-leaning self-placement. There has not, however, been a noticeable change over time in the correlation coefficients for gender, income, or any of the other demographic variables.

In sum, there are no signs of either polarization or sorting among Icelandic voters as evidenced by two main observations. First, the distribution of left–right scores has remained virtually unchanged over time. Second, the relationship between political orientation and various demographic variables such as gender, income, and education has not become stronger over time.

46 Hulda Thórisdóttir

TABLE 2.2 Bivariate correlation (Pearson's r) between left–right self-placement and demographic variables.

	1987	1991	1995	1999	2003	2007	2009	2013
Gender	−0.06*	−0.15*	−0.01	−0.10**	−0.10**	−0.16**	−0.13**	−0.11**
Age	0.00	−0.04	−0.05*	−0.01	0.00	0.01	−0.02	0.01
Family income	0.11**	0.11**	0.06*	0.12**	0.08**	0.14**	0.08*	0.18*
Education	−0.07*	0.038	0.00	0.05*	0.01	0.02	0.04	−0.03
Religiosity					0.08**	0.15**	0.05	0.14**

* $p < 0.05$; ** $p < 0.01$.

Left–right self-placement (0 = left to 10 = right), Gender (1 = male, 2 = female), Age in years, Family income (five equal categories, lowest through highest), Education (seven categories, except in 1987 when there were six), religiosity (1 = not at all, 4 = very religious).

Do Voters Perceive Polarization?—Issue 3

Even if no real polarization has taken place among Icelandic voters, this does not rule out the existence of perceived polarization. Perceived polarization is when voters *perceive* parties or people to have been shifting further away from the middle, even if attitude measurements indicate no such shifts. The tendency to overestimate the extremity of a political opponent's views can be viewed in the context of the false polarization effect (Dimdins & Montgomery, 2003). A study by Robinson, Keltner, Ward and Ross (1995) showed that respondents who labelled themselves as either pro-life or pro-choice on abortion, in actuality ranked closer to each other on the issue than they themselves presumed. More generally, both partisans and non-partisans tend to overestimate the polarization of partisans' views. In addition, what exacerbates the false polarization effect is that people are prone to believe that their own ideas are more in the middle than others' ideas. The tendency is to attribute the attitudes and behaviors of others to the ideological stance of the group they belong to, but to see one's own behavior as driven more by independent thought and less by group ideas and conformity (Pronin, 2007). This was, for example, demonstrated by Graham, Nosek and Haidt (2012) who showed that not only did both liberals and conservatives exaggerate how much the other group would espouse certain stereotypical values (moral values), but they also estimated that their own group would be more extreme on stereotypical traits than it actually was. As a result, even if voters for all parties have remained more or less stable in their ideological placement on the left–right scale across time, people may perceive polarization to have taken place. Thus, the third issue explored:

Question 3: Do we see perceived polarization among the Icelandic public in the sense that, even if no real polarization has taken place, people perceive other parties as having moved more toward the extremes over time?

In addition to rating their own left–right standing on a scale from 0–10, participants in the ICENES survey also placed all parties that had representatives elected to the parliament that year on that same scale. The number of parties ranged from about five to eight. In my analyses I only include parties that fielded candidates in at least three consecutive elections.

Figures 2.3 to 2.6 show the results for the five most prominent parties from 1987 until 2013. Again, we do not see big or consistent changes in the way the parties are perceived by their own voters or by the voters for other parties. All voters perceive the Independence Party as having moved to the left by just over half a point over time, which would be the opposite of perceived polarization. As a matter of fact, there seems to be remarkable consistency between voters for all parties in how they perceive the political stance of both their own and other parties.

A classic sign of polarization is, however, evident in this analysis—although this too has not changed over time. Voters for all parties see the Independence Party as standing further to the right than the self-placement of its own voters indicates (Figure 2.6), but this is especially true among voters of left-wing parties. That is, those voters are especially likely to place the Independence Party far to the right. This type of perceived polarization was expected to hold true for the leftmost party as well, the People's Alliance and later the Left–Greens. As can be seen from Figure 2.3, this does not seem to be the case, as voters for the Independence Party and the People's Alliance/Left–Greens show a remarkable level of alignment in their assessment. For the left- and rightmost parties, we also see a telltale sign of perceiving oneself as more reasonable and rational than most other people (Pronin, 2007). Voters for the People's Alliance/Left–Green Party, see themselves on average about one point closer to the middle than they perceive the party stance (Figure 2.3). The flipside picture emerges for the Independence Party, for which the average self-placement of its voters has hovered at just under 7.5, while at the same time they viewed their party as being considerably further to the right, at about 8 to 8.5, although the discrepancy seems to be diminishing over time (Figure 2.6). As expected, as can be seen in Figures 2.4 and 2.5, the two parties closer to the middle, the SDA and the Progressive Party, both show a very close alignment between voters' self-perception and their perception of their own parties. All lines form one cluster that the eye cannot detect as being different from each other in any noticeable way.

Of course, in reality, there does not have to be a close alignment between the average voter's self-placement on the left–right scale and his or her placement of the party's true policies or its political leaders, but such a misalignment should be viewed with concern by party leaders. It indicates either an image problem, a miscommunication of its political stance, or a true misalignment between the

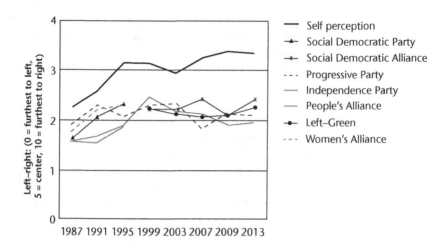

FIGURE 2.3 Perceptions of the People's Alliance/Left–Greens on the left–right scale by voters of each of the other parties. The solid black line graphs self-placement of People's Alliance/Left–Green voters. The graph shows that voters of the People's Alliance/Left–Greens place themselves closer to the middle than voters of any other party perceive them.

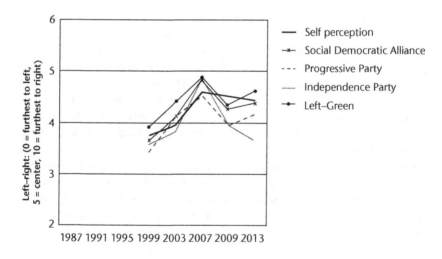

FIGURE 2.4 Perceptions of the SDA on the left–right scale by voters of each of the other parties. The solid black line graphs self-placement of SDA voters.

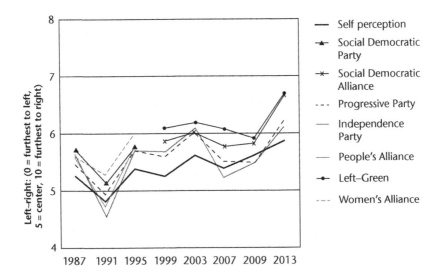

FIGURE 2.5 Perceptions of the Progressive Party on the left–right scale by voters of each of the other parties. The solid black line graphs self-placement of Progressive Party voters.

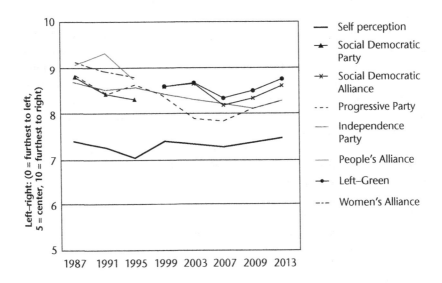

FIGURE 2.6 Perceptions of the Independence Party on the left–right scale by voters of each of the other parties. The solid black line graphs self-placement of Independence Party voters.

way it pursues politics and where its voters stand. To sum up what the data tells us about perceived party polarization among Icelandic voters over time, the story is yet again one of stability. There is no indication of voters increasingly viewing other parties than their own becoming more extreme on the left–right scale over time. There are, however, classic signs of falsely perceived polarization in the data as voters have a tendency to view the parties furthest to the left and right as being considerably more extreme than the voters of those parties see themselves.

Is There Polarization on Issue Positions?—Issue 4

Mason (2013) claims the debate on polarization is muddled by lack of conceptual clarity. She stresses the importance of distinguishing between *issue position polarization*, as evidenced by increasingly extreme opinions on political issues, and *behavioral polarization*, as evidenced by increased party allegiance and emotional attachment to political labels, without the underlying issue position polarization. This echoes the argument made by Converse and others that members of the political elite created ideological packages they then handed down to the public, who accepted them without fully, or even partially, understanding the content of the ideological package they had adopted as their own (Converse, 1964; Feldman, 1988, 2003; Fiorina, Abrams & Pope, 2005; Kinder, 1998).

The two final questions to be addressed in this study examine the stability of attitudes on particular political issues across time, and how they relate to the left–right dimension. Although this inquiry is somewhat limited by the low number of questions consistently asked since 1987, it will allow for some insight into the stability of political attitudes across time. Specifically, on six of the seven issues of taxes, environmental protection, NATO membership, prosperity of urban vs. rural areas, restrictions on agricultural imports, an EU application, and gender equality,[2] I will explore whether attitudes have moved or remained stable over time. That is, has the entire electorate perhaps shifted its position on the political issues and has what people perceive as left, right, and center on the scale changed accordingly? If we see consistent left- or right-wing shifts in attitudes toward political issues without the corresponding changes in people's self-placement on the overall left–right dimension, this will lend support to the idea that there is a disconnect between the meaning of left–right and real issue positions. Finally, an examination of attitudes toward these six political issues across time will provide for another opportunity to test for polarization, i.e., whether the correlation between left–right placement and these attitudes has grown stronger over time. The final two issues are:

Question 4a: Have attitudes toward taxes, environmental protection, NATO membership, prosperity of urban vs. rural areas, restrictions on agricultural imports, an EU application, and gender equality remained stable over time, or has there been a shift either to the left or the right?

Question 4b: Has the correlation between left–right self-placement and these political issues grown stronger over time, thus indicating polarization among the Icelandic electorate?

An analysis of the six questions on political attitudes asked most consistently across all eight studies can be seen in Figures 2.7a–f. As is noticeable from examining the black bars portraying the means for all six issues, only one shows a consistent change in overall attitudes over time. This is the question on whether progress in the capital area should be decreased in order to increase prosperity in the rural regions. Over time, respondents have become somewhat less likely to answer this question in the affirmative, at least partially due to the steady migration of people from the countryside to the capital area during this time. In 1980 about 53% of the population lived in the capital region but in 2013 that ratio was around 65% (Statistics Iceland, n.d.b). All other items show occasional fluctuations between surveys, but no trend is discernible.

An examination of the correlation between each issue and the left–right scale over time shows whether that issue seems be contributing more or less to ideological self-placement as the years go by. If the correlation between political issues and left–right placement is on the rise, it signifies a potential polarizing issue. The correlations are plotted as a line on the secondary axis in Figures 2.7a–f. We see that, as a rule, attitudes toward the environment have the strongest relationship with the left–right scale, hovering around r = 0.20. Other issues have either a lower or an inconsistent correlation. More importantly, we do not see—for any of the six items—that the relationship with left–right placement has been growing stronger over time. On the contrary, for attitudes toward EU membership and restrictions on agricultural imports, the relationship has been *weakening*. Again, it is not the scope of this chapter to examine which political issues play the biggest role in determining people's left–right self-placement. Each survey contained many more attitude items that tap into the political climate at the time than are used here. The six items used in this analysis were not chosen because they were believed to play the biggest role in determining left–right stance, but because they were the items most consistently asked throughout all seven surveys. Although the items cover a fairly broad spectrum of attitudes, they may or may not include items that most sharply divide the electorate into left and right at any given time. Finally, it has to be made clear that none of the attitude questions used in this study tap into real policy views; they do not ask, for example, *how much* income tax people think is appropriate, or *which particular measures* aimed at obtaining gender equality they favor or oppose. This analysis cannot, therefore, determine whether people's perception of what constitutes high or low taxes has changed toward the left, right, or center. What we do know is that these issues have not contributed to a changed political landscape and thus we see no indication in the data of increased issue polarization over time.

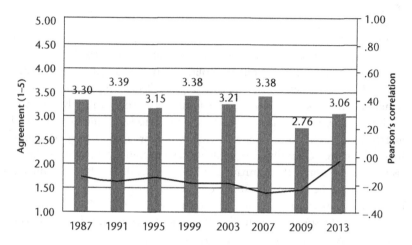

FIGURE 2.7a Environmental issues should be prioritized over economic growth.

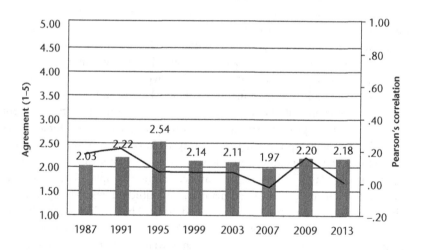

FIGURE 2.7b Taxes should be reduced.

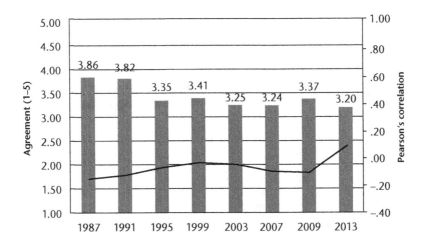

FIGURE 2.7c Decrease progress in capital area to increase prosperity in rural areas.

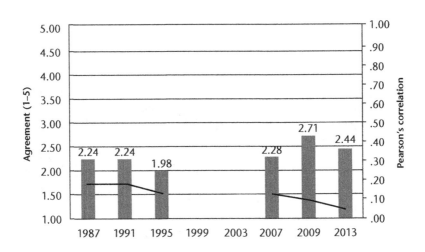

FIGURE 2.7d Attempts to ensure gender equality have gone too far.

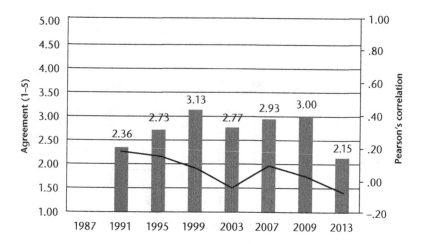

FIGURE 2.7e EU application is desirable.

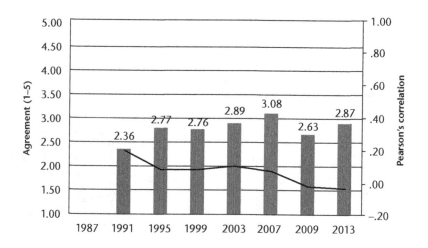

FIGURE 2.7f Ease restrictions on agricultural imports.

FIGURES 2.7a–f Attitudes toward six political issues across time. The grey bars show averages, the black line Pearson's correlation with left–right self-placement.

Conclusion

In this chapter I have examined the left–right political dimension in a stable, Western democratic state with a multi-party system during the years 1987 to 2013. The overarching picture to emerge is one of a stable, well-defined, left–right political landscape in the minds of Icelandic voters. There is no sign of the left–right dimension having lost its meaning over time as 75% to 91% of respondents each year are willing to place their own standing on the left–right dimension. The overall self-placement has been just right of center, or about 5.5 on a scale from 0 to 10.

Although Icelandic voters seem to understand and find the left–right scale meaningful, the electorate does not come across as very polarized. About 28% of respondents place themselves at the middle, with a steady tail-off to the left and right. Very few respondents place themselves in the two outermost categories on the left or right. Polarization or sorting is not rampant between social groups or political parties as correlations between left–right self-placement and several demographic variables is low to non-existent. Polarization was, in any case, not on the rise among Icelandic voters from 1987 to 2013. This is evident from two facts. First, the standard deviation of the distribution for left–right self-placement remained almost unchanged during the period. Second, self-placement of voters for all parties remained mostly unchanged over time, with only a slight right-leaning shift by the voters for two left-wing parties. False polarization was not widespread either, because there was a close alignment between how voters for a particular party perceived its left–right stance and how voters for other parties perceived it. This was true for all parties, left, right and center. Voters for the parties furthest left and right placed their political orientation closer to the middle than they placed their party, a sign of the human tendency to consider oneself more moderate and reasonable in opinion compared to others (Pronin, 2007).

Lastly, I examined whether systematic or obvious changes in six political attitudes could be found during the period. Results showed that while only attitudes toward cities vs. the countryside have been gradually moving in the same direction during the last 26 years, for most of the other attitudes there has not been a systematic change (although there may be spikes or dips in some years). A low to non-existent correlation between left–right placement and those political attitudes shows that issue polarization has not been on the rise as it pertains to the left–right dimension and these attitudes.

Just like any other stable Western democracy, Iceland has changed in many ways since 1987 due to both internal and international factors. The country has had its share of sharp economic downturns and exuberant upswings. It opened up an economy that was dominated by state-run enterprises and joined the European Economic Area in the early 1990s, thereby committing itself to free flow of capital and goods within the region. Despite these changes, the way people use the left–right scale has remained remarkably stable over time. This probably demonstrates both the stability and the flexibility of the left–right dimension (Jost, Glaser, Kruglanski, & Sulloway, 2003a, 2003b). It is flexible enough to incorporate new political issues that come to the forefront and thus remain relevant over time. At the same time it is stable in the sense that what was perceived as a left-wing party or a right-wing issue 25 years ago is still viewed the same way today.

Notes

1 INES is one of several international collaborations on national elections studies, including the Nordic Electoral Democracy, Comparative Studies of Electoral Systems, and True European Voter.
2 1) "Do you agree or disagree that progress in the capital area should be decreased in order to increase prosperity in the rural regions?"; 2) "Do you agree or disagree that taxes should be reduced, even though this would mean that public services would have to be cut, e.g., in health care, education, or social security—or are you indifferent on this question?"; 3) "Do you agree or disagree that restrictions on agricultural imports should be substantially relaxed—or are you indifferent on this question?" (This question was omitted in the 1987, 1991, and 1995 questionnaires.); 4) "Do you agree or disagree that in the next years action on environmental issues should be prioritized over attempts to increase economic growth?" (1 = strongly agree, 2 = tend to agree, 3 = no strong feeling either way, 4 = tend to disagree, 5 = strongly disagree.); 5) "Do you think that it is desirable or undesirable, that Iceland apply for membership of the European Union?" (1 = very desirable, 2 = rather desirable, 3 = neutral/not sure, 4 = rather undesirable, 5 = very undesirable. This question was omitted in the 1987 and 1991 questionnaires.); 6) "Regarding attempts to secure women equality with men, do you think things have gone too far, about right or not far enough?" (1 = gone much too far, 2 = gone a bit too far, 3 = about right, 4 = need to go a bit further, 5 = need to go much further. This question was omitted in the 1999 and 2003 questionnaires.).

References

Abramowitz, A. I. & Saunders, K. L. (2005). Why can't we all just get along? The reality of a polarized America. *The Forum, 3*, 1–22.

Abramowitz, A. I. & Saunders, K. L. (2008). Is polarization a myth? *Journal of Politics, 70*, 542–555.

Adams, I. (2001). *Political Ideology Today.* Manchester, UK: Manchester University Press.

Bell, D. (1960). *The End of Ideology.* Glencoe, IL: Free Press.

Bengtsson, Å., Hansen, K., Hardarson, Ó. P., Narud, H. M., & Oscarsson, H. (2013). *The Nordic Voter: Myths of Exceptionalism.* Colchester, UK: ECPR Press.

Brittan, S. (2012, April 12). The bogus distinction between left and right. *The Financial Times.* Retrieved November 20, 2012 from http://on.ft.com/HEWwek

Conover, P. J. & Feldman, S. (1981). The origin and meaning of liberal/conservative self identification. *American Journal of Political Science, 25*, 617–645.

Converse, P. E. (1964). The nature of belief systems in mass publics. In D. E. Apter (Ed.), *Ideology and DISCONTENT* (pp. 206–261). New York: Free Press.

Dimdins, G. & Montgomery, H. (2003). The false polarization effect in explanations of attitudinal behavior. *Current Research in Social Psychology, 8,* 275–302.

Feldman, S. (1988). Structure and consistency in public opinion: The role of core beliefs and values. *American Journal of Political Science, 32,* 416–440.

Feldman, S. (2003). Values, ideology, and the structure of political attitudes. In D. O. Sears, L. Huddy, & R. Jervis (Eds.), *The Oxford Handbook of Political Psychology* (pp. 477–508). New York: Oxford University Press.

Fiorina, M. P., & Abrams, S. J. (2008). Political polarization in the American public. *Annual Review of Political Science,* 11, 563–588.

Fiorina, M. P., Abrams, S. J., & Pope, J. (2005). *Culture War?.* New York: Pearson Education.

Fuchs, D. & Klingemann H. D. (1990). The left–right schema. In M. K. Jennings, J. W. van Deth (Eds.), *Continuities in Political Action: A Longitudinal Study of Political Orientations in Three Western Democracies.* Berlin: Walter de Gruyter.

Giddens, A. (1994). *Beyond Left and Right: The Future of Radical Politics.* Cambridge, UK: Polity Press.

Graham, J., Nosek, B. A., & Haidt, J. (2012). The moral stereotypes of liberals and conservatives: Exaggeration of differences across the political spectrum. *PloS one,* 7(12), e50092.

Grendstad, G. (2003). Reconsidering Nordic Party Space. *Scandinavian Political Studies, 26*(3), 193–217.

Hardarson, O. T. (e.d.). The Icelandic National Election Studies. Social Sciences Research Institute, University of Iceland.

Hjörvar, Helgi (2012, April 24). *Kastljós* [News program]. Reykjavik, Iceland: RUV (The Icelandic National Broadcasting Service).

Jennings, M. K. (1992). Ideological thinking among mass publics and political elites. *Public Opinion Quarterly, 56*(4), 419–441.

Jost, J. T. (2006). The end of the end of ideology. *American Psychologist, 61*(7), 651–670.

Jost, J. T., Glaser, J., Kruglanski, A. W., & Sulloway, F. (2003a). Political conservatism as motivated social cognition. *Psychological Bulletin, 129,* 339–375.

Jost, J. T., Glaser, J., Kruglanski, A. W., & Sulloway, F. (2003b). Exceptions that prove the rule: Using a theory of motivated social cognition to account for ideological incongruities and political anomalies. *Psychological Bulletin, 129,* 383–393.

Kerlinger, F. N. (1984). *Liberalism and Conservatism: The Nature and Structure of Social Attitudes.* Hillsdale, NJ: Erlbaum.

Kinder, D. R. (1998). Opinion and action in the realm of politics. In D. T. Gilbert, S. T. Fiske, G. Lindzey (Eds.), *The Handbook of Social Psychology, 2*: 778–867. Boston: McGraw-Hill.

Kirk, R. (1982). *The Conservative Reader.* Middlesex, UK: Penguin Books.

Knight, K. (1999). Liberalism and conservatism. In J. P. Robinson, P. R. Shaver, and L. S. Wrightsman (Eds.), *Measures of Political Attitudes* (pp. 59–158). San Diego, CA: Academic Press.

Kristinsson, G. H. (2007). *Íslenska stjórnkerfið.* Reykjavik: Háskólaútgáfan.

Lipset, S. (1960). *Political Man.* Garden City, NY: Doubleday.

Lipset, S. M. (1981). *Political Man* (expanded edition). Baltimore: Johns Hopkins University Press.

58 Hulda Thórisdóttir

McCarty, N., Poole, K. T., & Rosenthal, H. (2007). *Polarized America: The Dance of Ideology and Unequal Riches.* Cambridge, MA: MIT Press Books.

Mason, L. (2013). The rise of uncivil agreement: Issue versus behavioral polarization in the American electorate. *American Behavioral Scientist, 57*(1), 140–159.

Muller, J. Z. (2001). Conservatism: Historical aspects. In N. J. Smelser & P. B. Baltes (Eds.), *International Encyclopedia of the Social and Behavioral Sciences* (pp. 2624–2628). Amsterdam: Elsevier.

Müller, W. C. (1997). Inside the black box: A confrontation of party executive behaviour and theories of party organizational change. *Party Politics, 3*(3), 293–313.

Noël, A., & Thérien, J. P. (2008). *Left and Right in Global Politics.* Cambridge, UK: Cambridge University Press.

Pressan.is (2012, February 24). Fyrrverandi þingmaður áhyggjufullur: Liggur við slagsmálum í matsal Alþingis. Retrieved November 20, 2012 from http://www.pressan.is/m/Article.aspx?catID=7&ArtId=14062

Pronin, E. (2007). Perception and misperception of bias in human judgment. *Trends in Cognitive Sciences, 11*, 37–43.

Robinson, R., Keltner, D., Ward, A. & Ross, L. (1995). Actual versus assumed differences in construal: "Naïve realism" in intergroup perception and conflict. *Journal of Personality and Social Psychology, 68*, 404–417.

Statistics Iceland/Hagstofa Íslands (n.d.a). Results of general elections to the Althingi 1963–2009. Retrieved November 20, 2012 from http://www.statice.is/Statistics/Elections/General-elections

Statistics Iceland/Hagstofa Íslands (n.d.b). Population. Retrieved February 18, 2015 from http://www.statice.is/Statistics/Population

Stephensen, Ólafur (2012, April 26). Af stjórnmálamenningarástandi. *Fréttablaðið.* Retrieved November 20, 2012 from http://visir.is/af-stjornmalamenningarastandi/article/2012704269893

Wilson, G. D. (Ed.) (1973). *The Psychology of Conservatism.* London: Academic Press.

SECTION II

Psychological Mechanisms of Ideological Divides

3

IDEOLOGICAL DIFFERENCES IN THE EXPANSE OF EMPATHY

Adam Waytz, Ravi Iyer, Liane Young, and Jesse Graham

The American political landscape of the 21st century has largely been characterized by culture wars between liberals and conservatives. On policy issues as diverse as economic regulation, defense spending, abortion, marriage equality, and health care, ideological differences have become increasingly pronounced, as reflected in political legislation, public opinion, and news coverage. The 112th Congress, which governed from January 2011 through January 2013, is on record as the most ideologically polarized Congress ever (Carroll, Lewis, Lo, McCarty, Poole, & Rosenthal, 2013). Eight of the most ideologically divided years (as measured by presidential approval rating gaps between Democrats and Republicans) have occurred since 2004, making George W. Bush and Barack Obama the most polarizing presidents ever (Jones, 2013). This polarization is also evident in the political press that documents and spurs on this phenomenon, with media bias and media partisanship also approaching record levels (Groeling, 2013). One clear meme that exacerbates these divisions is the perceived "Empathy Gap," whereby liberals are seen as more caring (Davis, Smith, & Marsden, 2007; Iyer, Koleva, Graham, Ditto, & Haidt, 2012; Krauthammer, 2012; McCue & Gopoian, 2001), even as conservatives are equally generous with their time and money (Brooks, 2007).

As disagreement between left-wing individuals and right-wing individuals has grown, so too has psychological research attempting to document and explain this disagreement. A cursory search for the term "political psychology" in Google Scholar reveals 9,370 entries from 1900–2000, a figure that has more than doubled in just the first 14 years of the 21st century. Much of recent political psychology has indeed focused on explaining ideological differences in terms of cognition, perception, motivation, behavior, and psychological ability (see Jost, Federico, & Napier, 2009, and Stone et al., in press, for reviews). In line with this

62 Adam Waytz et al.

tradition of research, we suggest in this chapter that empathy, "other-oriented emotion elicited by and congruent with the perceived welfare of someone in need" (Batson, 2011, p. 11), is a primary factor that distinguishes liberals and conservatives. In a recent study of people's moral stereotypes about liberals and conservatives (comparing perceived to actual moral stances across a wide range of moral concerns), it was found that "the largest inaccuracies were in liberals' underestimations of conservatives' harm and fairness concerns, and liberals further exaggerated the political differences by overestimating their own such concerns" (Graham, Nosek, & Haidt, 2012, p. e50092). Although participants across the political spectrum (especially liberals) tended to stereotype conservatives as being relatively lacking in empathy with some evidence (described below) supporting this perception, we propose that liberals and conservatives do not differ in their capacity for empathy or willingness to empathize with others. Rather, the present research suggests that liberals and conservatives differ in terms of the *targets* toward whom they expend their empathy, with liberals expressing empathy to a greater degree toward larger social circles and conservatives expressing empathy toward smaller circles.

We begin by describing what is known about the relationship between ideology and empathy. We then summarize existing research on other psychological differences between liberals and conservatives that provide support for our existing hypotheses. Next, we describe preliminary studies testing these hypotheses, and provide suggestions for how our studies can inform work on political conflict.

Empathy and Ideology

Popular media representations of liberals and conservatives tend to depict liberals (and, by proxy, Democrats) as the far more empathic group of people. The term "bleeding heart liberal" commonly refers to individuals with liberal political leanings, and signifies the belief that liberals tend to sympathize excessively with the plight of the poor, the underprivileged, and others in need. Former Democratic president Bill Clinton epitomized this stereotype when he famously uttered, "I feel your pain" in 1992 (in fact Clinton made this remark angrily in the midst of a heated debate about the AIDS crisis). In 2006, the Democratic presidential candidate Barack Obama bemoaned the nation's "empathy deficit" in a commencement speech at Northwestern University.

Beyond anecdotal evidence, some empirical evidence also suggests that liberals are more empathic than conservatives. One piece of evidence for this comes from the General Social Survey (GSS; see Davis, Smith, & Marsden, 2007), a large-scale nationally representative survey of U.S. households collected by the National Opinion Research Center. From 2002 to 2004, the GSS administered a seven-item empathy scale that measured general empathy toward others (Davis, 1994; e.g., "I would describe myself as a pretty soft-hearted person") in conjunction

Ideological Differences in the Expanse of Empathy **63**

with numerous questions about support for various policies. Scores on this measure were positively related with support for policies that are typically supported by political liberals, including increased government spending for health care, Blacks, children, social security, welfare, and the poor; increased government efforts to help the poor, the sick, the elderly, and Blacks; increased efforts toward reducing wealth income inequality; and increased government action in general. These results suggest that individuals who endorse politically liberal policies are also those who report experiencing more empathy. Other empirical research that has employed measures of general empathy and measures of political ideology also shows that liberalism is correlated with self-reported empathy (Iyer et al., 2012; McCue & Gopoian, 2001).

Empirical research has also examined the association between empathic concern and social dominance orientation (SDO), an individual difference variable that reflects the endorsement of social hierarchy and that is also typically associated with political conservatism (Pratto, Sidanius, Stallworth, & Malle, 1994; Sidanius & Pratto, 2001). Numerous studies have confirmed that self-reported empathy and SDO are negatively associated with each other (Bäckström & Björklund, 2007; McFarland, 2010; Sidanius et al., 2013) and some research suggests that SDO is negatively associated with brain activity in regions associated with empathy (Cheon, Im, Harada, Kim, Mathur, Scimeca et al., 2011). Thus, the preference for social hierarchy, a key component of conservative ideology, has clearly been linked to lower empathy in general.

One additional domain of research that provides evidence for a relationship between empathy and political ideology is research employing life narrative interviews. In a study of liberal and conservative Christians (McAdams et al., 2008), participants were interviewed about major life events and their interviews were coded for various psychological themes. The life narratives of political conservatives tended to center on authority figures, moral rules, and self-discipline, whereas the life narratives of political liberals tended to center on nurturance, openness, and empathy. Liberals were more likely than conservatives to display the ability to sympathize with another individual's emotional state. Similarly, research on adolescents who describe themselves as liberal or conservative shows that liberals tend to describe themselves in more sympathetic terms (Eisenberg-Berg & Mussen, 1978). Consistent with work on self-reported empathy, this type of research suggests that liberals possess greater general empathy than conservatives.

Although the research on political ideology and empathy suggests differences in absolute empathy between liberals and conservatives, this research is not fully conclusive, as the vast majority of studies appear to assess empathy at a general level rather than empathy toward specific targets. We suggest the possibility that rather than liberals and conservatives differing in terms of the degree of empathy they possess, they instead differ in terms of the targets of that empathy. We next review existing evidence from a variety of research programs suggesting that

64 Adam Waytz et al.

liberals and conservatives expend their empathy toward more global and local targets, respectively. That is, liberals tend to empathize with larger, farther, less structured, and more encompassing social circles whereas conservatives tend to empathize with smaller, closer, more well-defined, and less encompassing social circles.

Cognitive–Motivational Styles

A broad program of research has suggested that differences in political stances between liberals and conservatives may stem from differences in more basic cognitive–motivational styles. A landmark article by Jost, Glaser, Kruglanski, and Sulloway (2003) reviewed evidence suggesting that conservatives exhibit a higher need for closure, order, and structure, a greater intolerance for ambiguity, and lower integrative complexity than liberals. This meta-analysis revealed that political conservatism might reflect stable individual differences in the tendency to seek safety, structure, and stability; to view ambiguity or changes to the status quo as threatening; and to exhibit closed-mindedness toward novelty. Political liberalism, on the other hand, thus reflected a greater comfort with lack of structure, greater openness to new experiences, and a stronger tendency to seek out novel situations.

These different cognitive–motivational profiles translate into different ways of viewing the social world as well. For example, high levels of intolerance to change, novelty, and instability contribute to group-centrism, a pattern behavior that manifests in high levels of adherence to group norms, ingroup preference, rejection of individuals who deviate from the group, and resistance to change within the group (Kruglanski, Pierro, Mannetti, & De Grada, 2006). Thus, based on these cognitive–motivational differences among liberals and conservatives, we would predict that the expression of empathy would follow a similar pattern. Conservatives, in their tendencies toward closure, order, and stability should expend empathy toward smaller, more well-defined, and less permeable social circles. Liberals, in their tendencies toward openness, tolerance for ambiguity, and desire for change should seek larger, less well-defined, and more permeable social circles.

Personality Traits

Research on the dominant personality traits of liberals and conservatives reveals a very similar pattern to the work on cognitive and motivational styles. A series of studies has revealed consistent findings on how "Big Five" personality traits map on to ideological positions, showing that liberals score higher on openness whereas conservatives score higher on conscientiousness (Carney, Jost, Gosling, & Potter, 2008; Goldberg & Rosolack, 1994; Jost, 2006; Rentfrow, Jost, Gosling, & Potter, 2009). Again, these findings suggest a greater willingness among liberals to extend empathy outward whereas the vigilance associated with conservatism suggests a greater tendency to extend empathy only toward one's inner social circle. More recent work has examined agreeableness among liberals and conservatives, showing that both liberals and conservatives exhibit this trait, but in different ways (Hirsh, DeYoung, Xu, & Peterson, 2010). Compassion, as one component of agreeableness, was more associated with liberalism, whereas politeness, as a separate component of agreeableness, was more associated with conservatism. This pattern of results suggests a similar dichotomy in suggesting that conservatives are more concerned with maintaining the social order through traditional rules and norms whereas liberals seem interested in compassion more broadly.

Motivational Orientations

Additional work suggesting ideological differences in the expanse of empathy concerns motivational orientations, specifically distinguishing between approach and avoidance motivation and between promotion and prevention focus. Regulatory focus theory (Higgins, 1997, 1998, 2000) suggests that people engage in self-regulatory maintenance through satisfying nurturance needs (the attainment of aspirations) or through safety needs (the attainment of security), and people differ in how much they focused on these two classes of needs. Focusing on satisfying nurturance needs constitutes a promotion focus, whereas focusing on satisfying security needs constitutes a prevention focus. People can be chronically high in prevention focus only, promotion focus only, or be high or low in both. Studies that have examined the association between ideology and regulatory focus have established consistent patterns between these constructs in that conservatism tends to be linked to a prevention focus, whereas liberalism tends to be linked to a promotion focus.

One set of studies demonstrated that individuals who either scored higher on prevention focus or who were experimentally induced to experience a prevention focus made more conservative choices about economic reform (Boldero & Higgins, 2011). Additional work has shown that a chronic or temporarily induced prevention focus is associated with an increased endorsement of moral values (e.g., loyalty, authority) typically associated with conservative ideology, whereas promotion focus is associated with an increased endorsement of moral values (e.g., harm, fairness) typically associated with liberal ideology (Cornwell & Higgins, 2013, 2014).

Related to this work, a recent model of morality has emerged that characterizes moral concerns across the political divide by similarly focusing on distinct motivational orientations. This model, the moral motives model (Janoff-Bulman & Carnes, 2013; see also Carnes & Janoff-Bulman, Chapter 6, this volume), suggests that orientations toward approach and avoidance (or inhibition; Carver, 2006), akin to promotion and prevention focus, produce different moral concerns toward the self, others, and groups. According to this model, the approach orientation produces moral concerns for industriousness, helping and fairness, and social justice and communal responsibility whereas the avoidance orientation produces moral concerns for self-restraint and moderation, refraining from harming others, and social order and communal solidarity. The moral concerns associated with approach orientation are more central to liberal ideology, whereas the moral concerns associated with avoidance orientation are more central to conservative ideology, consistent with previous work which has suggested that liberalism is based in approach motivation whereas conservatism is based in avoidance orientation (Janoff-Bulman, 2009; Janoff-Bulman, Sheikh, & Baldacci, 2008).

The sum of these studies on motivation suggests that conservatism is associated with motivational orientations toward preserving safety, security, and the status quo. Liberalism, on the other hand, is associated with motivational orientations toward seeking rewards and positive outcomes. When applied to empathic concern toward others, a pattern again emerges whereby conservatives tend to emphasize the importance of maintaining the security associated with group solidarity and loyalty whereas liberals focus on applying principles of justice more broadly. This pattern is again consistent with the idea that conservatives and liberals tend to prioritize smaller versus larger social circles, respectively.

Moral Foundations

Another prominent theory of morality as applied to political ideology is Moral Foundations Theory (Graham et al., 2013; Haidt, 2007; Haidt & Joseph, 2004; Haidt & Graham, 2007), which characterizes liberals and conservatives as diverging along two classes of intuitive moral values: individualizing values and binding values. Individualizing values primarily focus on individual people, specifically concerns about the rights of individuals to be treated fairly (fairness/ cheating) and protected from harm (care/harm). Binding values primarily focus on groups and institutions, and include concerns about support for one's ingroup (loyalty/betrayal), concerns about respect for authority and tradition (authority/ subversion), and concerns for acting in a sacred and pure manner (purity/ degradation). Extensive research now demonstrates that although both liberals and conservatives endorse these values, liberals prioritize individualizing values over binding values to a greater extent than do conservatives (Graham, Haidt, & Nosek, 2009; Graham et al., 2011). Across this research, liberals express more endorsement of statements that reflect concerns about harm and fairness (e.g., "It can never be right to kill a human being"), are less willing to compromise these values for money, and use rhetoric that reflects these values. Conservatives, on the other hand, show greater endorsement (relative to liberals) of statements that concern loyalty, authority, and purity (e.g., "It is more important to be a team player than to express oneself"), are less willing to compromise these values for money, and use rhetoric that reflects these binding values (Graham et al., 2009;

Graham et al., 2011). In line with the other research on ideology we have described, the work on moral foundations suggests that conservatives are more concerned with maintaining the structure, closeness, and order of their social ingroups, whereas liberals are concerned with the well-being of individuals more broadly.

Summary of Existing Research

Across numerous lines of research, the cognitive–motivational styles, personality traits, motivational orientations, and moral foundations of liberals and conservatives reveal a consistent pattern in how liberals and conservatives generally express empathy. Liberals tend to express their empathy outward, toward broader circles of individuals whereas conservatives tend to express their empathy inward, toward smaller and more well-defined social circles. Interestingly, this pattern appears even in programs of research that have traditionally been at odds with each other—Jost and colleagues' (2003) conceptualization of political conservatism, for example, has conflicted with conceptualizations from Moral Foundations Theory (Jost, 2012), yet both models provide a view of conservatives as more oriented toward smaller, defined groups with defined structures. Both of these models also suggest that liberals are more concerned with openness to a greater diversity of social practices and less concerned with strict group boundaries.

Empirical Investigation of Ideological Differences in the Expanse of Empathy

Despite the consistent pattern that appears to emerge across many lines of research, no research to our knowledge has explicitly tested the idea that liberals and conservatives expend empathy toward larger versus smaller social circles, respectively. Furthermore, no research has tested the counterpoint to the prevailing conventional wisdom that liberals possess and express *more* empathy than conservatives. We conducted a series of studies to test these hypotheses (Waytz, Iyer, Young, & Graham, in prep.). Across these studies, we asked people to indicate their political ideology and to answer questions measuring empathy and related constructs (such as moral concern, compassion, love, and identification) toward relatively smaller or larger social circles: family versus friends, the nation versus the world, and humans versus nonhumans (e.g., plants and animals). Across these studies, we found that conservatives tend to express their empathy toward family (versus friends), the nation (versus the world), and humans (versus nonhumans), whereas liberals showed the opposite pattern, preferring the larger groups.

As an initial test of whether liberals and conservatives differ in their distribution of empathy to larger versus smaller social circles, we experimentally tested whether people with different self-reported ideologies would report being empathic toward their friends versus their family members. In all studies,

68 Adam Waytz et al.

participants completed items online and indicated their political ideology on a seven-point scale from *very liberal* to *very conservative* (with additional options for libertarian, do not know/not political, and other, which we excluded). In this study, participants also completed the Interpersonal Reactivity Index (IRI; Davis, 1980), a measure that contains a subscale of empathic concern. Critically, we modified this empathic concern subscale to create three conditions to which participants were randomly assigned. In the baseline condition, participants completed the IRI in its normal format. In the *friends-oriented* condition, the questions that pertained to the empathic concern subscale were altered to be directed toward one's friends (e.g., "I often have tender, concerned feelings for people who are less fortunate than me" was changed to "I often have tender, concerned feelings for my friends who are less fortunate than me"). In the *family-oriented* condition, the questions in the empathic concern subscale were altered to be directed toward one's family, in a similar manner.

Consistent with prior studies, in the control condition, liberals reported more empathic concern than conservatives. Similarly, when the moral circle was expanded to one's friends, liberalism remained significantly associated with greater empathic concern. However, when the moral circle was restricted to one's family, ideology and empathic concern did not correlate significantly, suggesting for the first time that liberalism does not correspond to greater empathy across the board. These findings suggest that liberalism is associated with a greater tendency to extend empathy to people beyond one's family, whereas conservatism is not. However, this study does not definitively indicate whether conservatism is related to a more constricted sense of empathic concern or lower empathic concern overall (as suggested by the relationship between ideology and empathic concern in the control condition). We thus conducted a subsequent study to adjudicate between these two possibilities by employing a measure that captures love of family versus love of nonfamily specifically, and by assessing moral universalism and identification with all humanity.

Study 2 involved participants completing the love of humanity scale (Campos, Keltner, & Gonzaga, 2002), a measure that assesses four types of love: romantic love, love for friends, love for family, and love for all humanity (beyond friends and family). Ideology was unrelated to romantic love (a construct that lies somewhere in-between friendship and family relations, as in marriage), but was significantly related to love of family and love of friends, such that liberals reported more love of friends than conservatives but conservatives reported more love of family than liberals. This relationship is consistent with Study 1, suggesting that liberals extend their moral circle to friends whereas conservatives constrain their moral circle to the family. Of additional importance, liberal ideology was significantly correlated with love for all others, suggesting that liberalism is related toward a universal sense of compassion.

To build upon the finding that liberalism is related to a universal sense of compassion, Study 3 asked participants to complete the Schwartz Values Inventory

(Schwartz, 1992), which measures various values including universalism, the concept of peace, and equality for all. Conservative ideology was negatively correlated with universalism, again demonstrating that conservatism is negatively related to a universal love of others, whereas liberalism is positively related to this sense of universal compassion.

Although Studies 2 and 3 suggest liberalism correlates with empathy toward the world at large, and is consistent with the idea that liberals express empathy toward larger social circles, these studies do not explicitly compare empathy toward the world at large versus a smaller circle. Therefore, we conducted Study 4 to compare liberals' and conservatives' respective willingness to empathize with their nation versus all humanity. In Study 4, participants completed the Identification with All Humanity Scale (IWAHS; McFarland & Brown, 2008), which assesses how much people identify with their community, their country, and the world as a whole.

Political conservatism showed a small but significant correlation with identification with community and a more sizeable correlation with identification with country. Furthermore, liberalism correlated significantly with identification with the world as a whole. These findings demonstrate that whereas liberals identify with others in a more global sense, conservatives identify with others in a more local sense.

Studies 1–4 show that liberals and conservatives appear to differ in terms of the tendency to include socially dissimilar and distant others in their moral circles. This manifests at the level of family versus friends and nation versus world. These differences are unsurprising given the culture-war debates and well-known policy disagreements on issues that affect these specific circles of family, community, nation, and world (Graham et al., 2009; Hunter, 1991; Koleva et al., 2012).

Given these established differences, it is therefore possible that this difference in moral inclusion and exclusion extends to entities outside the boundaries of humanity, with liberals more likely to include nonhumans—animals, nature, and other entities—in their moral circles and conservatives more likely to restrict their moral circles to humans. To test whether this difference in moral circle size extends beyond humanity, we conducted subsequent studies to examine the relationship between political ideology and perceptions of nonhumans as capable of mental states such as feelings and consciousness.

In Study 5, we tested whether this relationship between ideology and moral concern for nonhumans manifests itself in anthropomorphism of nature, animals, and even technology. Anthropomorphism, the attribution of humanlike mental states to nonhumans (Epley, Waytz, & Cacioppo, 2007), is the basis for moral concern of nonhuman entities. Numerous studies now show that the more people attribute emotions to animals, nature, and technology, the less inclined they are to harm these entities (Bastian, Loughnan, Haslam, & Radke, 2012; Gray, Gray, & Wegner, 2007; Waytz, Cacioppo, & Epley, 2010). If conservative ideology (compared to liberal ideology) is linked to less inclusion of nonhumans

70 Adam Waytz et al.

in one's moral circle, then conservatives should be less likely to anthropomorphize than liberals.

Study 5 asked participants to complete the Individual Differences in Anthropomorphism Questionnaire (IDAQ; Waytz, Cacioppo, & Epley, 2010) and found that political conservatism was significantly and negatively correlated with anthropomorphism. These results suggest that ideology corresponds to the consideration of various nonhuman entities as humanlike. Given the relationship between humanization and moral concern (Waytz et al., 2010), we expected that this difference in anthropomorphism should manifest in a difference in moral concern as well. Our next step was to test the hypothesis that liberals are more likely to extend their moral circle to include nonhumans, whereas conservatives are more likely to restrict their moral circles to humans.

Importantly, although we have shown that liberals express greater moral concern for all humanity, our overarching prediction suggests that this expression is context-specific. That is, when all humanity represents a large circle (such as in comparison to one's nation), then liberals should show more (conservatives should show less) empathy toward humanity, but when humanity represents a smaller circle (such as in comparison to all living things), liberals should show less (conservatives should show more) empathy toward humanity. Study 6 examines this hypothesis directly.

In Study 6, participants completed a moral allocation task, in which they allocated 100 "moral units" (described as units representing the capacity for moral, prosocial, and generous behavior) among the following 16 categories. Nine of these categories comprised circles pertaining to humans only: immediate family; extended family; closest friends; distant friends; acquaintances; all people you have met; all people in your country; all people on your continent; all people in the world. Seven of these categories included nonhumans: all mammals; all amphibians, reptiles, mammals, fish, and birds; all animals including paramecia and amoebae; all animals in the universe, including alien lifeforms; all living things including plants and trees; all natural things in the universe including inert entities such as rocks; and all things in existence. We summed up scores for both categories to measure moral allocation to humans and nonhumans.

Participants completed two randomly ordered iterations of this task. In one, they were asked to allocate moral units how one should *ideally* divide them. In the other, they were asked to divide them as they *personally* do so in their daily lives. In addition, participants also completed a more general measure of the extent of their moral circle by clicking on rungs extending outward and representing the same categories as in the moral allocation task (see Appendix A). This measure allowed us to visualize the relative sizes of liberals' and conservatives' moral circles.

Political conservatism was significantly correlated with both personal moral allocation to humans only, and ideal moral allocation to humans only. In addition, the more liberal people were, the more they allocated equally to humans and nonhumans (in both their personal and ideal allocations). The more conservative people were, the more likely they were to prioritize moral concern for humans versus nonhumans. Finally, we assessed participants' clicks on the rung they felt best represented the extent of their moral circle. This qualitative measure demonstrated that liberals were most likely to select an outer rung whereas conservatives were most likely to select an inner rung. Overall, these results demonstrate that political conservatism is linked to a more enclosed moral circle that is exclusive to human beings and not to other animals or lifeforms. Liberal ideology is linked to a moral circle that includes nonhumans (and even aliens and rocks) as well. Study 6 also showed that the same differences emerge when asking about participants' ideal moral circles—that is, how big they think their moral circles *should* be, not necessarily how big they are. This suggests that liberals and conservatives, while having different sizes and patterns of allocations in their moral circles, both feel that their pattern is the right way to adjudicate moral concern in the world.

Of course, one major caveat to the interpretation of Study 6 is that we constrained the number of utiles (moral units) that participants could assign to each group, in effect forcing empathy to be zero-sum. To examine whether a similar pattern would emerge without this constraint, we conducted a final study, Study 7. In this study, participants completed the same personal moral allocation task as in Study 6, with one alteration: they were told that they could allocate any amount to any group, and any total amount overall.

Most important, we found no significant correlation between political ideology and absolute moral utiles allocated, consistent with the idea that liberals and conservatives do not differ in overall empathy when the targets of empathy are closely specified. Also, as in Study 6, conservatism was positively and significantly correlated with the percentage of moral utiles allocated toward humans, whereas liberalism was positively and significantly correlated with the percentage of moral utile allocation to nonhumans. Thus, even when participants are not constrained in their allocations (and when more allocations to nonhumans does not require less allocations to humans), the same pattern emerges such that liberals distribute empathy toward broader circles and conservatives distribute empathy toward smaller circles.

The seven studies show that across a variety of measures, liberals (relative to conservatives) empathize with friends compared to family, the world as a whole compared to the nation, and nonhumans compared to humans. Conservatives show the opposite pattern of results, again demonstrating that ideological differences do not correspond to differences in absolute levels of empathy, but rather correspond to differences in the *targets* of empathy.

Implications and Future Directions

The present work has implications for understanding political conflict and bridging the ideological divide. First and foremost, the recognition that liberals and conservatives both experience empathy, albeit toward different social targets, can enable political debates to be framed in terms of love rather than hate. Typically, in intergroup conflict, people expect that outgroup members' engagement in conflict is a product of dislike and animosity rather than positivity (Frey & Tropp, 2006; Kramer & Messick, 1998; Krueger, 1996), and people attribute negative outgroup behaviors to stable enduring characteristics (Pettigrew, 1979). Furthermore, liberals and conservatives in particular exaggerate each other's ideological extremity (Chambers & Melnyk, 2006; Graham, Nosek, & Haidt, 2012) and tend to view each other in negative terms (Krugman, 2007; Leo, 2002). These sort of pessimistic views toward outgroups can exacerbate intergroup conflict (Frey & Tropp, 2006), but recognition that political opponents are motivated by similar psychological experiences (i.e. empathy) might allow for increased opportunities for reconciliation.

In addition to generally reframing the broad conflict between liberals and conservatives in positive rather than negative terms, the present research also allows for specific policy debates central to this conflict to be construed in terms of empathy. For example, debate over immigration reform can be seen as a debate that pits strict empathy for U.S. citizens against empathy for individuals born outside the United States. Debate over diplomacy versus military deterrence strategies toward ostensible enemy countries can be seen as a debate regarding empathy toward foreign countries versus empathy toward one's own country and a desire to protect it at all costs. Even debates over global warming can be construed in terms of a moral concern for the environment versus exclusively caring for humans. Viewing these debates in terms of empathy has the potential to simplify the discussion surrounding them and to understand that the roots of each side's position lie in the shared goal of caring for others.

In addition to offering insights to ideological conflict, the present research offers numerous avenues for future research. One possibility is to examine the exact features of the particular social groups that evoke empathy from liberals versus conservatives, respectively. Although we have characterized the nature of family, nation, and humans compared to friends, the world, and nonhumans as differing in terms of size, they differ on a number of factors that are correlated with size. For example, these "small" groups are less diverse, less permeable, and more clearly hierarchical. "Larger" groups are inherently more diverse, more permeable, and less hierarchical. Future research can determine the influence of each of these factors on how ideology guides people to empathize with distinct social circles. A second question for future research to examine is whether ideological preferences for smaller versus larger social circles applies to novel social circles. The present studies demonstrate ideological preferences for relatively known circles and show that, for example, empathy for a given circle might differ in terms of whether it is construed as small or large. Although Studies 2 and 3 show that conservatives express more love of and identification with the nation, in Studies 6 and 7, no specific correlation emerges between ideology and moral concern toward the nation. This is likely because in Studies 6 and 7, nation is positioned among extremely small circles (e.g., one's immediate family) and extremely large circles (e.g., all existence). This result suggests that empathy toward any novel social circle that conservatives and liberals encounter will be determined by how large or small they construe the circle to be. A third avenue for future research is to determine causality between ideology and empathy toward circles of different sizes. The present research is largely correlational in nature, but we suspect that ideology contributes to different expressions of empathy just as the experience of empathy toward social circles of different sizes can influence ideological positions. Finally, future investigations of partisan perceptions of empathy as zero-sum or non-zero-sum could lead to ideological bridge-building interventions; after all, liberal and conservative allocations of empathy are only at odds if there is a fixed amount of empathy to go around. We welcome future research on these questions, and for now provide a framework for reinterpreting the ideological divide through the lens of empathy, which differs not in absolute amount between liberals and conservatives, but in how it is distributed.

References

Bäckström, M., & Björklund, F. (2007). Structural modeling of generalized prejudice: The role of social dominance, authoritarianism, and empathy. *Journal of Individual Differences, 28*(1), 10–17.

Bastian, B., Loughnan, S., Haslam, N., & Radke, H. R. (2012). Don't mind meat? The denial of mind to animals used for human consumption. *Personality and Social Psychology Bulletin, 38*(2), 247–256.

Batson, C. D. (2011). *Altruism in Humans.* Oxford, UK: Oxford University Press.

Boldero, J. M., & Higgins, E. T. (2011). Regulatory focus and political decision making: When people favor reform over the status quo. *Political Psychology, 32*(3), 399–418.

Brooks, A. C. (2007). *Who Really Cares: The Surprising Truth about Compassionate Conservatism—America's Charity Divide—Who Gives, Who Doesn't and Why it Matters.* New York: Basic Books.

Campos, B., Keltner, D., & Gonzaga, G. C. (2002, April). *Different Kinds of Love: How Love Experiences Differ across Relationships.* Poster presented at 2002 Western Psychological Association, Irvine, California, US.

Carney, D. R., Jost, J. T., Gosling, S. D., & Potter, J. (2008). The secret lives of liberals and conservatives: Personality profiles, interaction styles, and the things they leave behind. *Political Psychology, 29*(6), 807–840.

Carroll, R., Lewis, J., Lo, J., McCarty, N., Poole, K. & Rosenthal, H. (2013). Retrieved from http://voteview.com/dwnominate.asp

Carver, C. S. (2006). Approach, avoidance, and the self-regulation of affect and action. *Motivation and Emotion, 30*(2), 105–110.

Chambers, J. R., & Melnyk, D. (2006). Why do I hate thee? Conflict misperceptions and intergroup mistrust. *Personality and Social Psychology Bulletin, 32,* 1295–1311.

Cheon, B. K., Im, D. M., Harada, T., Kim, J. S., Mathur, V. A., Scimeca, J. M., & Chiao, J. Y. (2011). Cultural influences on neural basis of intergroup empathy. *Neuroimage, 57*(2), 642–650.

Cornwell, J. F., & Higgins, E. T. (2013). Morality and its relation to political ideology: The role of promotion and prevention concerns. *Personality and Social Psychology Bulletin, 39*(9), 1164–1172.

Cornwell, J. F., & Higgins, E. T. (2014). Locomotion concerns with moral usefulness: When liberals endorse conservative binding moral foundations. *Journal of Experimental Social Psychology, 50,* 109–117.

Davis, M. H. (1980). A multidimensional approach to individual differences in empathy. *JSAS Catalog of Selected Documents in Psychology, 10,* 85.

Davis, M. H. (1994). *Empathy: A Social Psychological Approach.* Madison, WI: WCB Brown and Benchmark.

Davis, J. A., Smith, T. W., & Marsden, P. V. (2007). General social surveys, 1972–2006 [Computer file]. Ann Arbor, MI: Inter-university Consortium for Political and Social Research.

Eisenberg-Berg, N., & Mussen, P. (1978). Empathy and moral development in adolescence. *Developmental Psychology, 14*(2), 185.

Epley, N., Waytz, A., & Cacioppo, J. T. (2007). On seeing human: A three-factor theory of anthropomorphism. *Psychological Review, 114*(4), 864–886.

Frey, F. E., & Tropp, L. R. (2006). Being seen as individuals versus as group members: Extending research on metaperception to intergroup contexts. *Personality and Social Psychology Review, 10*(3), 265–280.

Goldberg, L. R., & Rosolack, T. K. (1994). The Big Five factor structure as an integrative framework: An empirical comparison with Eysenck's PEN model. *The Developing Structure of Temperament and Personality from Infancy to Adulthood,* 7–35.

Graham, J., Haidt, J., & Nosek, B. A. (2009). Liberals and conservatives rely on different sets of moral foundations. *Journal of Personality and Social Psychology, 96*(5), 1029–1046.

Graham, J., Nosek, B. A., Haidt, J., Iyer, R., Koleva, S., & Ditto, P. H. (2011). Mapping the moral domain. *Journal of Personality and Social Psychology, 101*(2), 366–385.

Graham, J., Nosek, B. A., & Haidt, J. (2012). The moral stereotypes of liberals and conservatives: Exaggeration of differences across the political spectrum. *PloS one, 7*(12), e50092.

Graham, J., Haidt, J., Koleva, S., Motyl, M., Iyer, R., Wojcik, S., & Ditto, P. H. (2013). Moral Foundations Theory: The pragmatic validity of moral pluralism. *Advances in Experimental Social Psychology, 47,* 55–130.

Gray, H. M., Gray, K., & Wegner, D. M. (2007). Dimensions of mind perception. *Science, 315*(5812), 619.

Groeling, T. (2013). Media bias by the numbers: Challenges and opportunities in the empirical study of partisan news. *Political Science, 16*(1), 129–151.

Haidt, J. (2007). The new synthesis in moral psychology. *Science, 316*(5827), 998–1002.

Haidt, J., & Joseph, C. (2004). Intuitive ethics: How innately prepared intuitions generate culturally variable virtues. *Daedalus, 133*(4), 55–66.

Haidt, J., & Graham, J. (2007). When morality opposes justice: Conservatives have moral intuitions that liberals may not recognize. *Social Justice Research, 20*(1), 98–116.

Higgins, E. T. (1997). Beyond pleasure and pain. *American Psychologist, 52,* 1280–1300.

Higgins, E. T. (1998). Promotion and prevention: Regulatory focus as a motivational principle. *Advances in Experimental Social Psychology, 30,* 1–46.

Higgins, E. T. (2000). Making a good decision: Value from fit. *American Psychologist, 55*(11), 1217–1230.

Hirsh, J. B., DeYoung, C. G., Xu, X., & Peterson, J. B. (2010). Compassionate liberals and polite conservatives: Associations of agreeableness with political ideology and moral values. *Personality and Social Psychology Bulletin, 36*(5), 655–664.

Hunter, J. D. (1991). *Culture Wars: The Struggle to Define America.* New York, NY: Basic Books.

Iyer, R., Koleva, S., Graham, J., Ditto, P., & Haidt, J. (2012). Understanding libertarian morality: The psychological dispositions of self-identified libertarians. *PloS one, 7*(8), e42366.

Janoff-Bulman, R. (2009). To provide or protect: Motivational bases of political liberalism and conservatism. *Psychological Inquiry, 20*(2–3), 120–128.

Janoff-Bulman, R., & Carnes, N. C. (2013). Surveying the moral landscape: Moral motives and group-based moralities. *Personality and Social Psychology Review, 17*(3), 219–236.

Janoff-Bulman, R., Sheikh, S., & Baldacci, K (2008). Mapping moral motives: Approach, avoidance, and political orientation. *Journal of Experimental Social Psychology, 44,* 1091–1099.

Jones, J. M. (2013). Obams's fourth year in office ties as most polarized ever. Retrieved from http://www.gallup.com/poll/160097/obama-fourth-year-office-ties-polarized-ever.aspx

Jost, J. T. (2006). The end of the end of ideology. *American Psychologist, 61*(7), 651–670.

Jost, J. T. (2012). The righteous mind: Why good people are divided by politics and religion. *Science, 337*(6094), 525–526.

Jost, J. T., Glaser, J., Kruglanski, A. W., & Sulloway, F. J. (2003). Political conservatism as motivated social cognition. *Psychological Bulletin, 129*(3), 339–375.

Jost, J. T., Federico, C. M., & Napier, J. L. (2009). Political ideology: Its structure, functions, and elective affinities. *Annual Review of Psychology, 60,* 307–337.

Koleva, S., Graham, J., Haidt, J., Iyer, R., & Ditto, P. H. (2012). Tracing the threads: How five moral concerns (especially Purity) help explain culture war attitudes. *Journal of Research in Personality, 46,* 184–194.

Kramer, R. M. & Messick, D. M. (1998). Getting by with a little help from our enemies: Collective paranoia and its role in intergroup relations. In: *Intergroup Cognition and Intergroup Behavior.* C. Sedikides, J. Schopler, & C.A. Insko (Eds.). Mahwah, NJ: Lawrence Erlbaum Associates Publishers. Pp. 233–255.

Krauthammer, C. (2012). The empathy gap. Retrieved from http://www.washingtonpost.com/opinions/charles-krauthammer-the-empathy-gap/2012/09/06/b0ec930a-f85c-11e1-8b93-c4f4ab1c8d13_story.html

Krueger, J. I. (1996). Probabilistic national stereotypes. *European Journal of Social Psychology, 26,* 961–980.

Kruglanski, A. W., Pierro, A., Mannetti, L., & De Grada, E. (2006). Groups as epistemic providers: Need for closure and the unfolding of group-centrism. *Psychological Review, 113*(1), 84–100.

Krugman, P. (2007). *The Conscience of a Liberal.* New York, NY: Norton.

Leo, J. (2002). Ethics are made easy when anything goes. Retrieved from http://townhall.com/columnists/JohnLeo/2002/07/15/ethics_are_made_easy_when_anything_goes.

McAdams, D. P., Albaugh, M., Farber, E., Daniels, J., Logan, R. L., & Olson, B. (2008). Family metaphors and moral intuitions: How conservatives and liberals narrate their lives. *Journal of Personality and Social Psychology, 95*(4), 978–990.

McCue, C. P., & Gopoian, J. D. (2001). Dispositional empathy and the political gender gap. *Women & Politics, 21*(2), 1–20.

McFarland, S. (2010). Authoritarianism, social dominance, and other roots of generalized prejudice. *Political Psychology, 31*(3), 453–477.

McFarland, S., & Brown, D. (2008). Who believes that identification with all humanity is ethical?. *Psicología Política*, (36), 37–49.

Pettigrew, T. F. (1979). The ultimate attribution error: Extending Allport's cognitive analysis of prejudice. *Personality and Social Psychology Bulletin, 5*(4), 461–476.

Pratto, F., Sidanius, J., Stallworth, L. M., & Malle, B. F. (1994). Social dominance orientation: A personality variable predicting social and political attitudes. *Journal of Personality and Social Psychology, 67*(4), 741–763.

Rentfrow, P. J., Jost, J. T., Gosling, S. D., & Potter, J. (2009). Statewide differences in personality predict voting patterns in 1996–2004 US presidential elections. *Social and Psychological Bases of Ideology and System Justification, 1*, 314–349.

Schwartz, S. H. (1992). Universals in the content and structure of values: Theoretical advances and empirical tests in 20 countries. In: *Advances in Experimental Social Psychology*, M. Zanna (Ed.), San Diego, CA: Academic Press. Pp. 1–66.

Sidanius, J., & Pratto, F. (2001). *Social Dominance: An Intergroup Theory of Social Hierarchy and Oppression*. New York: Cambridge University Press.

Sidanius, J., Kteily, N., Sheehy-Skeffington, J., Ho, A. K., Sibley, C., & Duriez, B. (2013). You're inferior and not worth our concern: The interface between empathy and social dominance orientation. *Journal of Personality, 81*(3), 313–323.

Stone, S. J., Johnson, K. M., Bell, E., Meindl, P., Smith, B. J., & Graham, J. (in press). Political psychology. *WIREs Cognitive Science*.

Waytz, A., Cacioppo, J., & Epley, N. (2010). Who sees human? The stability and importance of individual differences in anthropomorphism. *Perspectives on Psychological Science, 5*(3), 219–232.

Waytz, A., Iyer, R., Young, L., & Graham, J. (in prep.). *Empirical Evidence for Ideological Differences in the Expanse of Empathy*. Unpublished manuscript.

Appendix A: Instructions for Circle Task

On the next page, we would like you to indicate the extent of your moral circle. By moral circle, we mean the circle of people or other entities for which you are concerned about right and wrong done toward them. This depiction demonstrates that people have different types of moral circles. At the innermost circle, some people care about their immediate family only, and at the outermost circle, people care about the entire universe—all things in existence. Please use the following scale and select a location that depicts the extent of your moral circle.

1 - all of your immediate family
2 - all of your extended family
3 - all of your closest friends
4 - all of your friends (including distant ones)
5 - all of your acquaintances
6 - all people you have ever met

Ideological Differences in the Expanse of Empathy **77**

7 - all people in your country
8 - all people on your continent
9 - all people on all continents
10 - all mammals
11 - all amphibians, reptiles, mammals, fish, and birds
12 - all animals on Earth including paramecia and amoebae
13 - all animals in the universe, including alien lifeforms
14 - all living things in the universe including plants and trees
15 - all natural things in the universe including inert entities such as rocks
16 - all things in existence

Please indicate a number that depicts the extent of your moral circle. Note that in this scale, the number you select includes the numbers below it as well. So, if you select 10 (all mammals), you are also including numbers 1–9 (up to 'all people on all continents') in your moral circle.

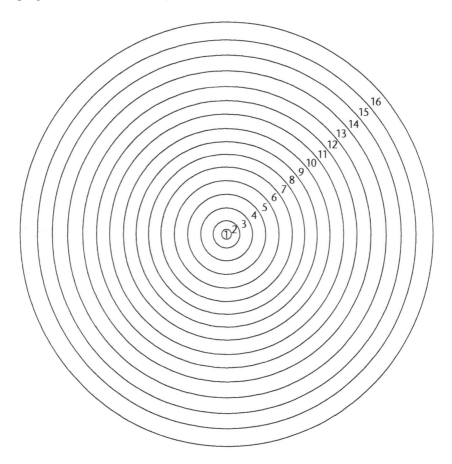

4

ARE CONSERVATIVES FROM MARS AND LIBERALS FROM VENUS?

Maybe Not So Much

Linda J. Skitka and Anthony N. Washburn

One of the most robustly replicated effects in political psychology is the "ideo-attribution effect," that is, the tendency for conservatives to explain social problems by referencing dispositional causes, such as people's lack of will power, personal discipline, self-reliance, or diminished moral standards, and liberals' tendency to explain the same problems by appealing to unjust social practices and structures. The ideo-attribution effect has been documented across a wide range of contexts, including explanations for poverty (Cozzarelli, Wilkinson, & Tagler, 2001; Furnham, 1982; Pandey, Sinha, Prakash, & Tripathi, 1982; Sniderman, Hagen, Tetlock, & Brady, 1986; Sniderman & Tetlock, 1986; Williams, 1984; Zucker & Weiner, 1993); wealth (Bobbio, Canova, & Manganelli, 2010); homelessness (Pellegrini, Queirolo, Monarrez, & Valenzuela, 1997; Skitka & Tetlock, 1992); unemployment (Gaskell & Smith, 1985; Skitka & Tetlock, 1992); crime (Carroll, Perkowitz, Lurigio, & Weaver, 1987); obesity (Crandall, 1994; Lantinga & Skitka, 1996; O'Brien, Hunter, & Banks, 2007); AIDS infections (Skitka & Tetlock, 1992, 1993); racial differences in success (Reyna, Henry, Korfmacher, & Tucker, 2006); foreign aggression (Sahar, 2008; Skitka, McMurray, & Burroughs, 1991; Skitka, Stephens, Angelou, & McMurray, 1993); and even explaining why people need assistance following natural disasters (Arceneaux & Stein, 2006; Skitka, 1999).

Ideological differences in the explanations for the causes of various social problems have important downstream consequences, including predicting people's willingness to support various public policies. For example, liberals generally favor increased spending on social programs, whereas conservatives oppose such spending, effects that are mediated by the different attributions liberals and conservatives make for why people need government assistance (e.g., Cozzarelli et al., 2001; Feather, 1985; Furnham, 1982; Griffin & Oheneba-Sakyi, 1993; Kluegel, 1990; Kluegel & Smith, 1986; Sniderman & Tetlock, 1986;

Williams, 1984). The goals of this chapter are to: (a) explore three competing explanations for the ideo-attribution effect, that is, the dispositional, ideological script, and motivated reasoning hypotheses; and (b) argue that political psychologists need to resist the tendency to assume that ideological differences always or even often arise from dispositionally different cognitive "wiring" of liberals and conservations.

The Dispositional Hypothesis

The dominant explanation for the ideo-attribution effect is that it is a consequence of stable individual differences in the ways that liberals and conservatives interpret their social worlds (the dispositional hypothesis). According to this argument, people vary in their baseline propensities to see the causes of others' behavior as rooted either in something about the person, or something about the person's situation. Individual differences in preferences for personal versus situational explanations for behavior subsequently lead people to adopt different positions and political identities. People who consistently perceive the causes of behavior as residing mostly within persons are more attracted to conservative beliefs and political orientation, whereas people who consistently perceive the causes of behavior to be the result of situational or institutional causes are more attracted to liberal beliefs and political orientation.

The conclusion that liberals and conservatives represent two very different kinds of people is consistent with a broader array of research that finds consistent associations of specific personality traits and reasoning styles with political orientation. Several decades of research on cognitive style constructs such as dogmatism (Rokeach, 1956), tolerance of ambiguity (Sidanius, 1978), flexibility–rigidity or close-mindedness (Jost, Glaser, Kruglanski, & Sulloway, 2003; Taylor, 1960) and integrative complexity (e.g., Russell & Sandilands, 1973; Scott, Osgood, & Peterson, 1979; Tetlock, 1981, 1983) indicates that, although there are certainly exceptions, conservatives are more dogmatic, intolerant of ambiguity, close-minded, and are more likely to think in terms of black and white than they are to be high in integrative complexity (see especially Jost et al., 2003). Some even argue that differences between liberals and conservatives are not superficial ones, and may be functionally "hard wired" in the brain (e.g., Amodio, Jost, Master, & Yee, 2007; Kanai, Feilden, Firth, & Rees, 2011; Schreiber et al., 2013). According to this view, conservatives are more likely to seize on first-pass dispositional attributions in part because their high needs for closure and cognitive rigidity prevent them from engaging in the more cognitively demanding and effortful process required to make a situational attribution (Gilbert, 1998; Gilbert & Krull, 1988; Gilbert, Pelham, & Krull, 1988). In summary, the dispositional hypothesis predicts that liberals and conservatives reason about and/or perceive their social worlds in very different ways, and that these differences run very deep into people's personalities and perhaps even their brain structure and function.

80 Linda J. Skitka and Anthony N. Washburn

Although the dispositional explanation for the ideo-attribution effect is certainly plausible, there are at least two other competing explanations that have not been given as much attention in the literature: the ideological script and motivated reasoning hypotheses. We review these in turn next.

The Ideological Script Hypothesis

The ideological script hypothesis reverses the causal order proposed by the dispositional hypothesis. Instead of differences in attributional thresholds leading people to self-identify as either liberal or conservative, the ideological script hypothesis proposes that identifying oneself as liberal or conservative leads people to adopt different explanations for social problems. Specifically, after self-identifying as either politically liberal or conservative, people may learn the corresponding attributional "party line." According to this hypothesis, attributions about the causes of social problems are *post hoc* explanations that justify a specific political point-of-view, rather than a dispositionally different way of interpreting the social world. Accordingly, this hypothesis predicts that ideologically patterned attributional differences should emerge only in contexts for which there is an easily accessible ideological script.

The ideological script hypothesis is consistent with the common image of citizens as "cognitive misers," with little or no political knowledge (e.g., Kam, 2005). People therefore use political parties and their platforms as a low effort heuristic for developing opinions about candidates and issues, or what some refer to as "System 1" style of reasoning (Kahneman, 2003; Stanovich & West, 2000). For example, candidate party affiliation shapes opinions about political candidates (Mondak, 1993a), something that even trumps whether the candidate actually endorses more party consistent policy positions (Skitka & Robideau, 1997). Similarly, information about party ties also shapes the direction of people's positions on various issues (e.g., Jacoby, 1988; Mondak, 1993b; Squire & Smith, 1988) and their perceptions of candidates' positions on various issues (Conover & Feldman, 1989; Feldman & Conover, 1983), something especially likely among people low rather than high in political awareness (Kam, 2005).

Zaller (1992) found that when liberal and conservative elites both supported the Vietnam War in 1964, people who attended to politics and current events showed similar non-partisan support for the war. By 1970, however, political elites had become much more divided about the war (liberals became increasingly against it, but conservatives continued to support the war effort), a division that was widely disseminated in the popular press. A subsequent division emerged among politically aware liberals and conservatives in the mass public. Similar patterns of results have been observed in public support for both World War II and the 2003 Iraq War (Berinsky, 2007). In other words, public opinion followed rather than shaped elite opinion, results that are also consistent with the notion that many people derive their opinions from the party line.

The ideological script hypothesis assumes that people do not really engage or take the time to understand the complexities of various policy positions largely because they lack the time, motivation, or ability to engage in more effortful "System 2" style of high effort systematic reasoning and analysis. They therefore rely on cognitive short cuts and heuristics, such as a party line script, when making these kinds of judgments. According to the ideological script hypothesis, we should therefore observe evidence of the ideo-attribution effect only in contexts in which elite or party opinion provides an easily accessible script.

The Motivated Reasoning Hypothesis

The dispositional and ideological script hypotheses both posit that liberals and conservatives arrive easily at their attributional conclusions, that is, that political opinions are the result of long-standing dispositional differences in modes of thinking and reacting to events (the dispositional hypothesis) or through the use of heuristics or low effect modes of thought and parroting of elite or party opinion (the script hypothesis). The motivated reasoning hypothesis paints a more nuanced picture of people's reasoning styles. Motivated reasoning refers to the tendency of people to conform their assessments of information to some goal other than accuracy (e.g., Kunda, 1990). The motivated reasoning hypothesis predicts that liberals and conservatives may be equally inclined to make personal attributions for why the poor are poor, why criminals engage in crime, and why fat people are fat. Where they may differ, however, is in their motivation to correct these first-pass attributions about the causes of behavior in domains where ideological differences have been observed. When attributional analysis yields a conclusion that is inconsistent with perceivers' core values or preferred conclusions, they will be motivated to engage in corrective processing. This effortful processing should lead them to consider the possibility of non-personal causes for why people might be poor, commit crimes, etc.

According to this hypothesis, people should be equally likely to make first-pass personal attributions about the causes of social problems—a notion consistent with Kluegel and Smith's (1986) assertion that individualism represents the dominant ideology in the United States. This hypothesis is also consistent with Gilbert and colleagues' (Gilbert, 1998; Gilbert & Krull, 1988; Gilbert, Pelham, & Krull, 1988) research on spontaneous trait inferences. According to Gilbert, people spontaneously infer personal causes for behavior, and only take into account situational information in a second, more effortful stage of reasoning, if they have sufficient motivation and cognitive resources to do so (Gilbert, 1998; Gilbert & Krull, 1988; Gilbert, Pelham, & Krull, 1988).

Similarly, Devine and her colleagues find that people automatically judge others in stereotypical terms (Devine, 1989; Devine, Monteith, Zuwerick, & Elliot, 1991). Low- and high-prejudiced people primarily differ in the extent to which they are motivated to correct these initial stereotypical judgments.

Low-prejudice people experience compunction because the automatically activated stereotypical judgments are inconsistent with their core values and beliefs about themselves as tolerant and egalitarian people. This compunction, in turn, motivates stereotype reasoning. High-prejudice people, in contrast, do not tend to adjust their initial stereotyped impression because they lack the motivation (i.e., compunction) to do so.

Taken together, these lines of theory and research converge on the hypothesis that perceivers may be motivated to adjust their initial attributions when the logical conclusions of a personal attribution conflict with their values. Figure 4.1 details a model of ideological reasoning based on an integration of these perspectives (note: the attributional side of the model was influenced by the explanation process model proposed by Anderson, Krull, & Weiner, 1996).

The model posits that when people notice an event or problem (e.g., they notice a delay in the checkout line they are in) they need to categorize or define

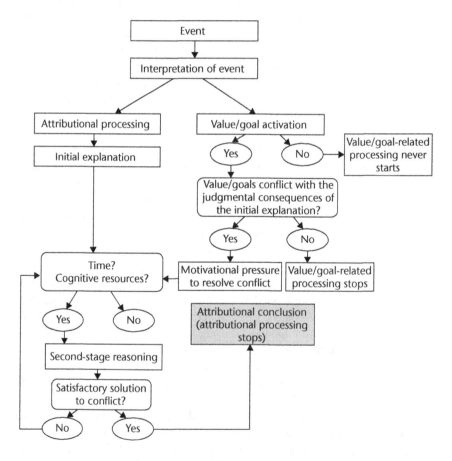

FIGURE 4.1 A motivated correction model of ideological reasoning.

what they have noticed (a person using food stamps). Even before perceivers engage in attributional analysis, their expectations will influence how they interpret a given event or problem (Ross & Nisbett, 1991). After interpreting the event, people generate an initial explanation, which we know from previous research is likely to be a trait inference or a personal attribution (Gilbert, 1998; Gilbert & Krull, 1988; Gilbert, Pelham, & Krull, 1988). This stage of reasoning is expected to happen in a very automatic way, based on people's expectations, previous experience, etc. The interpretation of the event, however, may simultaneously initiate another cognitive process, i.e., it might activate people's concerns with their core values. In short, some events may initiate dual processing. One process will be theoretically focused on attributional analysis, and another will be focused on making a judgment consistent with one's ideological values or goals. For example, witnessing a person using food stamps may lead to two separate thought processes: (a) an attributional chain of reasoning (why does this person need government assistance?); and (b) a chain of reasoning activated by values or goals, e.g., thoughts about unequal access to educational and job opportunities and humanitarian goals, or alternatively, thoughts about values associated with self-reliance and the protestant work ethic.

If initial attributional analysis and activated values lead to consistent conclusions, processing will stop. If activated values and initial attributions lead to inconsistent logical conclusions, however, people will be motivated to continue processing, presuming they have the time and cognitive resources to do so (cf. Devine, 1989; Devine, Monteith, Zuwerick, & Elliot, 1991). Unlike other inconsistent thoughts or beliefs, values are expected to provide an extra motivational component to lead people into System 2 reasoning because they are "shoulds" and "oughts" that are closely connected to people's self-concepts (e.g., Rokeach, 1973). When second-stage reasoning yields a satisfactory solution to the conflict between initial attributions and values, attributional processing will stop.

The motivated reasoning hypothesis therefore suggests that: (a) the observed tendency for liberals to prefer situational explanations and to be more likely to help people with internal-controllable causes of need in the contexts studied to date is a result of a cognitively effortful reasoning process; (b) we should observe ideological differences in preferences for personal versus situational attributions only in contexts where people are motivated by value conflict or other ideologically-based goals to engage in second-stage processing; and (c) liberals and conservatives are equally capable and likely to engage in second-stage processing should value conflict or other ideological goals provide the motivation to do so.

In summary, there are at least three different psychological accounts for why liberals and conservatives differ in their attributions and subsequent responses to various problems. The dispositional hypothesis is consistent with the idea that the "hard wiring" of liberals and conservatives basically differs. The ideological script hypothesis suggests that liberals' and conservatives' reasoning is essentially the

84 Linda J. Skitka and Anthony N. Washburn

same in these contexts; they are simply relying on different scripts. The motivated reasoning hypothesis similarly posits that liberals' and conservatives' reasoning is explained by very similar cognitive and motivational processes, and that context (such as the degree to which making a given attribution is consistent or inconsistent with people's values) will determine whether people make a dispositional or situational attribution in a given situation.

We turn next to a review of a number of studies that were designed to explicitly tease apart which of these explanations provides the clearest account for the ideo-attribution effect. The College Bowl and essay attribution studies tested whether the ideo-attribution effect only emerges in political behaviors (as predicted by the ideological script and motivated reasoning hypotheses) or if it also emerges when people make attributions for apoliticized phenomena (as predicted by the dispositional hypothesis). The repeated prompt study tests whether liberals and conservatives are equally or differentially likely to revise the attributions they make over time and with repeated prompting. The motivated reasoning hypothesis predicts that liberals should be more likely to show a revised pattern of response than conservatives (first making a personal attribution, followed by a situational revision), whereas the dispositional and script hypotheses would both predict no evidence of revision. The motivated reasoning hypothesis also argues that it should be cognitively effortful for liberals to make a situational attribution. The cognitive load study explicitly tests this hypothesis by examining whether the ideo-attribution effect goes away when people make judgments under conditions of high rather than low cognitive load. Finally, the strongest evidence in favor of the motivated reasoning hypothesis would be a demonstration that the effect reverses when conservative values are more consistent with making a situational than a personal attribution, and liberal values are more consistent with making a personal than a situational attribution. The Haditha and cougar studies tested whether the ideo-attribution effect reverses under these conditions.

The College Bowl Study

One way to tease apart whether the ideo-attribution effect is a consequence of dispositional differences, ideological scripts, or motivated reasoning is to test whether ideological differences in attributions emerge in less politicized contexts. We used an experimental paradigm designed to test hypotheses about attributional processes more generally rather than to explicitly test for ideological differences, that is, the College Bowl demonstration of the "fundamental attribution error" (the tendency for people to be inclined to make personal rather than situational attributions for others' behavior, Ross, 1977) to test whether liberals and conservatives would be differentially likely to make personal attributions in a less politicized context (Skitka, Mullen, Griffin, Hutchinson, & Chamberlin, 2002). Participants read a description of two students who were asked to participate in a quiz game. The students were described as volunteers for a classroom demonstration. The classroom instructor explained that their task was to play a game: one of them would be randomly assigned to the role of quizmaster, and the other would be assigned the role of contestant. The quizmaster's task was to generate five questions from his general knowledge, with the only requirement being that he had to know the correct answer, and then to pose these questions to the contestant. The story went on to describe the questions the quizmaster asked the contestant (which were in reality selected from the game Trivial Pursuit), and the contestant's answers. The contestant was described as getting only one out of the five answers correct.

If perceivers take into account the situational constraints of the game—that is, that the quizmaster and contestant roles were randomly assigned—they should realize that the quizmaster would have fared just as poorly as the contestant if their roles had been reversed. If, however, perceivers fail to take into account the situational constraints of the game, they are likely to rate the contestant as less intelligent than the quizmaster.

If liberals and conservatives dispositionally differ in their preferences or ability for making personal versus situational attributions, conservatives, but not liberals, should rate the contestant's intelligence as lower than the quizmaster's. The ideological script hypothesis, in contrast, predicts that liberals and conservatives will not differ in the attributions they make about the relative intelligence of the quizmaster and contestant, because there is no easily available ideological script for why people might perform well or poorly in the context of a College Bowl game.

The motivated reasoning hypothesis can also provide an account for why we might expect to see ideological differences in the College Bowl context. Academic debates about the malleability of intelligence have raged for years, and the arguments on the side of both nature and nurture have taken on a distinct ideological flavor. For example, Herrnstein and Murray (1996) argued in their controversial book *The Bell Curve* that inherited intelligence, not environment, is the primary determinant of a variety of social behaviors, including class, socio-economic level, crime, educational achievement, welfare, and even parental styles. Critics suggest that *The Bell Curve* represents a conservative political agenda masquerading as research (e.g., Gould, 1996; Kincheloe, Steinberg, & Gresson, 1997), with one critic going so far as to claim that it "lays the political, ideological, economic, and paramilitary groundwork for fascism" (Rosenthal, 1995, p. 44).

Simply quantifying intelligence has been argued (by liberals) to be an ideologically conservative effort to place individuals into "awkward, arbitrary categories" (Hitchens, 1994), and that efforts to assess human intelligence contradict the formal American commitment to equality (Hayman, 1998). These academic debates are not the substance of more popularized political discussion, and therefore are less likely to be absorbed as an ideological script than are, for example, attributions about the causes of poverty or crime. These academic debates, however, point to a fundamental tension between liberals' commitment to egalitarianism and making personal attributions for intelligence. In short, liberals' commitment to egalitarianism could lead them to be reluctant to report differences in perceived intelligence, a reluctance that may even extend to something like performance in a trivia game.

Results of the College Bowl study indicated that conservative participants rated the contestant significantly lower in intelligence than the quizmaster, whereas liberals saw the contestants as equal (and above average) in intelligence. The observation of ideological differences in this experimental context was therefore consistent with the predictions of both the dispositional and motivated reasoning hypotheses, but inconsistent with the ideological script hypothesis.

The Essay Attribution Study

Another test of the dispositional, script, and motivated reasoning hypotheses used an adaptation of Jones and Harris's (1967) attitude attribution paradigm. Jones and Harris had research participants guess the true opinion of another student after reading an essay the student, presumably, had written. In one condition of the study, participants were told that the author of the essay had freely chosen their essay position (either pro- or anti-Castro), thereby making it easy to guess the essayist's opinion. In the other condition, participants believed that the author had had no choice about the position to take in their essay, because they had been assigned their position as a participant in a debate. Although research participants perceived a smaller difference in opinion between the pro- and anti-Castro essayists in the no choice as compared to the choice condition, on the whole participants still assumed that the content of the essay reflected the author's true feelings even when the participant was given no choice about the position they took on the essay. In short, most people failed to take into account the situational constraints imposed on the participant in the no choice essay condition.

For our version of the study, we had all participants evaluate essays that were written under no choice conditions (Skitka et al., 2002). If the dispositional hypothesis is correct, political orientation should moderate participants' tendency to see a difference in the "true attitude" of participants randomly assigned to take a pro versus con position on a given issue. Conservatives should be less likely to take the situation into account (i.e., the random assignment of the position essayists were to take), and therefore should rely more on the essay content when guessing the essayists' true position on the issue than liberals. The ideological script hypothesis, however, predicts that the political orientation of the perceiver should have no impact on perceivers' attitude attributions, because there is no available ideological script to suggest what the authors' true attitudes should be. The motivated reasoning hypothesis also predicts an absence of ideological differences in attributed attitudes. Although liberal values might motivate corrected intelligence assessments, neither liberal nor conservative values or goals are implicated in attributing someone's true attitude based on reading an essay written under no choice conditions.

Results revealed no evidence of ideological differences in participants' ratings of the essayists' true attitudes. Liberals and conservatives both made correspondent inferences, that is, they inferred that the essayist's attitude was consistent with the position taken in the essay. Similar results emerged even when situational constraints were made especially salient to half of the participants by making them write an essay with no choice about the position to take before evaluating another essayist's true attitude. The results of the attitude attribution study are inconsistent with the dispositional hypothesis, but can be explained by either the script or the motivated reasoning hypotheses.

The Repeated Prompt Study

The 1987 pilot of the American National Election Study (ANES) survey included a number of open-ended items that used multiple probes (e.g., is there anything else you would like to add?) that allowed for the possibility for people to make different inferences as they reflected on the key question. Specifically, people were asked to consider the following:

> Some people feel the government in Washington should see to it that every person has a job and a good standard of living. Others think the government should just let each person get ahead on their own. Which is closer to the way you think about it?

Skitka et al. (2002) used this data to further test the implications of the dispositional, script and motivated reasoning hypotheses. The dispositional and ideological script hypotheses predict that conservatives' first and subsequent replies to this prompt would emphasize personal factors (e.g., laziness, the need to work hard), and that liberals' first and subsequent replies should emphasize situational or institutional barriers to getting ahead. In contrast, the motivated reasoning hypothesis predicts that liberals and conservatives should be similarly likely to make a personal inference in response to the first prompt, but that ideological differences would be more likely to emerge on the follow-up prompts. Conservatives' commitment to individualism and self-reliance should provide little motivation for them to think about situational impediments to getting ahead, so they should maintain a mostly consistent pattern of personal attributions across responses. Because liberals' commitment to egalitarian access to humanitarian assistance conflicts with notions like "people should get ahead on their own," liberals should be more likely than conservatives to subsequently correct their initial statements by making references to situational and institutional barriers that prevent some people from being able to do so.

As can be seen in Figure 4.2, liberals were: (a) less likely than conservatives to mention personal attributions; (b) more than twice as likely (19%) as conservatives (8%) to demonstrate a corrected pattern of response; and (c) most likely to

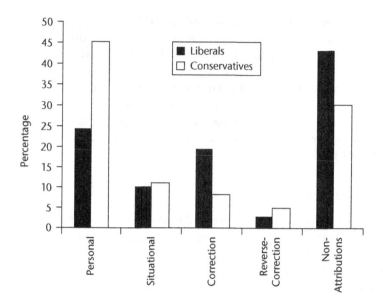

FIGURE 4.2 Attributional patterns as a function of political orientation.

spontaneously mention non-attributions when asked about social spending programs (usually references to humanitarian values). Conservatives were most likely to make references to personal attributions on their first and subsequent prompts. Although conservatives' reactions could be accounted for by a scripted or dispositional explanation, it is difficult to account for liberals' reactions using either of these frameworks. These results are therefore more consistent with the motivated reasoning than either the dispositional or script hypotheses.

The Cognitive Load Study

One key distinction between the dispositional and script hypotheses on the one hand, and the motivated reasoning hypothesis on the other, is the degree to which they posit that situational explanations in politicized contexts should be relatively effortful. If the ideo-attribution effect reflects an underlying dispositional tendency or a scripted response, then liberals' tendency to make situational attributions should be just as quick and easy as conservatives' dispositional inferences. If these inferences are the consequence of effortful motivated reasoning, however, then putting liberals under cognitive load should eliminate the ideo-attribution effect. To test this idea, Skitka et al. (2002) adapted another attributional judgment and decision making task used in prior research to explore ideological differences in willingness to provide public assistance (see Skitka & Tetlock, 1992, 1993). Specifically, research participants were asked to consider a number of claimants who varied in how they contracted AIDS and in their sexual orientation (the latter was included as a distractor variable). Participants' task was to decide as many or few of the claimants they thought should be given subsidized access to drug treatment. Previous research has found consistent evidence of ideological differences in willingness to help people with personal responsibility for their plight—another version of the ideo-attribution effect. Under conditions of no resource scarcity, liberals tend to help all who need assistance, regardless of why they need it. Conservatives, in contrast, withhold assistance from those personally responsible for their plight (Skitka & Tetlock, 1992, 1993).

The goal of this study was to see if cognitive load would attenuate previously observed ideological differences in willingness to help the personally responsible. Half of the participants made their judgments and allocation decisions while also engaged in a tone-tracking task (the high cognitive load condition), and half made their judgments and allocation decisions without the distraction of the tone-tracking task (the low cognitive load condition; Skitka et al., 2002). Results replicated previous research in the low cognitive load condition: liberals typically helped all claimants, whereas conservatives denied assistance to those who were personally responsible for contracting AIDS (i.e., who practiced unsafe sex despite knowing they were at risk). In the high cognitive load condition, however, liberals allocated assistance like conservatives: liberals and conservatives alike denied assistance to the personally responsible. In summary, the cognitive load study was consistent with the motivated reasoning, but not the dispositional or script hypotheses.

Can the Ideo-Attribution Effect be Reversed?

The motivated reasoning account for the ideo-attribution effect argues that value conflict motivates liberals to be more inclined to make situational attributions in some contexts, specifically, when their values conflict with making a personal attribution. One implication of this explanation for the ideo-attribution effect is that conservatives should be similarly motivated to make situational attributions when their values conflict with making a personal attribution. One limitation of previous research is that it has consistently tested hypotheses in contexts where liberals' values conflicted with making personal attributions, without testing whether the same effect would emerge when conservatives' values were at odds with doing so. To address this limitation, the next three studies tested hypotheses in contexts in which conservative values were more consistent with making a situational than a dispositional attribution for the target behavior.

One context we thought would be promising for testing whether the ideo-attribution effect could be reversed was that of authority misconduct. There are some hints in the literature that suggest that conservatives may be less punitive when responding to authority misconduct than liberals (Altemeyer, 1981). Because punitiveness is often shaped by attributions of personal responsibility (Carroll et al., 1987; Weiner, Graham, & Reyna, 1997), these findings may mean

90 Linda J. Skitka and Anthony N. Washburn

that conservatives may make weaker personal and stronger situational attributions for authority figures' misconduct. Conservatives' value commitments about respecting authority should conflict with holding authority figures personally responsible for their misconduct (e.g., Graham, Haidt, & Nosek, 2009), which could motivate them to override the default tendency to make a personal inference, and to make a situational one instead.

The Haditha Study (Version 1)

Morgan, Mullen, and Skitka (2010) asked research participants to make attributions for the real-world actions of U.S. Marines accused of killing 24 Iraqi civilians in Iraq. Participants read a news story that reported on the real-world case in which a Marine unit was attacked by a roadside bomb and one Marine was killed in Haditha, Iraq in November of 2005. The Marines suspected five men in the area were involved, and ordered them to lie on the ground. The men ran instead, and the Marines opened fire and killed them. They subsequently swept through nearby houses, and killed nineteen more people, including five women and four children.

After reading the news story, participants provided their attributions for the soldiers' behavior. It was possible for participants to either attribute the soldiers' actions as examples of "bad apples" (a personal inference) or take into account situational factors such as "the fog of war" (a situational inference). Consistent with the motivated reasoning hypothesis, conservatives made stronger situational attributions than liberals for the Marines' behavior—a reversal of the usual ideo-attribution effect.

The Haditha Study (Version 2)

Given that the results of the first Haditha study stand in such sharp contrast to so much research, it was especially important to replicate it. It would also be useful to compare whether these reactions are unique to authority figures, or if they generalize to explanations of non-authority figures who might have engaged in the same misconduct. The motivated reasoning hypothesis also predicts that value conflict should be driving the ideo-attribution effect and its reversal. To test whether value conflict plays a role in the ideo-attribution effect and its reversal, Morgan et al. (2010) designed a second study that manipulated whether the perpetrators of the Haditha slayings were Marines or Halliburton workers. In addition to measuring participants' attributions for the slayings, we also measured the relative salience of conservative values (e.g., respect for authority, security).

The reversal of the ideo-attribution effect emerged in the Marine but not the Halliburton condition. A moderated mediational analysis indicated that conservatives' higher sensitivity to salient conservative values (e.g., respect authority, security) in the Marine but not the Halliburton condition mediated the effect of political orientation on attributions. Higher levels of conservativism were associated with heigthened salience of conservative values in the Marine but not the Halliburton condition, which in turn explained the reversal of the usual ideo-attribution effect when explaining the Marines' but not the workers' behavior (Morgan et al., 2010). In short, conservatives made stronger situational attributions than liberals did for the Marines' behavior because doing so was more consistent with salient conservative values.

The Cougar Study

Because this was a first demonstration of a reversal of the ideo-attribution effect, it was important to establish that it would emerge in other settings in which conservatives should be more motivated to make situational than personal attributions. To do so, Morgan et al. (2010) used another real-world situation of possible authority misconduct. Residents in the Roscoe Village neighborhood of Chicago called the police in April of 2007 to report a large cat prowling the area. Police officers called to the scene discovered the cat was a 150-pound male cougar, that they subsequently tracked until it was cornered in a small alley. The police officers then opened fire, and shot the cougar more than a dozen times. Chicago residents engaged in a rather heated debate about whether the police responded appropriately to the incident. Police spokespersons claimed that the cougar posed a threat to public safety and could have injured or killed the police officers or others. Some residents, however, thought the police responded inappropriately and should have called in animal control officers who could have used a tranquilizer gun to capture the cougar instead of killing it (cougars are a protected species).

Participants were provided with a newspaper article that described the incident and were asked to make attributions for the police officers' behavior, and to report the degree to which specific conservative (e.g., safety, law and order) and liberal (e.g., mercy, protection of nature) values affected their judgments of it. Conservatives made stronger situational attributions for the police officers' behavior than did liberals, replicating the reversal of the ideo-attribution effect observed in the Haditha studies. Moreover, the perceived relevance of security and environmental values fully mediated the effects of political orientation on attributions for the police officers' behavior. Conservatives perceived greater relevance of security and respect for authority in this situation, which in turn predicted stronger situational attributions for the police officers' behavior. Liberals, in contrast, perceived greater relevance of mercy and environmental concerns, which in turn predicted stronger personal attributions for the police officers' behavior (Morgan et al., 2010).

In summary, the Haditha and cougar studies demonstrate that values-related reasoning motivates the ideo-attribution effect (and its reversal) and therefore supports the motivated reasoning account of the ideo-attribution effect. When conservative values conflict with making personal attributions, conservatives are more likely than liberals to make situational explanations for others' behavior. Conversely, when liberal values are more consistent with making personal than situational attributions for others' behavior, liberals are more likely than conservatives to make personal attributions for others' behavior.

Discussion

The goal of this chapter was to review research that has tested competing cognitive and motivational explanations for liberal and conservative approaches to understanding and reacting to social and personal behavior. Taken together, the results begin to paint a relatively coherent picture of how liberals and conservatives arrive at different explanations for phenomena like crime, poverty, or obesity. Liberals and conservatives appear to see the world in relatively similar ways, and to be equally likely to make first-pass personal attributions for the causes of others' actions or problems. However, liberals and conservatives diverge in their reactions when these first-pass judgments conflict with their ideological values or goals. In short, the results are more consistent with the motivated reasoning hypothesis than either a dispositional or ideological script hypothesis. Although the results of all eight studies reviewed here were consistent with the motivated reasoning hypothesis (see the summary presented in Table 4.1), the College Bowl and attitude attribution studies primarily ruled out the possibility that ideological differences in attributional proclivities are based either on stable underlying dispositional differences or the enactment of well-rehearsed ideological scripts. Although the results of these studies as a set could be explained in terms of motivated reasoning, the full implications of the motivated reasoning hypothesis were most persuasively tested by studies that demonstrated, for example, that the ideo-attribution effect disappeared under conditions of cognitive load, and in situations in which conservative values are more consistent with making a personal attribution the usual ideo-attribution effect reverses.

TABLE 4.1 Study results that were consistent with the dispositional, ideological script, and motivated reasoning hypotheses.

	Dispositional	Ideological script	Motivated reasoning
College Bowl	✓		✓
Attitude attribution		✓	✓
Repeated prompt			✓
AZT allocation			✓
Haditha I			✓
Haditha II			✓
Cougar			✓

Research on the psychology of ideology and other trait-like characteristics tend to focus more on differences than similarities of the groups or types being studied. Finding out that liberals and conservatives, for example, are more similar than they are different may not have the sex appeal of a story line more along the lines of "conservatives are from Mars, and liberals are from Venus," especially if the ways that the groups were thought to differ comfortably fits one's preferred conclusions. Academics are not immune either to: (a) the tendency to make the fundamental attribution error, that is, for their first-pass attributions for something like an ideological difference to be focused more on dispositional than situational causes (Gilbert, 1998; Gilbert & Krull, 1988; Gilbert, Pelham, & Krull, 1988; Ross, 1977); (b) motivated reasoning (Kunda, 1990); and therefore (c) accusations of possible liberal bias (e.g., Horowitz & Lehrer, 2002; Inbar & Lammers, 2012). It may be somewhat self-serving for political psychologists—who are mostly liberal (e.g., Horowitz & Lehrer, 2002; Inbar & Lammers, 2012; Klein & Western, 2004; Lindbolm, Szelényi, Hurtado, & Korn, 2005)—to conclude that liberals are dispositionally more cognitively flexible, nimble, and sophisticated than their conservative counterparts.

The dispositional hypothesis, however, is not the only possible account for ideological differences such as the ideo-attribution effect. Although there may be personality characteristics or dispositions that lead to observed differences, it is important not to begin and end with a dispositional explanation. It is important to consider the possibility that, instead, something about the context may lead liberals and conservatives to respond in different ways, and if the contextual cues were reversed, so too would the effect. Most previous demonstrations of the ideo-attribution effect tested hypotheses in contexts where conservatives were more likely than liberals to be motivated to make dispositional explanations for others' behavior. Testing hypotheses across a broader array of contexts reveals that what appeared to be a stable individual difference in cognitive style was instead being driven by exactly the same cognitive and motivational processes; when conservatives' motivational priorities were more consistent with making a situational explanation, conservatives were more likely than liberals to make situational attributions.

Several other labs have similarly started to examine whether standing assumptions that conservatives are figuratively from Mars and liberals are from Venus hold when one tests hypotheses across a broader range of contexts. Social psychological research, for example, generally finds that people on the political right are more prejudiced and politically intolerant than those on the left of specific ethnic or sexual minorities (see Sibley & Duckitt, 2008 for a recent meta-analysis). Much like the ideo-attribution effect, the dominant explanation for this ideological divide has been that liberals and conservatives are predisposed to be respectively tolerant and intolerant (an explanation that paints liberals in a more attractive light than conservatives, e.g., Hodson & Busseri, 2012; Jost et al., 2003; Sibley & Duckitt, 2008). Other research, however, that tested hypotheses using a much broader range of possible targets of prejudice or intolerance—including groups that liberals are more likely to dislike than conservatives—found weak or no support for an ideological asymmetry in prejudice and political intolerance (Lambert & Chasteen, 1997; McCloskey & Chong, 1985; Yancey, 2010). Conservatives do express more prejudice and intolerance than liberals when evaluating targets associated with liberal values or worldviews, or targets liberals are more inclined to want to protect than conservatives (e.g., pro-choice advocates and people on welfare). That said, liberals express more prejudice and intolerance than conservatives do when evaluating targets associated with conservative values or worldviews, or targets that conservatives are more inclined to want to protect than liberals (e.g., pro-life advocates and Tea Party supporters, Chambers, Schlenker, & Collisson, 2013; see also Crawford & Pilanski, in press; Wetherell, Brandt, & Reyna, 2013 for similar results). In short, explicit tests of the stimulus generalizability of previously assumed ideological asymmetries in prejudice and intolerance indicated that previous conclusions were premature and too one-sided (see Brandt, Reyna, Chambers, Crawford, & Wetherell, in press for a review).

New research also calls into question the common assumption that conservatives (more than liberals) believe that people should blindly obey authorities. Frimer, Wright, and Gaucher (2013) found that liberals and conservatives both see obedience as a moral good when the authority making the orders aligns with their own ideological views. People on the political right see obedience to conservative authorities to be morally good, but obedience to liberal authorities to be morally suspect. Conversely, people on the political left see obedience to liberal authorities as morally good, but obedience to conservative authorities as morally suspect. For reasons that are not yet well understood, however, both liberals and conservatives see the general idea of an authority as someone on the political right rather than the left. The general tendency for liberals to be more skeptical about obeying authorities, therefore, has little to do with obedience per se, and everything to do with their skepticism about the authorities' ideological commitments. Regardless, beneath the surface of liberals' and conservatives' beliefs about the moral appropriateness of obedience, is the same underlying process. Liberals and conservatives are equally "groupish" about authorities and obedience, so long as those authorities are members of their own ideological tribe.

In a similar fashion, many researchers have argued that conservatives are more willing than liberals to deny the validity of scientific evidence for politically relevant social and economic issues (e.g., Feygina, Jost, & Goldsmith, 2010; McCright & Dunlap, 2011a, 2011b; Mooney, 2012), most prominently, global warming (Dunlap, 2008; Gallup Poll, 2009). However, more recent social science research has found that people on both the left and the right are motivated to evaluate the credibility of scientific evidence in ways that bolster their ideological preferences (Kahan, 2013; Kahan, Jenkins-Smith, & Braman,

2011; Peterson, Skov, Serritzlew, & Ramsoy, 2013). For example, liberals often dispute scientific evidence that indicates that nuclear waste can be safely disposed of without risk to the environment (Braman, Kahan, Slovic, Gastil, & Cohen, 2007; Jenkins-Smith, Silva, & Murray, 2009; Newport, 2012) and see scientists who cite evidence of the safety of nuclear waste disposal as less trustworthy than scientists who acknowledge risks (Kahan, Jenkins-Smith, & Braman, 2011). Liberals are also more likely than conservatives to be skeptical about the safety of the gas drilling technique known as fracking, and its possible effects on water quality (Mooney, 2012; Pew Research Center, 2012), despite considerable evidence of its safety with respect to the water table [e.g., after extensive study, the Environmental Protection Agency issued a 2004 report that concluded, "the injection of hydraulic fracturing fluids into CBM (coalmethane) wells poses no threat to USDWs" (underground source of drinking water)"].[1]

The most persuasive evidence of ideological symmetry in science denial, however, is the finding that liberals and conservatives interpret raw scientific data—i.e., the very same numbers—in completely different ways depending on whether the findings bolster (e.g., for liberals, gun control decreases crime; for conservatives, gun control increases crime) or conflict with their preferred ideological conclusions, effects that do not emerge in a non-politicized control condition (Kahan, Peters, Dawson, & Slovic, 2013). In summary, science denial appears to be an equal opportunity sport driven by motivated reasoning. When conservative values or policy preferences conflict with scientific findings, conservatives are more likely than liberals to deny the validity, trustworthiness, or utility of that scientific evidence. Conversely, when liberal values or policy preferences conflict with scientific claims, liberals are more likely than conservatives to deny the science behind those claims.

In conclusion, although liberals and conservatives may differ in the priorities they hold dear, the same cognitive and motivational processes nonetheless drive the way they interpret and react to their social worlds. In most ways, conservatives and liberals are more similar than they are different, even if they find different groups, policies, or premises differentially preferable or objectionable. Both those on the political left and right are motivated to make attributions for others' behavior in ways that are consistent with their values, to be prejudiced and intolerant of those who do not share their worldview, and to be skeptical of science that challenges their core assumptions. Before making claims about essential differences between liberals and conservatives it is especially important to carefully consider whether one has been sufficiently attentive to the contexts in which they have been observed, and to consider whether different patterns of results might be observed in contexts in which the politicized values are not salient, or when the motivational priorities of liberals and conservatives are reversed.

Note

1 Definitions of acronyms were not in the original quote. Liberal anxiety about fracking may have been fed by a documentary film *Gasland* (2010) in which a man was shown setting a match to his tap water and the water igniting into flame. Investigations of this and other cases depicted in the documentary by the Colorado Oil and Gas Information System (COGIS, a branch of the Colorado Department of Natural Resources) determined that the methane in the wells was not a result of oil or gas activity in the area (COGCC statement, undated). Although correlational and still being studied, there is some emerging evidence that fracking may lead to an increase in earthquake activity (Ellsworth, 2013).

References

Altemeyer, B. (1981). *Right-Wing Authoritarianism.* Winnipeg, Canada: University of Manitoba Press.

Amodio, D. M., Jost, J. T., Master, S. L., & Yee, C. M. (2007). Neurocognitive correlates of liberalism and conservatism. *Nature Neuroscience, 10*(10), 1246–1247.

Anderson, C. A., Krull, D. S., & Weiner, B. (1996). Explanations: Processes and consequences. In E. T. Higgins & A. W. Kruglanski (Eds.), *Social Psychology: Handbook of Basic Principles* (pp. 271–296). New York: Guilford Press.

Arceneaux, K., & Stein, R. M. (2006). Who is held responsible when disaster strikes? The attribution of responsibility for a natural disaster in an urban election. *Journal of Urban Affairs, 28,* 43–53.

Berinsky, A. J. (2007). Assuming the costs of war: Events, elites, and American public support for military conflict. *Journal of Politics, 69*(4), 975–997.

Bobbio, A., Canova, L., & Manganelli, A. M. (2010). Conservative ideology, economic conservatism, and causal attributions for poverty and wealth. *Current Psychology, 29*(3), 222–234.

Braman, D., Kahan, D. M., Slovic, P., Gastil, J., & Cohen, G. L. (2007). The second national risk and culture study: Making sense of—and making progress in—the American culture war of fact. *GW Law Faculty Publications & Other Works, 211.* Retrieved on January 6, 2014 from http://scholarship.law.gwu.edu/faculty_publications/211

Brandt, M. J., Reyna, C., Chambers, J. R., Crawford, J. T., & Wetherell, G. (in press). The ideological-conflict hypothesis: Intolerance among both liberals and conservatives. *Current Directions in Psychological Science.*

Carroll, J. S., Perkowitz, W. T., Lurigio, A. J., & Weaver, F. M. (1987). Sentencing goals, causal attributions, ideology, and personality. *Journal of Personality and Social Psychology, 52,* 107–118.

Chambers, J. R., Schlenker, B. R., & Collisson, B. (2013). Ideology and prejudice: The role of value conflicts. *Psychological Science, 24,* 140–149.

COGCC (Colorado Oil and Gas Conservation Commission) (no date). Statement of the Colorado Oil and Gas Conservation Commission on *Gasland,* retrieved January 8, 2014 from http://cogcc.state.co.us/library/GASLAND%20DOC.pdf

Conover, P. J., & Feldman, S. (1989). Candidate perception in an ambiguous world: Campaigns, cues, and inference processes. *American Journal of Political Science, 33,* 912–940.

Cozzarelli, C., Wilkinson, A. V., & Tagler, M. J. (2001). Attitudes toward the poor and attributions for poverty. *Journal of Social Issues, 2*, 207–228.

Crandall, C. S. (1994). Prejudice against fat people: Ideology and self-interest. *Journal of Personality and Social Psychology, 66*, 882–894.

Crawford, J. T., & Pilanski, J. M. (in press). Political intolerance, right and left. *Political Psychology*.

Devine, P. G. (1989). Stereotypes and prejudice: Their automatic and controlled components. *Journal of Personality and Social Psychology, 56*, 5–18.

Devine, P. O., Monteith, M. J., Zuwerick, R. J., & Elliot, A. J. (1991). Prejudice with and without compunction. *Journal of Personality and Social Psychology, 60*, 817–830.

Dunlap, R. (2008). Partisan gap on global warming grows. *Gallup Poll*. Retrieved August 5, 2008, from http://www.gallup.com/ poll/107593/Partisan-Gap-Global-Warming-Grows.aspx

Ellsworth, W. L. (2013). Injection-induced earthquakes. *Science, 341,* DOI: 10.1126/science.1225942.

Environmental Protection Agency (2004). Evaluation of impacts to underground sources of drinking water by hydraulic fracturing of coalbed methane reservoirs study. Retrieved January 7, 2014 from http://water.epa.gov/type/groundwater/uic/class2/hydraulicfracturing/wells_coalbedmethanestudy.cfm

Feather, N. (1985). Attitudes, values, and attributions: Explanations of unemployment. *Journal of Personality and Social Psychology, 48*, 876–889.

Feldman, S., & Conover, P. J. (1983). Candidates, issues and voters: The role of inference in political perception. *The Journal of Politics, 45*(4), 810–839.

Feygina, I., Jost, J. T., & Goldsmith, R. E. (2010). System justification, the denial of global warming, and the possibility of "system-sanctioned change." *Personality and Social Psychology Bulletin, 36*, 326–338.

Frimer, J. A., Wright, J. C., & Gaucher, D. (2013). *Do Conservatives Really Moralize Obedience to Authority?* Paper presented at the Society for Personality and Social Psychology annual conference, Austin TX, US.

Furnham, A. (1982). Why are the poor always with us? Explanations for poverty in Great Britain. *British Journal of Social Psychology, 21*, 311–322.

Gallup Poll. (2009, October 30). *Environment*. Retrieved on January 6, 2014 from http://www.gallup.com/poll/107593/partisan-gap-global- warming-grows.aspx

Gaskell, G., & Smith, P. (1985). An investigation of youths' attributions for unemployment and their political attitudes. *Journal of Economic Psychology, 6*(1), 65–80.

Gilbert, D. T. (1998). Speeding with Ned: A personal view of the correspondence bias. In J. M. Darley & J. Cooper (Eds.), *Attribution and Social Interaction: The Legacy of Edward E. Jones*. Washington, DC: APA.

Gilbert, D. T., & Krull, D. S. (1988). Seeing less and knowing more: The benefits of perceptual ignorance. *Journal of Personality and Social Psychology, 54*, 193–202.

Gilbert, D. T., Pelham, B. W., & Krull, D. S. (1988). On cognitive busyness: When person perceivers meet persons perceived. *Journal of Personality and Social Psychology, 54*, 733–740.

Gould, S. J. (1996). *The Mismeasure of Man* (revised and expanded edn.). New York, NY: W. W. Norton and Co.

Graham, J., Haidt, J., & Nosek, B. A. (2009). Liberals and conservatives rely on different sets of moral foundations. *Journal of Personality and Social Psychology, 96*(5), 1029–1046.

Griffin, W. E., & Oheneba-Sakyi, Y. (1993). Sociodemographic and political correlates of university students' causal attributions for poverty. *Psychological Reports, 73*, 795–800.

Hayman, R. L. Jr. (1998). *The Smart Culture: Society, Intelligence and the Law*. New York: New York University Press.

Herrnstein, R. J., & Murray, C. (1996). *The Bell Curve: Intelligence and Class Structure in American Life*. New York: Free Press Books.

Hitchens, C. (1994). Let's lose the race (reflection on the wrong-headedness of the resurgent ideology of genetically determined IQ). *New Statesman & Society, 7*, 24.

Hodson, G., & Busseri, M. A. (2012). Bright minds and dark attitudes: Lower cognitive ability predicts greater prejudice through right-wing ideology and low intergroup contact. *Psychological Science, 23*, 187–195.

Horowitz, D., & Lehrer, E. (2002). Political bias in the administrations and faculties of 32 elite colleges and universities. Center for the Study of Popular Culture. Retrieved January 2, 2014 from http://www.studentsforacademicfreedom.org/news/1898/lackdiversity.html

Inbar, Y., & Lammers, J. (2012). Political diversity in social and personality psychology. *Perspectives on Psychological Science, 7*, 496–503.

Jacoby, W. G. (1988). The impact of party identification on issue attitudes. *American Journal of Political Science, 32*, 643–661.

Jenkins-Smith, H. C., Silva, C. L., & Murray, C. (2009). Beliefs about radiation: Scientists, the public and public policy. *Health Physics, 97*, 519–527.

Jones, E. E., & Harris, V. A. (1967). The attribution of attitudes. *Journal of Experimental Social Psychology, 3*, 1–24.

Jost, J. T., Glaser, J., Kruglanski, A. W., & Sulloway, F. J. (2003). Political conservatism as motivated social cognition. *Psychological Bulletin, 129*(3), 339–375.

Kahan, D. M. (2013). Ideology, motivated reasoning, and cognitive reflection. *Judgment and Decision Making, 8*, 407–424.

Kahan, D. M., Jenkins-Smith, H., & Braman, D. (2011). Cultural cognition of scientific consensus. *Journal of Risk Research, 14*, 147–174.

Kahan, D. M., Peters, E., Dawson, E. C., & Slovic, P. (2013). Motivated numeracy and enlightened self-government. *Yale Law School Public Law & Legal Theory, Public Working Paper, 116*. Retrieved on January 6, 2014 from http://papers.ssrn.com/sol3/Delivery.cfm/SSRN_ID2319992_code45442.pdf?abstractid=2319992&mirid=1

Kahneman, D. (2003). A perspective on judgment and choice: Mapping bounded rationality. *American Psychologist, 58*(9), 697–720.

Kam, C. D. (2005). Who toes the party line? Cues, values, and individual differences. *Political Behavior, 27*, 163–182.

Kanai, R., Feilden, T., Firth, C., & Rees, G. (2011). Political orientations are correlated with brain structure in young adults. *Current Biology, 21*(8), 677–680.

Kincheloe, J. L., Steinberg, S. R., & Gresson, A. D. (1997). *Measured Lies: The Bell Curve Examined*. New York: St. Martins Press.

Klein, D. B., & Western, A. (2004). How many Democrats per Republicans at UC-Berkeley and Stanford? Voter registration data across 23 academic departments. Retrieved January 2, 2014 from http://papers.ssrn.com/sol3/papers.cfm?abstract_id=664045

Kluegel, J. R. (1990). Trends in Whites' explanations of the Black-White gap in socioeconomic status, 1977–1989. *American Sociological Review, 55*(4), 512–525.

Kluegel, J. R., & Smith, E. R. (1986). *Beliefs about Inequality*. New York: Aldine Publishing.

Kunda, Z. (1990). The case for motivated reasoning. *Psychological Bulletin, 108*, 480–498.

Lambert, A. J., & Chasteen, A. L. (1997). Perceptions of disadvantage versus conventionality: Political values and attitudes toward the elderly versus Blacks. *Personality and Social Psychology Bulletin, 23*, 469–481.

Lantinga, S. B., & Skitka, L. J. (1996, July). *Antifat Attitudes: Reliability, Replicability and an Extension.* Paper presented at the eighth annual American Psychological Society Conference, San Francisco, US.

Lindbolm, J. A., Szelényi, K., Hurtado, S., & Korn, W. S. (2005). *The American College Teacher: National Norms for the 2004–2005 HERI Faculty Survey.* Los Angeles: University of California, Los Angeles, Higher Education Research Institute.

McCloskey, H., & Chong, D. (1985). Similarities and differences between left-wing and right-wing radicals. *British Journal of Political Science, 15*, 329–363.

McCright, A. M., & Dunlap, R. E. (2011a). Cool dudes: The denial of climate change among conservative white males in the United States. *Global Environmental Change, 21*, 1163–1172.

McCright, A. M., & Dunlap, R. E. (2011b). The politicization of climate change and polarization in the American public's views of global warming, 2001–2010. *The Sociological Quarterly, 52*, 155–194.

Mondak, J. J. (1993a). Public opinion and heuristic processing of source cues. *Political Behavior, 15*(2), 167–192.

Mondak, J. J. (1993b). Source cues and policy approval: The cognitive dynamics of public support for the Reagan agenda. *American Journal of Political Science, 37*, 186–212.

Mooney, C. (2012). *The Republican Brain: The Science of Why They Deny Science—and Reality.* Hoboken, NJ: John Wiley & Sons, Inc.

Morgan, G. S., Mullen, E., & Skitka, L. J. (2010). When values and attributions collide: Liberals' and conservatives' values motivate attributions for alleged misdeeds. *Personality and Social Psychology Bulletin, 36*, 1241–1254.

Newport, F. (2012, March 26). *Americans Still Favor Nuclear Power a Year after Fukushima: Majority Also Still Sees Nuclear Power as Safe.* Retrieved on January 6, 2014 from http://www.gallup.com/poll/153452/americans-favor-nuclear-power-year-fukushima.aspx

O'Brien, K. S., Hunter, J. A., & Banks, M. (2007). Implicit anti-fat bias in physical educations: Physical attributes, ideology, and socialization. *International Journal of Obesity, 31*, 308–314.

Pandey, J., Sinha, Y., Prakash, A., & Tripathi, R. C. (1982). Right–left political ideologies and attribution of the causes of poverty. *European Journal of Social Psychology, 12*, 327–331.

Pellegrini, R. J., Queirolo, S. S., Monarrez, V. E., & Valenzuela, D. M. (1997). Political identification and perceptions of homelessness: Attributed causality and attitudes on public policy. *Psychological Reports, 80*, 1139–1148.

Peterson, M. B., Skov, M., Serritzlew, S., & Ramsoy, T. (2013). Motivated reasoning and political parties: Evidence for increased processing in the face of party cues. *Political Behavior, 35*, 831–854.

Pew Research Center (2012, March 19). *As Gas Prices Pinch, Support for Oil and Gas Production Grows: Those Aware of Fracking Favor Its Use.* Retrieved on January 6, 2014 from http://www.people-press.org/2012/03/19/as-gas-prices-pinch-support-for-oil-and-gas-production-grows/1

Reyna, C., Henry, P. J., Korfmacher, W., & Tucker, A. (2006). Attributional stereotypes as cues for deservingness: Examining the role of principled conservatism in racial policy. *Journal of Personality and Social Psychology, 90,* 109–128.

Rokeach, M. (1956). Political and religious dogmatism: An alternative to the authoritarian personality. *Psychological Monographs: General and Applied, 70*(18), 1–43.

Rokeach, M. (1973). *The Nature of Human Values.* New York: Free Press.

Rosenthal, S. J. (1995). The Pioneer Fund: Financier of fascist research. *American Behavioral Scientist, 39,* 44–61.

Ross, L. (1977). The intuitive psychologist and his shortcomings. In L. Berkowitz (Ed.), *Advances in Experimental Social Psychology* (Vol. 10, pp. 173–220). San Diego, CA: Academic Press.

Ross, L., & Nisbett, R. E. (1991). *The Person and the Situation: Perspectives on Social Psychology.* New York: McGraw-Hill.

Russell, G. W., & Sandilands, M. L. (1973). Some correlates of conceptual complexity. *Psychological Reports, 33,* 587–593.

Sahar, G. (2008). Patriotism, attributions for the 9/11 attacks, and support for war: Then and now. *Basic and Applied Social Psychology, 30,* 189–197.

Schreiber, D., Fonzo, G., Simmons, A. N., Dawes, C. T., Flagan, T., Fowler, J. H., & Paulus, M. P. (2013). Red brain, blue brain: Evaluative processes differ in Democrats and Republicans. *PLoS One, 8*(2), e52970.

Scott, W. A., Osgood, D. W., & Peterson, C. (1979). *Cognitive Structure: Theory and Measurement of Individual Differences.* Washington, DC, US: Winston & Sons.

Sibley, C. G., & Duckitt, J. (2008). Personality and prejudice: A meta-analysis and theoretical review. *Personality and Social Psychology Review, 12,* 248–279.

Sidanius, J. (1978). Intolerance of ambiguity and socio-politico ideology: A multidimensional analysis. *European Journal of Social Psychology, 8*(2), 215–235.

Skitka, L. J. (1999). Ideological and attributional boundaries on public compassion: Reactions to individuals and communities affected by a natural disaster. *Personality and Social Psychology Bulletin, 25,* 793–808.

Skitka, L. J., & Tetlock, P. E. (1992). Allocating scarce resources: A contingency model of distributive justice. *Journal of Experimental Social Psychology, 28,* 491–522.

Skitka, L. J., & Tetlock, P. E. (1993). Providing public assistance: Cognitive and motivational processes underlying liberal and conservative policy preferences. *Journal of Personality and Social Psychology, 65,* 1205–1223.

Skitka, L. J., & Robideau, R. L. (1997). Judging a book by its cover: The effects of candidate party label and issue stands on voting behavior. *Journal of Applied Social Psychology, 27,* 967–982.

Skitka, L. J., McMurray, P. J., & Burroughs, T. E. (1991). Willingness to provide post-war aid to Iraq and Kuwait: An application of the contingency model of distributive justice. *Contemporary Social Psychology, 15,* 179–188.

Skitka, L. J., Stephens, L. J., Angelou, I. N., & McMurray, P. J. (1993). Willingness to provide post-war aid to Iraq and Kuwait: A one-year follow-up. *Contemporary Social Psychology, 17,* 33–37.

Skitka, L. J., Mullen, E., Griffin, T., Hutchinson, S., & Chamberlin, B. (2002). Dispositions, ideological scripts, or motivated reasoning? Understanding ideological differences in attributions for social problems. *Journal of Personality and Social Psychology, 83,* 470–487.

Sniderman, P. M., & Tetlock, P. E. (1986). Interrelationship of political ideology and public opinion. In M. G. Hermann (Ed.), *Political Psychology: Contemporary Problems and Issues* (pp. 232–260). San Francisco, CA: Jossey-Bass.

Sniderman, P. M., Hagen, M. G., Tetlock, P. E., & Brady, H. E. (1986). Reasoning chains: Causal models of policy reasoning in mass publics. *British Journal of Political Science, 16*, 405–430.

Squire, P., & Smith, E. R. (1988). The effect of partisan information on voters in nonpartisan elections. *Journal of Politics, 50*(1), 169–179.

Stanovich, K. E., & West, R. F. (2000). Individual differences in reasoning: Implications for the rationality debate? *Behavioral and Brain Sciences, 23*(5), 645–665.

Taylor, I. A. (1960). Similarities in the structure of extreme attitudes. *Psychological Monographs, 74*(2), 1–36.

Tetlock, P. E. (1981). Personality and isolationism: Content analysis of senatorial speeches. *Journal of Personality and Social Psychology, 41*, 737–743.

Tetlock, P. E. (1983). Cognitive style and political ideology. *Journal of Personality and Social Psychology, 45*, 118–126.

Weiner, B., Graham, S., & Reyna, C. (1997). An attributional examination of retributive versus utilitarian philosophies of punishment. *Social Justice Research, 10*(4), 431–452.

Wetherell, G., Brandt, M. J., & Reyna, C. (2013). Discrimination across the ideological divide: The role of perceptions of value violations and abstract values in discrimination by liberals and conservatives. *Social Psychological and Personality Science, 4*(6), 658–667.

Williams, S. (1984). Left–right ideological differences in blaming victims. *Political Psychology, 5*, 573–581.

Yancey, G. (2010). Who has religious prejudice? Differing sources of anti-religious animosity in the United States. *Review of Religious Research, 52*, 159–171.

Zaller, J. R. (1992). *The Nature and Origins of Mass Opinion*. New York: Cambridge University Press.

Zucker, G. S., & Weiner, B. (1993). Conservatism and perceptions of poverty: An attributional analysis. *Journal of Applied Social Psychology, 23*, 925–943.

5

MORAL COHERENCE AND POLITICAL CONFLICT

Peter H. Ditto and Brittany S. Liu

We do not always think about morality. But when we do, we think Dick Cheney.

This is not meant as a partisan statement. On the contrary, we see the former Vice President's moral beliefs as illustrating an all-too-human pattern that readers of any political persuasion will recognize.

On virtually every issue of the day, Mr. Cheney's views epitomize the conservative end of the political spectrum. He is a strong supporter of military intervention abroad and aggressive interrogation of terrorist suspects at home. He is pro-business and anti-taxes, an enthusiastic supporter of gun rights but hostile toward abortion rights, and dismissive of scientific research documenting the dangers of global climate change.

But there is one issue where Mr. Cheney's views are surprisingly liberal. In 2009 he declared his support for same-sex marriage. It is challenging to construct a principled ideological view that can integrate this one anomalous attitude with Mr. Cheney's otherwise overwhelmingly conservative constellation of political beliefs. The former Vice President has shown a libertarian streak at times, but his staunch opposition to drug law liberalization, aggressive support for foreign military intervention, and commitment to a powerful executive branch make a principled explanation for his same-sex marriage position seem implausible.

On the other hand, Mr. Cheney's moral belief system becomes instantly understandable once we know that his daughter Mary is openly lesbian, married to a woman and parent to two of his grandchildren. The desire to view one's children in a positive light is a tendency that most people (and any parent) will recognize immediately. This tendency should make questioning the morality of his daughter's chosen lifestyle uncomfortable, and inconsistent with the knowledge that she is otherwise very much the morally-upstanding woman that he raised and continues to love very much. Indeed, Mr. Cheney is not the only politician whose feelings about same-sex marriage have evolved, oftentimes evoked by the discovery that a child, another family member, or a close friend is gay. The arc of moral reasoning may be long, but it often seems to bend toward viewing those we love (including ourselves) in a positive light.

In this chapter we will argue for this view that moral and political beliefs arise from an intuitive process infused with emotion and thus subject to extraneous affective influences. We will describe research demonstrating how these processes can alter reasoning in ways that lead political partisans to see their moral views as grounded in principle and supported by facts. We will also discuss how this tendency to "factualize" moral intuitions, compounded by our insensitivity to our own susceptibility to this tendency, contributes to political conflict by creating mirror image misperceptions in which both liberals and conservatives come to see their political adversaries as hypocritical and intellectually challenged. Our overarching goal is to better understand the psychological factors contributing to the hyper-partisan state of contemporary American politics by situating them within our current scientific understanding of moral reasoning processes. And even more broadly, we will show how these processes affecting moral reasoning can be seen as yet another example of a long recognized tendency for people to confuse what they value with what they believe is true.

Thinking from the Top Down

If you asked a group of average people why they hold their particular position on some moral political issue such as capital punishment, many would likely tell you a story about reasoning. They might describe some basic values and principles they learned as a child or adolescent, and how through a thoughtful process of logical consideration they applied those principles, informed by basic facts about the world, to generate their opinions.

Some opinions may actually be formed through this kind of reasoned analysis, combining principles and facts to form a considered position on the matter at hand. But a crucial lesson learned from decades of social psychological research is that quite often the process proceeds in precisely the opposite fashion.

Beginning with work by Piaget (1953), Bartlett (1958), Bruner (1957), and others (e.g., Allport, 1955) on schema-based processing and perceptual sets, and continuing with huge bodies of research on priming (e.g., Bargh & Chartrand, 1999), expectancy confirmation processes (e.g., Darley & Fazio, 1980) and motivated reasoning (e.g., Kunda, 1990), psychologists have demonstrated repeatedly that perception and judgment processes are organized and directed as much by higher-order concepts, expectancies, and motivations than by specific aspects of the target stimulus. In a seminal paper, Haidt (2001) identified moral reasoning as particularly susceptible to this kind of top-down reasoning process. Challenging the rationalist view that had dominated moral psychology during the previous decades (Kohlberg, 1969; Turiel, 1978), Haidt argued that when ordinary people form moral judgments, they are seldom the product of some reasoned, principle-based analysis. Instead, moral evaluations result primarily from "gut" intuitions, implicit feelings that some act is morally good or morally bad. When moral reasoning occurs, Haidt (2001, 2007, 2012) posits that it is almost always due to social demands to explain or defend our moral intuitions to others, in which case "reasoning" operates in a post hoc fashion guided by, and providing justification for, those pre-existing moral intuitions.

Stated another way, what people colloquially refer to as "reasoning" more closely resembles arguing than rational deliberation (Mercier & Sperber, 2011), and people are more aptly characterized as intuitive lawyers than intuitive scientists (Baumeister & Newman, 1994; Ditto, Pizarro, & Tannenbaum, 2009; Tetlock, 2002). People may prefer to see their reasoning as bottom-up, rationally moving from evidence to conclusions, but research clearly shows that the process flows the other way as well, with desired or expected conclusions organizing cognitive processes from the top down in a way that privileges evidence for exactly the conclusions that people prefer or expect (Ditto & Lopez, 1992; Kunda, 1990). Just as attorneys are motivated by professional duty to only present evidence that supports their client's claims, everyday people are subject to a variety of motivations that can lead them to recruit evidence selectively to support their favored verdicts.

Moral Coherence and Factualization

But how does one recruit evidence to support a moral view? How can a father like Mr. Cheney, motivated to see his daughter's life choices in a positive light, generate reasons to support the morality of same-sex marriage?

It is important to first note two key differences between motivated reasoning and legal argumentation. Attorneys are fully cognizant that they are choosing evidence selectively to present a case in support of a particular conclusion. With motivated reasoning, however, the individual's explicit motivation is to see the world accurately, as it would do people little good to know that they had simply constructed a view of the world that was "rigged" to conform to their hopes and desires. Instead, preferences affect information processing in subtle ways that advantage preferred conclusions even when people feel that they are approaching the judgment problem in good faith (e.g., Ditto & Lopez, 1992; Ditto, Scepansky, Munro, Apanovitch, & Lockhart, 1998; Norton, Vandello, & Darley, 2004). Attorneys are also free to gather and present in trial any evidence that supports their position, no matter how implausible, one-sided, or internally inconsistent their argument might be. In contrast, because people faced with everyday judgments are interested (at least explicitly) in forming an accurate view of the world, a view that fits logically with other facts they understand to be true, what they come to believe is constrained by this "reality." People do not believe whatever they want to believe no matter its implausibility (Ditto & Lopez, 1992;

Kunda, 1990; Pyszczynski & Greenberg, 1987). Instead, motivated reasoning produces what is best construed as a compromise between what the individual wishes were true and what can plausibly be believed based on the available data (Ditto, 2009; Festinger, 1957; Heider, 1958).

A theoretical perspective that captures this nuanced process well is that of explanatory coherence (Read, Vanman, & Miller, 1997; Thagard, 2004). Coherence-based models posit that individuals construct beliefs through a process of parallel constraint satisfaction (e.g., Simon, Krawezyk, & Holyoak, 2004). They resemble classic cognitive consistency theories, but reject simplifying assumptions about linear causation in favor of a more dynamic view in which beliefs, feelings, goals, and actions all influence one another, and are adjusted iteratively toward a point of maximal internal consistency or "coherence." That is, very much consistent with the image of motivated reasoning sketched out above, coherence-based models depict people as striving in good faith to integrate and make sense of the information available to them, but doing so in a way that includes influence from both the bottom up (e.g., adjusting conclusions to fit facts) and the top down (e.g., adjusting facts to fit conclusions).

There is little reason to think that moral judgments are immune from coherence pressures. For example, research has shown that beliefs about the extent to which an action is controllable and intentional influence moral evaluations of that action (Shaver, 1985; Weiner, 1995). This is the normative, bottom-up process. Studies have also shown, however, that the reverse causal flow occurs; moral evaluation of an action can influence the extent to which perceivers infer that it must have been controlled and intended (Alicke, 2000; Knobe, 2003; Walster, 1966).

We believe that a similar process of mutual influence operates in moral justifications more generally. There are two primary ways that moral evaluations are justified. The first is by tying an act to a broad, underlying principle or rule. This is the essence of what philosophers refer to as deontological morality, in which certain acts are seen as inherently right or inherently wrong, independent of their consequences. For example, an individual may assert that a particular act of terrorism is morally wrong because it violates the principle that combatants should never intentionally target and kill innocent civilians. According to a deontological ethic, this principle is broad and inviolate, and should apply even if intentionally killing a small number of civilians might result in highly beneficial outcomes such as saving the lives of many more civilians than were killed in the original attack.

The second primary way to justify a moral belief makes precisely the opposite claim: that the morality of acts is fundamentally about consequences. This moral view encompasses a variety of related positions that are broadly referred to as consequentialist or utilitarian, according to which acts are judged as moral to the extent that they maximize positive outcomes. For example, an individual may assert that the use of atomic weapons against Japan in World War II was morally justified, despite the horrific death toll, because hastening a Japanese surrender saved many more lives than were lost in Hiroshima and Nagasaki.

As in the examples above, deontological and consequentialist logic often produce competing moral conclusions, and the tension between them provides the dynamic underlying classic moral dilemmas such as the well-known trolley problem (Foot, 1994). They are similar, however, in that both provide a rationale for moral evaluations that resembles the kinds of justifications typically provided for more objectively verifiable descriptive judgments. That is, descriptive statements are justified with some fact-based rationale, e.g., "Smoking cigarettes is bad for your health *because* it increases your chances of heart and lung disease." Both deontological and consequentialist rationales allow moral justifications to assume a similar structure, e.g., "Terrorism is morally wrong *because* it is never justified to kill innocent civilians" or "Dropping atomic bombs on Japan was morally justified *because* it saved more civilian lives than it cost."

To the extent that individuals ground their moral intuitions in either broad principle or a favorable cost–benefit analysis, moral judgments become subjectively *factualized*—experienced less like arbitrary preferences and more like rational, defensible, "objective" assessments (Ditto & Liu, 2012). Importantly, this should be true whether the moral evaluation was actually generated from the bottom up based on principle or cost–benefit analyses, or whether these rationales are generated post hoc (from the top down) to explain a gut moral intuition.

Let us return now to the predicament of our former Vice President. Emotional preferences are not generally considered reasonable justifications for moral judgments. As Mr. Cheney struggles—just as countless fathers and mothers have before him—to reconcile his conservative moral sensibilities with his affection for his daughter, he should feel more comfortable to the extent that he can ground his intuitive desire to embrace his daughter's lifestyle in broad moral principle (e.g., a libertarian ethic that prioritizes individual freedom) or recruit facts suggesting that same-sex marriage has few social costs relative to its many social benefits (e.g., it promotes stable families without posing a threat to the well-being of children or heterosexual marriage).

In the following sections we will review empirical evidence that the judgments of political partisans show both of these patterns, relying on principle selectively to support intuitively palatable moral evaluations, and recruiting facts selectively to make actions that feel moral seem effective and beneficial as well.

The Problem with Principle

The job of the U.S. Supreme Court is to uphold the fundamental principles of justice enumerated in the U.S. Constitution. Arguably the most fundamental of those fundamental principles is the freedom of speech guaranteed in the First Amendment. It is striking then, albeit not completely surprising, that in an analysis of over 50 years of Supreme Court decisions involving First Amendment claims (Epstein, Parker, & Segal, 2013), substantial ideological bias was revealed: liberal justices were more receptive than conservative justices to First Amendment arguments protecting liberal-friendly speech (e.g., public employee whistle-blowing), but conservative justices were more receptive than liberal ones to similar arguments protecting conservative-friendly speech (e.g., a club's right to exclude gay members).

Presidents, pundits, and jurists all want to be seen as people of principle. The term implies an individual of high character, whose judgments about difficult moral issues are not made haphazardly, but rather reflect deeply held commitments that cannot be breached even when the immediate benefits of violating the principle seem obvious. But this is precisely the problem with principle. Principles are by definition broad, widely applicable rules that should not be applied nor ignored selectively, and their ability to provide intellectual grounding for specific moral judgments derives directly from this generality. But generality is what makes principled judgment both intellectually and emotionally challenging. The same general rule that explains and justifies a desirable course of action in one case will often compel less palatable action in another. And yet, if one relies on a given principle only when it is convenient, the normative status of the principle as a justification for any specific moral claim is weakened, and the door is opened to charges of intellectual incoherence or hypocrisy.

Anecdotal evidence of the selective use of principle in political speech is too voluminous to fully recount here. Democrats tout the virtues of the Senate filibuster as an essential right of the minority party when Republicans are in control (calling attempts to amend it the "nuclear option"), then vote to limit its applicability a few years later when they have regained the majority in the Senate. Republicans unsurprisingly showed exactly the opposite pattern of preferences (Seitz-Wald, 2012). Perhaps most iconically, the Presidency of the U.S. was decided in *Bush v. Gore* with the five most conservative Supreme Court Justices (whose previous court decisions frequently favored state-sovereignty over federal intervention) deciding in this case that it was appropriate to overturn the Florida State Supreme Court's ruling (virtually guaranteeing the election of George W. Bush), while the four more liberal (and historically more federalism-friendly) justices favored allowing the state court's ruling to stand. Political flip-flopping of this kind is so regular that showing back-to-back video of politicians making conflicting appeals to principle is a central feature of the popular and influential comedy program *The Daily Show with Jon Stewart*.

Anecdotes and TV shows are not controlled experiments, of course, but the selective use of principle is exactly what would be expected from a moral coherence perspective. Rather than using principle to generate specific moral preferences from the bottom up, it will often be the case that political partisans selectively recruit particular principles from the top down based on whether or not that principle coheres with (and thus reinforces) their intuitive moral reaction to that specific set of circumstances. Because similar situations can generate quite different moral preferences, this top-down privileging of intuition-reinforcing principles will frequently result in individuals offering one principle to justify their desired course of action in one situation, but rejecting the applicability of that very same principle in a seemingly similar situation.

A number of experiments have now shown just this kind of selective use of principle by political partisans (Knowles & Ditto, 2012; Uhlmann, Pizarro, Tannenbaum, & Ditto, 2009). The basic approach in each study was to present participants with a moral dilemma in which they must choose between an action consistent with a deontological rationale (i.e., refusing to engage in a morally questionable act for a greater good) and one consistent with a consequentialist action (i.e., agreeing to engage in a morally questionable act for a greater good). Importantly, the scenario included extraneous information that would be expected to evoke differing intuitive reactions to the action alternatives depending on the participant's political ideology.

In one study, for example (Uhlmann et al., 2009, Study 1a), college students were presented with a modified version of the footbridge dilemma in which the morality of pushing one man to his death to save the lives of many others must be assessed. Half of the participants were faced with a decision about whether to push a man named "Tyrone Payton" into the path of an oncoming train to save "100 members of the New York Philharmonic," while the other half had to decide whether to push a man named "Chip Ellsworth III" to save "100 members of the Harlem Jazz Orchestra." The goal, of course, was to lead participants to infer that in the first case their decision involved whether to sacrifice one African-American life to save 100 that were mostly White, and in the second case whether to sacrifice one White life to save 100 that were mostly African-American. After reading the scenarios, participants completed a series of scales assessing their endorsement of consequentialism as a general moral principle (e.g., "It is sometimes necessary to allow the death of an innocent person in order to save a larger number of innocent people").

The results revealed that there was a tendency for all participants to be more likely to invoke a consequentialist justification for sacrificing a man with a stereotypically White American name than one with a stereotypically African-American name. When participant's political orientation was entered into the regression, however, a significant interaction effect was found. Students endorsing a conservative political ideology showed a non-significant reversal of the overall trend, expressing slightly greater support for consequentialism when considering the fate of Tyrone than Chip. As students became more liberal, however, they were increasingly likely to invoke a consequentialist rationale for sacrificing Chip's life, but a deontological rationale for saving Tyrone's. The same interaction pattern was replicated in another study using a more diverse sample and the lifeboat dilemma, in which participants must choose whether to throw a dying man (again, named either Chip or Tyrone) overboard to save the other passengers in a sinking lifeboat (Uhlmann et al., 2009, Study 1b). Liberals were again more likely to sacrifice Chip than Tyrone, whereas conservatives showed a slight tendency in the opposite direction.

These studies provide evidence of the selective use of principle, at least among political liberals. All participants were faced with the identical moral dilemma of deciding whether to sacrifice one man's life for the lives of many others. When the individual to be sacrificed was apparently African-American, liberals were expected to be particularly squeamish about sacrificing his life for the lives of a larger group of people that seemed likely to be mostly White. In this case, liberals more than conservatives endorsed the deontological principle that sacrificing one life to save many is not morally justified. However, when the same choice had to be made involving a White (and seemingly patrician) victim and a mostly African-American group of individuals to be saved, liberals' squeamishness was expected to dissipate, and in fact, liberals were found to be more likely than conservatives to reject the deontological rationale and endorse instead the consequentialist principle that the potential to save many African-American lives does justify the sacrifice of a single White one.

The obvious question that arises from the Chip–Tyrone studies is why political conservatives showed little evidence of principle switching. Given the distain for racial prejudice found among most Americans, and American college students in particular, conservatives were not expected to show a full reversal of the pattern found in liberals. Moral Foundations Theory (Graham et al., 2013), as well as a wealth of other research, suggests that race, with its deep connotations of inequality and victimization, is a particular moral hotspot for political liberals. Because political conservatives, on the other hand, are not as sensitized to race as their liberal counterparts, they were not expected to favor White lives over African-American ones, but simply to lack liberals' highly accessible intuitions regarding inequality and thus to respond in a more even-handed fashion to the Chip and Tyrone scenarios (both affectively and cognitively) than would liberals.

This does not mean, however, that conservatives are more principled than liberals, no matter what Republican politicians' and pundits' public devotion to principled decision-making would have one believe. It is quite possible to find issues that evoke conservative moral intuitions more so than liberal ones. For example, just as racial and other underrepresented minorities act as sacred "totems" to the liberal tribe, the U.S. military has a similar totemic quality for political conservatives. Moral Foundations Theory posits that conservatives place greater moral value than liberals on ingroup loyalty, and for many political conservatives, patriotism is a sacred value and the American military represents the ultimate symbol of national pride. Conservatives should, therefore, be more likely than liberals to give the American military moral leeway in evaluating their behavior, and to make a moral distinction between the lives of Americans and those of non-Americans.

To examine this prediction, Uhlmann et al. (2009, Study 3) presented participants with one of two military scenarios. Half of the participants received a scenario describing American military leaders deciding to carry out an attack on Iraqi insurgent leaders in order to prevent the future deaths of American troops. The other half read about Iraqi insurgent leaders deciding to carry out an attack on leaders of the American military in order to prevent future deaths of Iraqi insurgents. In both cases, it was explicitly stated that the attackers (whether American or Iraqi) neither wanted nor intended to cause civilian casualties, but in both cases the attack did. As in the Chip–Tyrone study, participants then expressed their endorsement of consequentialist moral principles. Perhaps not surprisingly, there was an overall tendency such that as political conservatism increased, so did a more permissive (i.e., consequentialist) view of any kind of collateral damage. More to the point, however, conservatives were significantly more likely to endorse consequentialist principles after reading about American-caused casualties than after reading about Iraqi-caused casualties. Liberals, on the other hand, showed a non-significant tendency in the opposite direction, viewing Iraqi-caused casualties in consequentialist terms, but being slightly more deontological when collateral damage was caused by American soldiers. Importantly, Uhlmann and colleagues (2009) replicated this effect in a follow up experiment (Study 4) by non-consciously priming participants with words related either to patriotism (e.g., American, loyal) or multiculturalism (e.g., diversity, equal). When reading about American-caused casualties, participants who were primed with patriotism were more likely to endorse consequentialist collateral damage than participants primed with multiculturalism. Replacing a non-manipulated individual difference variable (political ideology) with an experimental manipulation provides important evidence for the causal role of moral intuition in selective principle use.

As a moral issue, collateral damage scenarios pit deontological and consequentialist logics against one another in much the same way as the trolley or lifeboat dilemmas. Together, Uhlmann et al.'s (2009) data suggest that if the right moral button is pushed, political partisans—whether conservative or liberal—will invoke whichever of these moral stances best supports their ideologically-based moral intuitions. Liberals are consequentialists when considering White lives but show a deontological reluctance to sacrifice an African-American one. Conservatives can justify civilian casualties caused by American military action as a necessary evil, while condemning the morality of Iraqi soldiers when their actions inadvertently cause similar civilian carnage.

From a moral coherence perspective, selective reliance on principle does not represent a conscious, strategic attempt to build an argument for one's chosen moral position the way that an attorney deliberately builds a one-sided case in her client's favor. Rather, individuals prompted to explain or defend a moral choice (as they are asked to do in psychological experiments, and more importantly, in political debates, discussions, and negotiations) attempt to make sense of their feelings and thoughts on the matter. Because most people find both deontological and consequentialist rationales intuitively plausible (i.e., to almost anyone except moral philosophers, sometimes the ends seem to justify the means and sometimes they do not), they are likely to find most plausible whichever moral stance fits coherently with their preferred moral conclusion. If people actually applied principles consistently to moral judgments in a bottom-up fashion—always approaching moral quandaries as either principled deontologists or principled consequentialists for example—we would expect considerable consistency in the moral rationales offered across morally similar situations. But because moral principles are often recruited *from* specific moral situations rather than applied *to* them, people will often offer what seem like logically incompatible rationales for arguably identical moral judgments.

But what if it was argued that the moral rationales offered by Uhlmann et al.'s (2009) participants were not necessarily incompatible, but rather that these individuals might be consciously relying on nuanced, situation-specific moral rules? That is, perhaps our participants were not recruiting general moral principles selectively, but rather were naïve particularists (Dancy, 1993, 2004) cognizant of the fact that they were using different moral rules to evaluate African-American versus White or American versus Iraqi lives.

There are two primary reasons to discount this particularist explanation for the observed data (see Ditto et al., 2009, or Uhlmann et al., 2009, for a more detailed treatment of this concern). First, 92% of participants in Uhlmann et al.'s Chip–Tyrone lifeboat study said after the fact that their responses would not have differed if the target person was of another race, and 87% of participants in a pilot study reported by these same researchers explicitly rejected the idea that race was a relevant moral factor in life or death decisions.

Second, if participants in Uhlmann et al.'s (2009) studies were consciously using different moral rules to evaluate the worth of White versus African-American lives, then they should report differing responses across the Chip and Tyrone scenarios if both scenarios were judged together in a within-subjects design, just as they gave differing responses when this information was manipulated in a between subjects design. In fact, when Uhlmann and colleagues conducted a within-subjects version of the Chip and Tyrone study (Study 2), participants' responses were almost perfectly consistent across the two versions (r = .9). This consistency produced a particularly striking pattern for liberals, as it led them to demonstrate a complete reversal of their initial bias. Liberal participants evaluating the first scenario replicated the results of the initial Chip–Tyrone study: consequentialism was endorsed more strongly when deciding the fate of Chip than Tyrone. When these same liberal participants then read the alternative scenario (those reading about Chip first then read about Tyrone, and vice versa), they were suddenly more consequentialist toward Tyrone than Chip. Participants seemed to perceive a strong constraint to remain consistent in their use of moral principles across the two scenarios, as would be the case if one believed the principle being applied was a general one. This pronounced carry-over effect, together with participants' explicit rejection of race as a relevant moral consideration, provides strong support for our moral coherence account.

112   Peter H. Ditto and Brittany S. Liu

There seems to be solid evidence to believe that political partisans recruit principles selectively to support ideologically palatable conclusions. This selectivity serves to ground moral intuitions as exemplars of broad moral principle, making moral opinions feel like moral facts, and may even affect the judgments of the ostensibly principle-minded occupants of the highest court in the land (Epstein et al., 2013; Furgeson, Babcock, & Shane, 2008). American justice is frequently said to be blind, but it may be more accurate to say that it often sees the world through red- or blue-colored glasses.

What Is Moral Is Effective

Perhaps the most striking feature of the venomous culture war raging in contemporary American politics is the dramatic difference in factual beliefs between the liberal and conservative factions. Belief in the reality of global climate change is the most obvious example, but red and blue America show factual divergences in any number of areas, including whether gun possession promotes or reduces gun violence, whether social welfare programs promote or discourage economic growth, and the effectiveness of "enhanced" interrogation techniques in combatting terrorism, just to name a few.

Almost certainly the new media environment contributes to this divergence. Advances in television and computer technology have opened up a world teeming with entertainment and information options, many carefully tailored to fit specific consumer interests (Arceneaux & Johnson, 2013). A host of print publications, television news shows, and internet sites are clearly labeled for partisan consumption and allow citizens to expose themselves selectively to information congenial to their political inclinations (Arceneaux & Johnson, 2013; Iyengar, Hahn, Krosnick, & Walker, 2008; Sunstein, 2007).

But ideological selectivity does not end with exposure. Media silos are never completely impermeable, and we are all exposed on occasion to factual information that challenges our preferred beliefs about the state of national and world affairs. Such information is not likely to be processed in an even-handed manner. Beginning with Lord, Ross, and Lepper's (1979) highly influential demonstration of what they termed "biased assimilation" processes, a long tradition of research has confirmed that strong attitudes and ideological commitments guide information processing such that scientific data and other fact-based information that challenge one's political preferences is subjected to more intense critical scrutiny than is more politically congenial information (Crawford, Jussim, Cain, & Cohen, 2013; Kahan, 2013; Kahan, Jenkins-Smith, & Braman, 2011; Kopko, Mckinnon, Budziak, Devine, & Nawara, 2011; Munro & Ditto, 1997; Scurich & Shniderman, in press; Taber & Lodge, 2006). Some have even argued that because of our skeptical approach to information that challenges our political beliefs, exposure to such information can actually backfire, reinforcing rather than diminishing the challenged belief (Lord et al., 1979;

Nyhan & Reifler, 2010; Redlawsk, 2002; but see also Miller, McHoskey, Bane, & Dowd, 1993).

It seems likely that both selective exposure and selective interpretation processes contribute to the fact war between the liberal and conservative wings of American politics. But the question most relevant to us here is why political partisans are attracted to certain kinds of facts and not others. That is, what is it, specifically, that makes certain factual beliefs reinforce certain political beliefs?

If you examine closely the various fact gaps between liberals and conservatives, many of them share a particular quality: political partisans favor facts suggesting that the policies they believe are the most morally praiseworthy are also the most pragmatically beneficial. For example, many conservatives see gun ownership as an important moral right, and also tend to believe that increasing gun ownership will lead to decreases in criminal activity (e.g., Lott, 1998). Liberals, on the other hand, are more morally disapproving of gun ownership, and also tend to believe that it increases rather than decreases crime (e.g., Anglemyer, Horvath, & Rutherford, 2014). Conversely, liberals tend to see social welfare programs (e.g., the minimum wage, unemployment insurance) as both morally admirable and economically stimulative, whereas conservatives often view them as simply rewarding the unproductive, and thus both morally dubious and economically counterproductive.

This psychological link between morality and effectiveness is interesting because an essential aspect of moral evaluation is its conceptual independence from pragmatic considerations. The very essence of deontological judgment, for example, is that some actions are seen as morally wrong (e.g., pushing a person in front of an oncoming trolley) even when engaging in those actions would result in the best consequences (e.g., one person dying rather than five). Similarly, behavioral scientists describe some values as "sacred" or "protected," meaning that they are given disproportionate or even infinite weight in decision-making, and thus distort rational, utilitarian cost–benefit considerations (e.g., Atran, Axelrod, & Davis, 2007; Baron & Spranca, 1997; Bartels & Medin, 2007; Tetlock, 2003). In short, morality is about doing what is right, not doing what is best, and although consequentialist morality serves to conflate these two standards to an important degree (essentially defining what is right *as* what is best), virtually every ordinary person—and all but the most dogged consequentialist philosophers (e.g., Singer, 1993)—would acknowledge that there are substantial limits on the extent to which beneficial ends can justify any means (e.g., harvesting a healthy person's organs to save the lives of numerous others).

But consider the issue from a coherence perspective. When people's moral intuitions conflict with cold, cost–benefit calculations, one option is to acknowledge and accept this conflict, maintaining, for example, that capital punishment is morally wrong even though it deters future crime. A half century of psychological research, however, has demonstrated that this kind of cognitive conflict is psychologically unstable, and that mental systems evolve naturally toward reducing conflict by changing, adding, or altering the importance of the component cognitions (Cooper, 2007; Festinger, 1957; Read et al., 1997). In coherence terms, believing that capital punishment is morally wrong but practically effective is more complicated and less coherent than a view in which one's moral and pragmatic beliefs about capital punishment are affectively consistent. Because the implicit nature of moral intuitions makes them difficult to change, coherence pressures should primarily operate toward bringing beliefs about the costs and benefits of capital punishment in line with its moral evaluation, likely via the biased assimilation processes so well documented in political judgment (Lord & Taylor, 2009). People who believe capital punishment is morally wrong should be inclined to believe evidence suggesting that it is also an ineffective deterrent or that it involves substantial costs such as frequent wrongful executions, and find flaws in evidence to the contrary. People more comfortable with the morality of the death penalty on the other hand, should show the opposite pattern of acceptance and skepticism (Lord et al., 1979).

Like the selective use of moral principle, the selective recruitment of facts—a process we have referred to in the past as motivated consequentialism (Liu & Ditto, 2013)—should help to factualize moral intuitions by grounding them in a highly intuitive economic logic. It may be difficult to argue for the morality of gun ownership on its own terms, but it becomes much easier when armed with facts suggesting that it produces tangible benefits like reducing crime.

If this kind of motivated consequentialism occurs, people's beliefs should show a natural pattern such that acts perceived as moral should also be perceived as having relatively few costs and many benefits. To test this prediction, we (Liu & Ditto, 2013, Study 2) surveyed over 1,800 participants recruited from the website *YourMorals.org* regarding their beliefs about four controversial social issues, two of which were morally more objectionable to political conservatives than liberals (embryonic stem cell research, promoting contraception use in sexual education classes) and two of which were more morally objectionable to political liberals than conservatives (enhanced interrogations of terrorist suspects, capital punishment). Across all four issues, there were substantial positive associations between participants' judgments of an issue's morality and their factual beliefs about its effectiveness. For instance, the more strongly participants believed that embryonic stem cell research was morally acceptable, the more they believed such research would lead to cures for conditions like Alzheimer's Disease. Likewise, the more strongly participants believed that educating teens about contraception was morally wrong, the less effective they believed condoms were in preventing sexually-transmitted infections and the more they believed that these programs encouraged teens to have sex. These results held for perceptions of both the costs and benefits of each issue and after controlling for political orientation, gender, how informed participants said they were on an issue, and how morally convicted participants felt about an issue.

This psychological connection between morality and effectiveness is quite consistent with the operation of top-down moral coherence processes, but it might also be expected if the majority of our respondents were simply bottom-up consequentialists, deciding, for example, that stem cell research is morally acceptable precisely *because* it is effective. To partially address this issue, participants in the Liu and Ditto (2013) study were asked to rate whether each policy was inherently (i.e., deontologically) immoral, that is, immoral even if it achieved good consequences. This makes the findings more puzzling from a rationalist perspective in that participants were in essence saying that a policy like stem cell research was immoral even it did not produce negative consequences, but that it also just happened to produce negative consequences as well.

Of course, the ideal way to address issues of causal influence is to do it experimentally, manipulating participants' moral evaluation of an act and observing the effect of that manipulation on factual beliefs about the act. Accordingly, we asked undergraduate students to participate in a study on political beliefs in exchange for extra course credit (Liu & Ditto, 2013, Study 3). Participants were first asked to agree or disagree with statements assessing their beliefs about the inherent morality of the death penalty (e.g., "In terms of morality, it doesn't matter if the death penalty discourages would-be criminals, it is still morally wrong"), as well as factual statements about the death penalty (e.g., "The death penalty is an effective deterrent that prevents people from committing crimes"). They were then randomly assigned to either read an essay arguing that the death penalty is inherently morally wrong, or one arguing that the death penalty is inherently morally acceptable. These essays were designed to sway participants' moral evaluations, without referencing deterrence, effectiveness, or negative consequences of the death penalty. For example, the pro-death penalty essay (ostensibly authored by a priest who had worked with death row inmates) argued that the death penalty is the best and most fair means of achieving justice for murder and that favoring the death penalty underscored the value of human life. The anti-death penalty essay (ostensibly written by a police officer who had witnessed many gruesome murders) argued instead that the death penalty is inhumane and barbaric and that peace cannot be achieved by responding to violence with more violence. After reading the essays, participants answered the same moral judgment and factual belief questions they had answered previously.

As anticipated, the essays made a small, but statistically significant, impact on participants' evaluations of the death penalty's inherent morality. Compared to their pre-essay judgments, participants rated the death penalty as more inherently moral after reading the pro-death penalty essay, and as more inherently immoral after reading the anti-death penalty essay. More importantly, the essays were also effective at changing participants' factual beliefs about the consequences of capital punishment, such as whether capital punishment deterred people from committing crimes like murder, or whether it frequently led to wrongful executions of innocent people. Participants saw the death penalty as more effective (that is, as having greater benefits and fewer costs) after reading the pro-death penalty essay, and less effective after reading the anti-death penalty essay. It is worth emphasizing that participants changed their factual beliefs about capital punishment despite the fact that the essays were comprised of purely principle-based arguments and never mentioned any costs or benefits associated with it. Furthermore, mediation analyses supported the causal role of moral belief change in factual belief change.

Together, the results of the Liu and Ditto (2013) studies illustrate another way that moral coherence processes serve to fortify the differing moral intuitions of political partisans, and help to explain the factual gulf seen between liberals and conservatives in the U.S. It is impressive to see someone take a moral stand, arguing that engaging in some act, like waterboarding suspected terrorists, is morally wrong despite the fact that it might be practically advantageous. But taking such a stand is psychologically challenging given the essential conflict it entails between moral impulse and a rational cost–benefit analysis. Our assertion is that such conflict tends to resolve itself by individuals selectively recruiting factual beliefs to bring cost–benefit analyses in line with moral evaluations. Believing that the most moral course of action is also the most beneficial course of action grounds moral evaluations in consequentialist logic, making them feel less like intuitions or opinions and more like justified beliefs, backed by facts and reason. The factual differences that mark the battle lines of the American culture war are best understood as each side's assertion that the policies they believe are *moral* also happen to be the most *effective*.

Coherence and the Culture War

In the preceding sections we have described two lines of research suggesting that political partisans factualize their moral intuitions by creating coherent moral narratives in which policies that feel morally right are seen as grounded in principle and likely to produce optimal utilitarian outcomes. We believe this factualization process contributes to political conflict in two different ways, one intrapersonal and the other interpersonal.

At an intrapersonal level, moral coherence processes serve to fortify moral intuitions by transforming them into moral beliefs. In a sense, people are both moral intuitionists and moral realists. Our beliefs about right and wrong often derive from affective reactions rather than deliberative logic, but as many before us have noted, people approach the world as naïve realists—believing that their perceptions reflect the external world as it is—with little appreciation for how top-down processes shape subjective impressions (e.g., Ross & Ward, 1996). Committed partisans of the left and right hold differing moral views (Graham et al., 2013) and one can imagine a political world in which these are treated as simply legitimate differences of moral opinion. However, to the extent that these opinions are experienced as crucial matters of principle, or as justified beliefs about what policy will produce the most beneficial outcomes, our feelings about moral right and wrong become things that can themselves be factually right or wrong (Goodwin & Darley, 2008), with one's own side's moral beliefs almost inevitably perceived as right and those of one's opponents equally inevitably perceived as wrong (in both senses of those words).

It is not hard to imagine that our natural tendency to integrate moral intuitions into coherent narratives about the "facts" of the world serves to reinforce partisan's beliefs in the validity of their side's policy positions and makes negotiated settlement of morally sensitive political issues considerably more difficult. It is hard for political opponents to find a middle ground when both sides view compromise as an abdication of principle and their own side's policy positions as demonstrably more effective than their opponents' policies (based on "objective" evidence).

But consider too how the factualization processes we describe are likely to be perceived and responded to at an interpersonal level. People are notorious for recognizing biased judgment in others, while failing to recognize it in themselves (Pronin, 2007). This suggests that while we are unlikely to appreciate the selective nature of our own side's use of principle and facts, that selectivity should be much more obvious to our political adversaries (just as theirs is more obvious to us). This differential sensitivity to bias seems likely to contribute to common and pernicious political stereotypes.

People who justify a given policy based on one principle, but reject that principle in a seemingly similar case, appear (and perhaps are) hypocritical. Charges of hypocrisy are a common insult hurled by both sides of the political aisle in American politics (just google Democratic or Republican hypocrisy—the images are the best part). An interesting manifestation of this recognition is the tendency of both sides to respond to political controversies by constructing counterfactuals implying the other side's double standards (e.g., "If a Republican made that remark, he would be vilified!"; "George W. Bush took far more vacation days when he was in office than President Obama has!").

The selective use of facts can foment similar negative perceptions. When another person adamantly believes a particular fact to be true that you just as adamantly believe is untrue, your first reaction would likely be to question that person's intelligence. Disparaging the intellectual competence of political adversaries is, of course, a common (and much enjoyed) pastime for partisans of both political persuasions. A similar and only slightly more benign response is to see individuals with differing factual beliefs as deluded victims of their own side's political propaganda (e.g., both liberal and conservative pundits are fond of using the Jonestown-inspired imagery that the other side must be "drinking the Kool-Aid").

The crucial point is that moral coherence effects can contribute to political conflict both by reinforcing and reifying the opposing moral positions held by each side, and by contributing to both sides' unflattering perception of their political opponents as unprincipled, unintelligent, and under the influence of a manipulative political elite. Importantly, a key dynamic in both processes is our differential sensitivity to bias in ourselves versus others. An interesting implication

118 Peter H. Ditto and Brittany S. Liu

of the bias blind spot perspective (Pronin, 2007), as well as research on "motivated skepticism" (Ditto & Lopez, 1992; Ditto et al., 1998), is that when political partisans on one side point out instances of bias in the other side, they will often be correct. Where both liberals and conservatives most clearly miss the mark is in their belief that they and their political brethren are immune to the partisan biases that they see so clearly, and complain about so loudly, in the other side.

Conclusions

Philosopher John Rawls was exceedingly clear about what he thought was required to govern a pluralistic society justly (Rawls, 1971). He argued that when a collection of people includes those of different moral or religious beliefs, political transactions should be restricted to a common intellectual currency that all sides would find persuasive: arguments based on universally-held values, evidence, and reason. Arguments based on the superiority of one moral position over another are acceptable in private thought and discussion, according to Rawls, but should be avoided in the public sphere where universal participation in decision-making is the ideal and where the decisions that are made affect the society as a whole.

Superficially, political discourse in the U.S. holds well to Rawls' idealized notion of public reason. Politicians and pundits make principled arguments for their favored policies and cite data to support how implementation of those policies will improve the lives of everyday citizens. But the research reported here suggests that in important ways public reason in contemporary American politics is little more than an illusion. Democrats and Republicans argue their positions citing principles they tout as universal and facts they believe are true, but the principles and facts they choose to utilize are shaped to support the superiority of their own particular moral sensibilities. Politicians of the left and right argue about runaway spending or intrusive regulation, framing them as general principles of effective governing, but a close look reveals that both sides are more than happy to spend money on government programs they see as moral (e.g., Democrats on social welfare, Republicans on defense) and to regulate behavior they see as immoral (e.g., discrimination for Democrats, abortion for Republicans). What seems like rational argumentation and cost–benefit consideration is just a veneer, hiding what in many ways is just a good old-fashioned clash of competing moral visions.

Perhaps this is stated too strongly, particularly given the notion at the heart of coherence-based models that judgments reflect bottom-up as well as top-down influences, and Rawls' recognition that his ideal of public reason was subject to many practical challenges similar to those discussed in this chapter (Rawls, 1997). But Rawls' ideas are important because they can be seen as a continuation of the Enlightenment project of admonishing people to distinguish empirically verifiable facts from inherently subjective values. David Hume was the first to discuss in detail the tendency of even the most sophisticated thinkers to blur this line between fact and value (Hume, 1740/1985), observing his fellow philosophers inappropriately draw prescriptive conclusions from descriptive statements in what he termed the is–ought problem.

This chapter makes a similar argument about the pervasive human tendency to blur the distinction between descriptive and prescriptive judgment, but the research we describe illustrates the opposite conceptual confusion, what we sometimes refer to as the other is–ought problem (Ditto & Liu, 2012). Where Hume was concerned primarily about the tendency to infer how the world ought to be from how the world is, our central concern is with the converse tendency to infer how the world is from how (each of us believes) it ought to be. Both are important fallacies and the psychological dynamic underlying both of them—the desire for consistency between our descriptive and prescriptive views of the world—is itself wonderfully consistent with the logic of explanatory coherence.

The world makes most sense when what we value coheres with what we believe to be true. At an individual level, this tendency to construct morally coherent worlds likely provides some measure of comfort to people, like our former Vice President, as they struggle to reconcile the various and often contradictory threads of their moral, political, and personal beliefs. At a societal level, however, the consequences of moral coherence processes are less comforting. As the data clearly show (at least to us), the tendency to confuse what we value with what we believe is an important source of the conflict, distrust, and mutual recrimination underlying the dysfunctional state of contemporary American politics.

References

Alicke, M. (2000). Culpable control and the psychology of blame. *Psychological Bulletin, 126*, 556–574.

Allport, F. H. (1955). *Theories of Perception and the Concept of Structure.* New York: Wiley.

Anglemyer, A., Horvath, T., & Rutherford, G. (2014). The accessibility of firearms and risk for suicide and homicide victimization among household members: A systematic review and meta-analysis. *Annals of Internal Medicine, 160*, 101–110.

Arceneaux, K., & Johnson, M. (2013). *Changing Minds or Changing Channels? Partisan News in an Age of Choice.* Chicago: University of Chicago Press.

Atran, S., Axelrod, R. & Davis, R. (2007). Sacred barriers to conflict resolution. *Science, 317*, 1039–1040.

Bargh, J. A., & Chartrand, T. L. (1999). The unbearable automaticity of being. *American Psychologist, 54*, 462–479.

Baron, J., & Spranca, M. (1997). Protected values. *Organizational Behavior and Human Decision Processes, 70*, 1–16.

Bartels, D. M., & Medin, D. L. (2007). Are morally-motivated decision makers insensitive to the consequences of their choices? *Psychological Science, 18*, 24–28.

Bartlett, F. (1958). *Thinking: An Experimental and Social Study.* New York: Basic Books.

Baumeister, R. F., & Newman, L. S. (1994). Self-regulation of cognitive inference and decision processes. *Personality and Social Psychology Bulletin, 20*, 3–19.

Bruner, J. S. (1957). On perceptual readiness. *Psychological Review, 64*, 123–152.

Cooper, J. (2007). *Cognitive Dissonance: Fifty Years of a Classic Theory*. Thousand Oaks, CA: Sage.

Crawford, J. T., Jussim, L., Cain, T. R. & Cohen, F. (2013). Right-wing authoritarianism and social dominance orientation differentially predict biased evaluations of media reports. *Journal of Applied Social Psychology, 43*, 163–174.

Dancy, J. P. (1993). *Moral Reasons*. Oxford, UK: Blackwell Publishing.

Dancy, J. P. (2004). *Ethics without Principles*. Oxford, UK: Clarendon Press.

Darley, J. M., & Fazio, R. H. (1980). Expectancy confirmation processes arising in the social interaction sequence. *American Psychologist, 35*, 867–881.

Ditto, P. H. (2009). Passion, reason, and necessity: A quantity of processing view of motivated reasoning. In T. Bayne & J. Fernandez (Eds.), *Delusion, Self-Deception, and Affective Influences on Belief Formation* (pp. 23–53). New York: Psychology Press.

Ditto, P. H., & Lopez, D. F. (1992). Motivated skepticism: Use of differential decision criteria for preferred and nonpreferred conclusions. *Journal of Personality and Social Psychology, 63*, 568–584.

Ditto, P. H., & Liu, B. (2012). Deontological dissonance and the consequentialist crutch. In M. Mikulincer & P. Shaver (Eds.), *The Social Psychology of Morality: Exploring the Causes of Good and Evil* (pp. 51–70). Washington, DC: American Psychological Association.

Ditto, P. H., Scepansky, J. A., Munro, G. D., Apanovitch, A. M., & Lockhart, L. K. (1998). Motivated sensitivity to preference-inconsistent information. *Journal of Personality and Social Psychology, 75*, 53–69.

Ditto, P. H., Pizarro, D. A., & Tannenbaum, D. (2009). Motivated moral reasoning. In D. M. Bartels, C. W. Bauman, L. J. Skitka, and D. L. Medin (Eds.), *The Psychology of Learning and Motivation* (Vol. 50, pp. 307–338). Burlington: Academic Press.

Epstein, L., Parker, C. M., & Segal, J. A. (2013). Do justices defend the speech they hate? In-group bias, opportunism, and the First Amendment. Working paper presented at the 2013 annual meeting of the American Political Science Association, Chicago, IL.

Festinger, L. (1957). *A Theory of Cognitive Dissonance*. Stanford, CA: Stanford University Press.

Foot, P. (1994). The problem of abortion and the doctrine of double effect. In B. Steinbock & A. Norcross (Eds.), *Killing and Letting Die* (2nd edn., pp. 266–279). New York: Fordham University Press.

Furgeson, J. R., Babcock, L., & Shane, P. M. (2008). Behind the mask of method: Political orientation and constitutional interpretive preferences. *Law and Human Behavior, 32*, 502–510.

Goodwin, G. P., & Darley, J. M. (2008). The psychology of meta-ethics: Exploring objectivism. *Cognition, 106*, 1339–1366.

Graham, J., Haidt, J., Koleva, S., Motyl, M., Iyer, R., Wojcik, S. P., & Ditto, P. H. (2013). Moral foundations theory: The pragmatic validity of moral pluralism. *Advances in Experimental Social Psychology, 47*, 55–130.

Haidt, J. (2001). The emotional dog and its rational tail: A social intuitionist approach to moral judgment. *Psychological Review, 108*, 814–834.

Haidt, J. (2007). The new synthesis in moral psychology. *Science, 316*, 998–1002.

Haidt, J. (2012). *The Righteous Mind: Why Good People are Divided by Politics and Religion.* New York: Pantheon.

Heider, F. (1958). *The Psychology of Interpersonal Relations.* New York: Wiley.

Hume, D. (1985). *A Treatise of Human Nature.* Penguin: London. (Original work published 1739–1740)

Iyengar, S., Hahn, K., Krosnick, J., & Walker, J. (2008). Selective exposure to campaign communication: The role of anticipated agreement and issue public membership. *Journal of Politics, 70,* 186–200.

Kahan, D. M. (2013). Ideology, motivated reasoning, and cognitive reflection. *Judgment and Decision Making, 8,* 407–424.

Kahan, D. M., Jenkins-Smith, H., & Braman, D. (2011). Cultural cognition of scientific consensus. *Journal of Risk Research, 14,* 147–174.

Knobe, J. (2003). Intentional action and side-effects in ordinary language. *Analysis, 63,* 190–193.

Knowles, E. D., & Ditto, P. H. (2012). Preference, principle, and political casuistry. In J. Hanson (Ed.), *Ideology, Psychology, and Law* (pp. 341–379). New York: Oxford University Press.

Kohlberg, L. (1969). Stage and sequence: The cognitive-developmental approach to socialization. In D. A. Goslin (Ed.), *Handbook of Socialization Theory and Research* (pp. 347–489). Chicago: Rand McNally.

Kopko, K. C., Mckinnon, S., Budziak, J., Devine, C. J., & Nawara, S. P. (2011). In the eye of the beholder? Motivated reasoning in disputed elections. *Political Behavior, 33,* 271–290.

Kunda, Z. (1990). The case for motivated reasoning. *Psychological Bulletin, 108,* 480–498.

Liu, B. S., & Ditto, P. H. (2013). What dilemma? Moral evaluation shapes factual beliefs. *Social Psychological and Personality Science, 4,* 316–323.

Lord, C. G., & Taylor, C. A. (2009). Biased assimilation: Effects of assumptions and expectations on the interpretation of new evidence. *Social and Personality Psychology Compass, 3/5,* 827–841.

Lord, C. G., Ross, L., & Lepper, M. R. (1979). Biased assimilation and attitude polarization: The effects of prior theories on subsequently considered evidence. *Journal of Personality and Social Psychology, 37,* 2098–2109.

Lott, J. R. (1998). *More Guns, Less Crime.* Chicago: University of Chicago Press.

Mercier, H., & Sperber, D. (2011). Why do humans reason? Arguments for an argumentative theory. *Behavioral and Brain Sciences, 34,* 57–111.

Miller, A. G., McHoskey, J. W., Bane, C. M., & Dowd, T. G. (1993). The attitude polarization phenomenon: Role of response measure, attitude extremity, and behavioral consequences of reported attitude change. *Journal of Personality and Social Psychology, 64,* 561–574.

Munro, G. D., & Ditto, P. H. (1997). Biased assimilation, attitude polarization, and affect in reactions to stereotype-relevant scientific information. *Personality and Social Psychology Bulletin, 23,* 636–653.

Norton, M. I., Vandello, J. A., & Darley, J. M. (2004). Casuistry and Socials category bias. *Journal of Personality and Social Psychology, 87,* 817–831.

Nyhan, B., & Reifler, J. (2010). When corrections fail: The persistence of political misconceptions. *Political Behavior, 32,* 303–330.

Piaget, J. (1953). *The Origin of Intelligence in the Child.* New York: Routledge.

Pronin, E. (2007). Perception and misperception of bias in human judgment. *Trends in Cognitive Sciences, 11,* 37–43.

Pyszczynski, T. & Greenberg, J. (1987). Toward and integration of cognitive and motivational perspectives on social inference: A biased hypothesis-testing model. In L. Berkowitz (Ed.), *Advances in Experimental Social Psychology* (Vol. 20, pp. 297–340). New York: Academic Press.

Rawls, J. (1971). *A Theory of Justice.* Cambridge, MA: Harvard University Press.

Rawls, J. (1997). The idea of public reason revisited. *Chicago Law Review, 64,* 765–807.

Read, S. J., Vanman, E. J., & Miller, L. C. (1997). Connectionism, parallel constraint satisfaction processes, and gestalt principles: (Re)introducing cognitive dynamics to social psychology. *Personality and Social Psychology Review, 1,* 26–53.

Redlawsk, D. (2002). Hot cognition or cool consideration: Testing the effects of motivated reasoning on political decision making. *Journal of Politics, 64,* 1021–1044.

Ross, L., & Ward, A. (1996). Naive realism in everyday life: Implications for social conflict and misunderstanding. In T. Brown, E. Reed, & E. Turiel (Eds.), *Values and Knowledge* (pp. 103–135). Hillsdale, NJ: Lawrence Erlbaum.

Scurich, N., & Shniderman, A. (in press). The selective allure of neuroscientific explanations. *PLOSone.*

Seitz-Wald, A. (November 27, 2012). Filibuster reform: The Senate is filled with hypocrites. *Salon.* Retrieved September 3, 2015, from http://www.salon.com/2012/11/27/plenty_of_hypocrisy_to_go_around_on_filibuster_reform

Shaver, K. G. (1985). *The Attribution of Blame.* New York: Springer-Verlag.

Simon, D., Krawezyk, D. C., & Holyoak, K. J. (2004). Construction of preferences by constraint satisfaction. *Psychological Science, 15,* 331–336.

Singer, P. (1993). *Animal Liberation,* 2nd edn. London: Thorsons.

Sunstein, C. R. (2007). *Republic.com 2.0.* Princeton, NJ: Princeton University Press.

Taber, C. S., & Lodge, M. (2006). Motivated skepticism in the evaluation of political beliefs. *American Journal of Political Science, 50,* 755–769.

Tetlock, P. E. (2002). Social functionalist frameworks for judgment and choice: Intuitive politicians, theologians, and prosecutors. *Psychological Review, 109,* 451–471.

Tetlock, P. E. (2003). Thinking about the unthinkable: Coping with secular encroachments on sacred values. *Trends in Cognitive Science, 7,* 320–324.

Thagard, P. (2004). *Coherence in Thought and Action.* Boston: MIT Press.

Turiel, E. (1978). Social regulations and domains of social concepts. In W. Damon (Ed.), *New Directions for Child Development. Vol. 1. Social Cognition* (pp. 45–74). New York: Gardner.

Uhlmann, E. L., Pizarro, D. A., Tannenbaum, D., & Ditto, P. H. (2009). The motivated use of moral principles. *Judgment and Decision Making, 4,* 476–491.

Walster, E. (1966). Assignment of responsibility for an accident. *Journal of Personality and Social Psychology, 3,* 73–79.

Weiner, B. (1995). *Judgments of Responsibility: A Foundation for a Theory of Social Conduct.* New York: Guilford Press.

6

RESTRAINING SELF-INTEREST OR ENABLING ALTRUISM

Morality and Politics

Nate C. Carnes and Ronnie Janoff-Bulman

In a recent congressional session, Democrats advocated an extension of unemployment benefits while Republicans argued for major cuts to the food stamp program. Conservative state legislatures have passed ever-more restrictive laws limiting women's access to legal abortion, while legislatures in liberal states have worked to grant marriage equality regardless of sexual orientation. It seems that politics has become markedly more polarized and predictable, as Republicans have aligned themselves with conservative positions and Democrats with liberal positions (Pew Research Center, 2014). Outside of Washington, psychologists have focused increasing attention on political ideology. Researchers have found that conservatives have stronger physiological reactions to threatening noises and images than liberals (Oxley, Smith, Alford, Hibbing, Miller, Scalero, et al., 2008), have more fixed responses and less neurocognitive sensitivity to response conflicts than liberals (Amodio, Jost, Master, & Yee, 2007), and attentionally and physiologically are more oriented to aversive (unpleasant) stimuli than liberals, who are more oriented to appetitive (pleasant) images (Dodd, Balzer, Jacobs, Gruszczynski, Smith, & Hibbing, 2012). Relatedly, liberals are more open to novel stimuli, whereas conservatives learn negative stimuli better than positive stimuli (Shook & Fazio, 2009). Differences in political ideology are found both in the psychological laboratory and in the political agendas of the left and right. In this chapter we link these differences through an exploration of motivation and morality, and in particular their confluence in moral motivation.

Our claim is that liberal–conservative differences reflect distinct moral orientations that are based in different motivational systems. The distinct motivations are reflected in the above-noted results of psychological research focused on attentional, physiological, and learning responses of liberals and conservatives. In past work we have linked these basic motivations to differences in morality, and specifically moral motives and moral regulation, which in turn are associated with different policy positions and preferences for liberals and conservatives (Janoff-Bulman, 2009; Janoff-Bulman & Carnes, 2013; Janoff-Bulman, Sheikh, & Baldacci, 2008). Here our intention is not only to further explain these links, but also to begin addressing why these links from motivation to morality to politics might exist at all. The answer, we suggest, centers on the functional role morality plays in facilitating social life.

The Fundamental Motivational Distinction and Two Systems of Moral Regulation

Across the varied domains of psychology, from neuroscience to clinical psychology, and cognitive to social psychology, researchers and theorists have distinguished between two motivational orientations, best understood as basic approach versus avoidance (Carver, 2006; Carver & Scheier, 1998; Gray, 1982, 1990; Higgins, 1997, 1998; for reviews, see Carver & Scheier, 2008, and Gable, Reis, & Elliot, 2003). These motivations regulate behavior through behavioral activation versus inhibition and typically involve different end-states; more specifically, approach motivation activates behavior through a focus on positive outcomes (i.e., rewards and gains), whereas avoidance motivation inhibits behavior through a focus on negative outcomes (i.e., punishments and losses).

Janoff-Bulman and colleagues (Janoff-Bulman, 2009; Janoff-Bulman & Carnes, 2013; Janoff-Bulman, Sheikh, and Baldacci, 2008) proposed that conservatives are more sensitive to negative outcomes and inhibition-based avoidance motivation whereas liberals are more sensitive to positive outcomes and activation-based approach motivation, propositions we address more fully below. Why these differences might account for left–right politics, and their manifestation in support for particular social policies, is not readily apparent. We think the missing link is morality, and particularly work linking morality with these motivational differences.

It is generally recognized that morality evolved in order to facilitate cooperation and coordinate social life (Darwin, 1998/1871; de Waal, 1996; Haidt, 2007; Wilson, 1975). There is a rich body of empirical work that suggests that although we can be self-interested (Ariely, 2008, 2012; Baron, 2007; Bersoff, 1999; de Mesquita, Smith, Siverson, & Morrow, 2003; Haidt, 2012; Leary, 2005; Lerner, Tetlock, Schneider, & Shanteau, 2003), we are also genuinely altruistic (Batson, 1998; Bowles, 2006; Boyd, 2006; de Waal, 2008; Harbaugh, Mayr & Burghart, 2007; Keltner, 2009; Nowak & Highfield, 2011; Rilling, Gutman, Zeh, Pagnoni, Berns, & Kilts, 2002; Sober & Wilson, 1998; Warneken & Tomasello, 2006; Wilson, 2012). Humans have both a self-interested side and an altruistic side (or at least a groupish side; see Haidt, 2012) to their nature, a conclusion consistent with the work of primatologist Frans de Waal (1996, 2005, 2008), who calls us the bipolar ape because we have the capacity for both great cruelty and great kindness.

An array of evolutionary mechanisms have been theorized to help explain cooperation and altruism, including kin selection (Hamilton, 1964), reciprocal altruism (Trivers, 1971), indirect reciprocity (Alexander, 1987), cultural evolution (Richerson & Boyd, 2005), and group selection (Kesebir, 2012; Nowak, Tarnita, & Wilson, 2010). Wilson (2012) has argued that individual-level selection forces shaped the self-interested side of our nature, whereas group-level selection forces shaped the more altruistic side. Richerson and Boyd (2005) also argue that group selection shaped human nature, but they rely heavily on gene-culture coevolution. It is plausible that cultural evolution is sufficient to explain much of the variation we observe in human behavior. Regardless, genetic evolution, cultural evolution, and coevolution all lead to the same maxim that morality is for social life.

Following from this body of work on human nature, Janoff-Bulman and Carnes (2013) characterized morality as interlocking sets of psychological processes that work together to both suppress self-interest and enable altruism in order to make social life possible. This differs in a subtle but important way from the definition proposed by Haidt and Kesebir (2010), which argues that moral systems make cooperative social life possible by suppressing selfishness; here the role of morality in directing our better natures toward altruism is omitted. Janoff-Bulman and Carnes (2013) provide a framework called the Model of Moral Motives (MMM) that fits neatly with a definition of morality that recognizes both self-interest and altruism. It organizes the moral domain according to the fundamental motivational distinction discussed above—approach versus avoidance or behavioral activation versus inhibition.

MMM distinguishes between prescriptive morality, based in approach motivation, and proscriptive morality, based in avoidance motivation (Janoff-Bulman, Sheikh, and Hepp, 2009; also see Janoff-Bulman, 2009; Janoff-Bulman & Carnes, 2013). Prescriptive morality focuses on what we should do and emphasizes providing for well-being, whereas proscriptive morality focuses on what we should not do and emphasizes protecting from harm. Prescriptive morality requires engaging in helpful behaviors and thus involves activation of the psychological mechanisms behind altruism in order to establish a motivation to do something good. On the other hand, proscriptive morality is restrictive and entails overcoming temptation and desire; it involves inhibition of the psychological mechanisms behind self-interest in order to restrain a motivation to do something bad (Janoff-Bulman and Carnes, 2013).

Janoff-Bulman et al. (2009, seven studies reported) found that proscriptive morality is condemnatory and strict, whereas prescriptive morality is commendatory and not strict; proscriptive morality is represented in concrete terms linguistically, emphasizes transgressions, is responsive to threat, is mandatory, and focuses on blameworthiness, whereas prescriptive morality is represented in

126 Nate C. Carnes and Ronnie Janoff-Bulman

abstract terms linguistically, emphasizes good deeds, is not responsive to threat, is discretionary, and focuses on credit-worthiness. Interestingly, this distinction reflects the negativity bias, but in the moral domain (for reviews see Baumeister, Brataslavsky, Finkenauer, & Vohs, 2001; Rozin & Royzman, 2001; Vaish, Grossmann, & Woodward, 2008).

Broadly speaking, prescriptive morality is the motivation to provide (i.e., increase well-being) and proscriptive morality is the motivation to protect (i.e., minimize harm). Proscriptive and prescriptive moralities form the foundation for the moral motives; however, the nature of these moral motives changes depending on the context regarding what is being protected or provided for, or the foci of moral concern. Thus, Janoff-Bulman and Carnes (2013) present these moral motives at three levels of analysis or alternatively three kinds of social contexts: the self, the other, and the group (see Figure 6.1).

The self-focused moral motives are proximally concerned with self-regulation, but have distal ramifications for the group that help make social life possible. Prescriptive morality directed toward the self manifests as Industriousness or self-reliance, but this ethic of hard work and persistence ultimately contributes to the group's resources. Proscriptive morality directed toward the self manifests as Self-Restraint or moderation, but this ethic of self-control also serves to protect the group's resources. Next, the other-focused moral motives regulate interpersonal relationships and facilitate social life in dyads and small bands where others are specified and known. This moral context is focused on people as individuals who have close ties, reputation information, or past behavior to rely on. Prescriptive morality directed toward the other entails Helping and Fairness. Proscriptive morality directed toward the other entails Not Harming either physically or by taking advantage of another person. Finally, the group-focused moral motives regulate the group itself and render collective life as social beings possible. This moral context is focused on people as deindividuated group members. Prescriptive

	Self (Personal)	Other (Interpersonal)	Group (Collective)
Proscriptive Morality	Self-Restraint	Not Harming	Social Order
Prescriptive Morality	Industriousness	Helping/Fairness	Social Justice

FIGURE 6.1 Model of moral motives.

morality directed toward the group involves Social Justice, which emphasizes communal responsibility and equality. Proscriptive morality directed toward the group involves Social Order, which stresses communal solidarity and conformity (Janoff-Bulman & Carnes, 2013).

There are surely different ways of thinking about the many different moral principles people employ in navigating their social worlds. If we were to zoom out and take a broader perspective, we might argue that morality comes down to not harming and helping (Carnes & Janoff-Bulman, 2012); indeed, Gray, Young, and Waytz (2012) argue that harm is at the core of morality, as the essence of the phenomenon involves an intentional agent and a suffering patient. Perhaps we could zoom further in—taking a narrower or more concrete perspective—and distinguish between intentional and unintentional harms or procedural and distributional fairness. However, the approach we have taken is aimed at specifying general moral principles with discrete functions and a reasonable basis in psychological processes. We have examined how the moral motives are based in the fundamental approach–avoidance motivational distinction and a social context (for a more detailed discussion, see Janoff-Bulman & Carnes, 2013), but we now return to politics and the relationship between moral motives and political orientation.

Politics and Group Morality

The self-focused cells (Self-Restraint and Industriousness) and other-directed cells (Not Harming and Helping/Fairness) of MMM both involve the self-regulation of moral behavior—that is, how individuals should (or should not) conduct themselves regarding right and wrong in order to be moral. Interestingly, although the group-focused cells of Social Order and Social Justice implicate self-regulation, they are more centrally focused on social regulation—how the group should (or should not) conduct itself in order to be moral. Social regulation involves group-level norms, laws, and standards that develop to regulate the behavior of group members, whose compliance is expected. The question of what makes a society moral is really an inquiry into social regulation, and in turn becomes a question about group-based moral motives. This group or societal focus is the domain of politics, and it is therefore not surprising that it is in advocacy of Social Order or Social Justice, and not the other four moral motives, that we find strong associations with political orientation (Janoff-Bulman & Carnes, 2014). Before turning to these relationships, we take a closer look at the two group-focused moral motives.

As a proscriptive morality based in avoidance motivation, Social Order most fundamentally serves to protect the group from threats and dangers, from both inside and outside the group. These can be physical threats to safety or psychological threats to identity. Here conformity is important as a sign of group allegiance and loyalty, and in turn serves to maximize group cohesion and solidarity. In contrast, Social Justice is a prescriptive morality that focuses on providing for the group. This moral motive involves the activation of group-based efforts to help, based predominantly on equality-oriented distributional principles. Here group bonds are strengthened through a sense of shared communal responsibility.

Past work on distinct moral principles has been dominated by Moral Foundations Theory (MFT) as proposed by Haidt and his colleagues (Haidt, 2007, 2012; Haidt & Graham, 2007; Haidt & Joseph, 2004, 2007). According to MFT there are two individualizing foundations, Care/Harm and Fairness/Reciprocity, and three binding foundations: Ingroup/Loyalty, Authority/Respect, and Purity/Sanctity. The individualizing foundations are essentially about individuals and contractual approaches to morality, whereas the three other foundations approach morality by binding people into groups. In relating MFT to politics, Haidt, Graham, Nosek and colleagues (Graham, Haidt & Nosek, 2009; Graham, Nosek, Haidt, Iyer, Koleva, & Ditto, 2011; Haidt, 2012; Haidt & Graham, 2007) note that liberals rely on the individualizing foundations, whereas conservatives rely on all five foundations, including both the individualizing and the binding foundations. Another way of understanding these differences is to recognize that according to MFT, liberals do not have a group-based (i.e., binding) morality.

From the perspective of MMM, all three of the MFT binding moralities are subsumed by Social Order; that is, each is essentially a means of ensuring greater Social Order. In recent research we found supporting evidence for this, because the three MFT binding foundations were highly associated with Social Order, but not at all associated with Social Justice (Carnes, Lickel, & Janoff-Bulman, 2014). In other words, we maintain that in MFT the domain of group-focused morality is incomplete, and a group morality that might be associated with the political left has simply been overlooked. Social Justice may seem akin to MFT's Fairness/Reciprocity, but Fairness/Reciprocity involves interpersonal (individualizing) fairness that is based on considerations of another's perceived deservingness; it requires specific knowledge of individuals' attributes (e.g., merit, need). In contrast, Social Justice is based in group-level considerations focused on the overall distribution of outcomes in the group and entails a priori constraints on the nature of this distribution in the direction of greater equality (see Brickman, Folger, Goode, Schul, 1981 on the "qualitatively different principles" involved in microjustice and macrojustice). Fairness is input-based and implicates estimates of proportionality, whereas Social Justice is outcome-based and involves recognition of shared group membership (Janoff-Bulman & Bharadwaj, 2015).

In our own research we have found that there are two distinct group-focused, binding moralities that are differentially associated with the political left and right. More specifically, Social Order is highly associated with political conservatism, and Social Justice is highly associated with political liberalism. For example, in two recent online samples (N's = 311 and 295) we found Social Order and political conservatism positively correlated at .415 and .434, and political conservatism and Social Justice negatively correlated at −.481 and −.385 (all *p* < .001); in other words, political conservatism was strongly associated with Social Order, and political liberalism was strongly associated with Social Justice (Janoff-Bulman & Carnes, 2014; also see Carnes, Lickel, & Janoff-Bulman, 2014). There appears to be a binding, but different group morality for both liberals and conservatives, and the pattern of associations seems quite predictable when we return to the proscriptive/avoidance versus prescriptive/approach bases of these group-focused moralities.

More specifically, considerable research in recent years has provided evidence of distinct motivational orientations associated with the two sides of the political spectrum. The attentional and physiological differences between the political left and the right mentioned at the beginning of the chapter can be understood in terms of these basic motivational differences. Approach versus avoidance motivation can explain physiological differences in sensitivity to threats, learning differences regarding negative stimuli, and attentional differences regarding appetitive versus aversive stimuli. For example, a robust literature supports a positive association between cognitive rigidity and conservatism (e.g., Altemeyer, 1998; Chirumbolo, 2002; Fibert & Ressler, 1998; Joe, Jones, & Ryder, 1977; Jost, Napier, Thórisdóttir, Gosling, Palfai, & Ostafin, 2007; for a review, see Jost, Glaser, Kruglanski, & Sulloway, 2003). In addition, research on self-regulation suggests that avoidance motivation is associated with cognitive rigidity whereas approach motivation is associated with cognitive flexibility (e.g., Crowe & Higgins, 1997; Förster, Friedman, Özelsel, & Denzler, 2006; Friedman & Förster, 2005; Semin & Fiedler, 1988). Connecting these two literatures, Rock and Janoff-Bulman (2010) found that conservatism (but not liberalism) was more strongly associated with cognitive rigidity when participants were primed with avoidance motivation.

In addition, across a number of studies, researchers have found that conservatives are more reactive to threat, focus on losses more than gains, have greater disgust sensitivity, and are more likely to be the product of restrictive parenting; in contrast, liberals focus on gains more than losses, are more open to experience, engage in more exploratory behaviors, and are more apt to be the product of egalitarian parenting (e.g., Amodio, Jost, Master, & Yee, 2007; Block & Block, 2006; Fraley, Griffin, Belsky, & Roisman, 2012; Inbar, Pizarro, & Bloom, 2009; Inbar, Pizarro, Iyer, & Haidt, 2011; Janoff-Bulman, Carnes, & Sheikh, 2014; Kanai, Feilden, Firth, & Rees, 2011; Lavine, Burgess, Snyder, Transue, Sullivan, Haney, & Wagner, 1999; McAdams, Albaugh, Farber et al., 2008; McCrae, 1996; Oxley, et al., 2008; Shook & Fazio, 2009). More broadly, in a recent review Hibbing, Smith, and Alford (2014) concluded that conservatives, but not liberals, exhibit a "negativity bias," which is consistent with a general avoidance orientation. Liberals' greater openness and exploration are consistent with a general approach orientation. These broad motivational differences between the political left and right parallel the differences found in espousal of Social Justice and Social Order, for the proscriptive group-based morality (Social Order) is strongly associated with political conservatism, whereas the prescriptive group-based morality (Social Justice) is strongly associated with political liberalism.

A group morality based on Social Order engenders a sensitivity to threats from outside and within, and a related focus on who is in the group and who is not; the upshot is a relatively restrictive group categorization that emphasizes common social identity. A group morality based on Social Justice involves a sensitivity to the distribution of outcomes within the group and greater categorization inclusivity that emphasizes interdependence and common goals (Janoff-Bulman & Carnes, 2013; also see van der Toorn, Napier, & Dovidio, 2014). Consistent with proscriptive morality more generally, a Social Order morality is strict and condemnatory and emphasizes group homogeneity and behavioral conformity. Strict norm adherence, which emphasizes the importance of behaviors as social identity markers, is evident in conservatives' social regulation of lifestyles and personal behaviors such as abortion and same-sex marriage. Consistent with prescriptive morality more generally, a Social Justice group morality is commendatory and more lenient, with a focus on greater equality in providing public goods. Not surprisingly, then, the social regulation of liberals focuses on the distribution of societal resources, evident in an emphasis on programs involving welfare, health care, and affirmative action.

It is interesting that in the public mind conservatism is often associated with deregulation and a push for eliminating government involvement in society's affairs. Yet this is clearly a false perception when considering the broad range of human behavior. It is interesting to note that a very wide array of social issues, from stem cell research to public funding of day care (and including hot button issues such as abortion, same-sex marriage, capital punishment, affirmative action, and public funding of health care) factor into two distinct groups of issues that are essentially about personal behaviors and lifestyles versus public goods and social welfare (Janoff-Bulman et al., 2008; also see Lewis-Beck, Jacoby, Norpoth, & Weisberg, 2008). Both liberals and conservatives espouse government regulation, but differ in the desired domain of such regulation. That is, liberals want regulation when economics and social goods are involved, whereas conservatives want regulation in the domains of lifestyles and personal behaviors. Thus liberals want the free market regulated, and conservatives want abortion and same-sex marriage regulated. The political left and right also have preferred domains of autonomy, where the government should leave people alone. Not surprisingly, these are the domains of lifestyles and personal behaviors for liberals and the domains of public goods and economics for conservatives.

What about libertarians? Conservatives score high on Social Order and low on Social Justice, whereas liberals score high on Social Justice and low on Social Order. Both groups have a group-focused, binding morality, but these moralities differ. There is a group that appears to lack a group-based morality, and it is not liberals, as proposed by Haidt, Graham, and colleagues (e.g., Graham et al., 2009, 2011; Haidt, 2012; Haidt & Graham, 2007). Instead it is libertarians, who are low on both Social Order and Social Justice (see Janoff-Bulman & Carnes, 2014; also see Janoff-Bulman, Sheikh, & Baldacci, 2008). Libertarians espouse a highly individualistic morality and do not want social regulation in any domain, be it economics and public goods or lifestyles and personal behaviors. They choose to rely solely on the individualizing moralities that are self- and other-focused rather than group-focused.

The current political climate would no doubt lead us to view Social Order and Social Justice moralities as necessarily conflictual, particularly given politicians' apparent desire to avoid compromise at all costs these days, despite the necessity of compromise for a functioning political system. When southern Democrats were conservative and northern Republicans were liberal, there was compromise within and across party lines. Today the political parties are essentially monolithic in terms of conservatism and liberalism and wholly aligned with either a Social Order or Social Justice morality (for a review see Janoff-Bulman & Parker, 2012). Yet these moralities can and should be understood apart from their associations with politics. A closer look at the possible functions of these distinct moralities may ultimately inform a more successful polity, so we now turn to what these moral motives might actually do in social groups.

Functional Morality

William James originally stated, "My thinking is first and last and always for the sake of my doing" (1890), but Fiske (1993) famously paraphrased this as "Thinking is for doing." So it is for morality as well—morality is for doing. The idea that morality serves some kind of functional role in human social life dates back at least to Darwin, but is also a relatively popular concept in moral psychology today (e.g., Greene, 2014; Haidt, 2007; Haidt & Kesebir, 2010; Richerson & Boyd, 2005). A likely starting point in the natural history of our moral prescriptions and proscriptions is the family, specifically parent–child relationships, as human parents must provide for and protect their children for an extended period of development. Here morality helps provide the motivational energy to facilitate parenting in response to a specific adaptive problem, in this case the extended and vulnerable development of human children and adolescents. As human groups expanded to include extended kin and eventually strangers, new adaptive problems arose that people had to find a way to navigate. It is our contention that further moral motives developed, through whatever means, be they cultural or genetic, to facilitate some workable solution to the challenges and threats of this sociality.

For example, trading with unrelated strangers in some ancestral environment may offer enticing benefits—such as access to scarce resources or cultural innovations—that an individual might find hard to come by acting alone.

However, with this opportunity comes the possibility of exploitation or violence, unless there is some sort of mechanism that can reasonably assuage these threats and concerns. A moral proscription against harm and a moral prescription for fairness, especially when paired with reputation, sanctioning, and bystander influence, could function as the mechanisms that assuage such threats and concerns, allowing individuals to reap the benefits of trade and sociality. A great deal more empirical work is needed on the functional role of morality in groups in order to move beyond such "just-so stories," but some recent research is beginning to address this problem and reveals some fascinating insights into what morality can do (see e.g., Rand & Nowak, 2013).

Social coordination is one kind of problem facing human sociality. Coordination, or mutualistic collaboration, involves instances of collaboration in which actors benefit themselves and others simultaneously. Examples of coordination include getting everyone to drive on the right side of the road, convincing protesters to meet at a particular time and place, and even commanding different military forces to attack together. The challenge of coordination is not motivational, because there is no conflict of interest per se; rather, the challenge is epistemological because actors must come to a common understanding (e.g., which side of the road to drive on, where to meet, what to write) and know that other actors are aware of this common understanding (Thomas, DeScioli, Haque, & Pinker, 2014). Thomas et al. (2014) found that people were more willing to engage in risky coordination in a coordination game when they possessed common knowledge (i.e., everyone knows X), as opposed to private knowledge or shared knowledge, because this form of knowledge allows people to arrive at the common understanding needed to solve coordination problems. Norms, as informal rules of behavior, are a form of common knowledge that could facilitate coordination in much the same way. Another solution to coordination problems involves leadership and followership; Van Vugt and Kurzban (2007) found that most people coordinated in a coordination game when they played the game sequentially with one player making a decision first and the other player following the "leader" (for a review, see Van Vugt, Hogan, & Kaiser, 2008; see also Cartwright, Gillett, & Van Vugt, 2013). If everyone does what the leader or authority says, then everyone can arrive at the common understanding needed to solve coordination problems without possessing common knowledge. In this sense, simple heuristics like "follow the leader" or "do what others do" provide non-taxing solutions when common knowledge is absent.

Interestingly, recent cross-cultural work on tight and loose societies also posits a link between norms and social coordination. Tight societies are characterized by very strong norm adherence, a low tolerance for deviant behavior, and strict punishment for norm violations (Gelfand et al., 2011). Tight societies typically have a history of severe challenges (e.g., ecological and historical threats), and "the need for strong norms and the sanctioning of deviant behavior...help humans coordinate their social action for survival" (Gelfand, 2012, p. 421). If norms can facilitate social coordination, it is not surprising that strict or mandatory norms might be even better at facilitating social coordination. Norms that are mandatory can serve as a kind of common knowledge, because they help us confidently predict how other people will behave and guide our own behavior.

Strict norms, conformity, and obedience are precisely what Social Order morality emphasizes in the service of social regulation. In fact, Carnes and Janoff-Bulman (2014) recently found that Social Order morality is positively associated with the belief that people need strict rules and authority to guide their behavior. Adding moral weight to simple heuristics like "do what others do" and "follow the leader" is likely to facilitate coordination in just the same way that making norms strict and mandatory facilitates coordination. All of these factors help us predict what others will do with some confidence and arrive at a common understanding. Although more research is needed to test this hypothesis, we believe one of the important things Social Order morality does is help solve the problem of social coordination.

Another kind of problem facing human sociality is social cooperation. Cooperation, or altruistic collaboration, involves instances of collaboration in which actors benefit others at a cost to themselves. Examples of cooperation include everything from students sharing the burden of a group project, to communities regulating environmental pollution in order to protect public goods, and to nation-states bilaterally disarming nuclear weapon stockpiles. In contrast to social coordination in which the central challenge is epistemological, the core challenge of cooperation is motivational; actors need to know something about the intentions and motivations of other social actors (Thomas et al., 2014; Yamagishi & Yamagishi, 1994). One way of knowing the intentions of others is to lean on past behavior and reputation; indeed, an expansive literature supports the dual role of reputation and punishment in facilitating cooperative behavior in economic games modeling social cooperation (e.g., Fehr & Gächter, 2002). However, people in Western societies tend to cooperate even when reputational information is absent and there is no real threat of punishment (Henrich, Boyd, Bowles, Camerer, Fehr, & Gintis, 2004).

One reason why people continue to cooperate may be that in the absence of prior information, many individuals presume that other social actors are benevolent and trustworthy; that is, many people are generally trusting of others. Trust refers to the belief that others are well-meaning and will abide by "ordinary ethical rules" (Messick & Kramer, 2001, p. 91). If you can assume that others are benevolent and will cooperate, then it would be perfectly reasonable to cooperate. Indeed, Bicchieri, Xiao, and Muldoon (2011) found that while trusting others is not a social norm, being trustworthy is. When someone places trust in you, there are strong norms around reciprocating that trust. Importantly, Ishii and Kurzban (2008) found that those high in general trust are more willing to cooperate in public goods games. Just as distrusting others may lead to a negative spiral of fewer interactions with others and greater distrust (see Yamagishi & Yamagishi,

1994), trusting others may lead to a positive spiral of more (presumably positive) interactions with others and greater trust. Interestingly, strict norms mandating cooperation would likely undermine this positive spiral. It stands to reason that trust and beliefs about human benevolence may help solve the problem of social cooperation.

A related but distinct predictor of cooperation is prosociality. Research on Social Value Orientation (SVO) classifies people according to whether they are concerned with their own outcomes (individualists), concerned with relative advantage (competitors), or concerned with joint outcomes (prosocials) in settings of interdependence (Messick & McClintock, 1968; Van Lange, 1999). Balliet, Parks, and Joireman (2009) conducted a meta-analysis on 82 studies investigating the relationship between SVO and cooperation in social dilemmas and found that prosocials are more cooperative than either competitors or individualists (for a review, see Parks, Joireman, & Van Lange, 2013). If you are concerned with the outcomes of others, then it is certainly more likely that you would act to benefit them than if you were simply concerned with your own outcomes.

In many ways, prosociality builds off of general trust because believing that other people are essentially good and benevolent can lead to the imperative that one is responsible for those others. In fact, Janoff-Bulman and Carnes (2013) argue that Social Justice is rooted in a positive view of human nature and the belief that others are basically altruistic. In recent research Carnes and Janoff-Bulman (2014) found that Social Justice, which moralizes our responsibility to provide for those who are worse off or vulnerable, is positively associated with general trust in people and beliefs about human benevolence. Although more research is needed to test this hypothesis, we believe one of the things that Social Justice morality does is help solve the problem of social cooperation.

An important facet of functional morality is that moral principles are relatively specific solutions to relatively specific problems; there is no single moral principle in our toolbox that can solve every challenge we face equally well. For example, Social Justice may not be a particularly good solution to social coordination, and Social Order may not be a good solution to social cooperation. There is some evidence to support this hypothesis. Balliet and Van Lange (2013) conducted a meta-analysis on the relationship between trust and cooperation in social dilemmas and found that the degree of conflicting interests in the social dilemma moderated the relationship; the relationship between trust and cooperation became stronger when the conflict of self-interest in the game was high and much weaker when the conflict of self-interest was low. Trust is a solution to cooperation, which is defined by its mixed-motive structure of conflicting self-interests. Believing that others are benevolent or not does not matter when there is no motivational challenge. Trust-based Social Justice may be relatively specific to social cooperation problems, and not social coordination problems.

Similarly, leadership and authority may not be particularly suited to solve cooperation problems. A large literature on power, which is the ability to control or influence other social actors, suggests that power does indeed corrupt; experiencing greater psychological power is associated with acting more self-interestedly (e.g., Fiske, 1993; Galinsky, Gruenfeld, & Magee, 2003; Galinsky, Magee, Inesi, & Gruenfeld, 2006; Keltner, Gruenfeld, & Anderson, 2003; Kipnis, 1972, 1976). It stands to reason that although authority figures may be very helpful for facilitating social coordination in which there is no motivational challenge, authority figures may act self-interestedly and actually restrict social cooperation in which there is by definition a motivational challenge. In the same vein, Fehr and Gächter (2000) found that explicit disincentives (i.e., strict norms) actually undermine trust-based cooperation because they crowd-out intrinsic incentives. The benefits of conformity-based Social Order may be relatively specific to social coordination problems, and not social cooperation problems.

Balanced Morality

The rows of the six cells of MMM represent proscriptive versus prescriptive morality, manifestations of approach versus avoidance motivation in the moral domain. Interestingly, in each of the first two columns of the model, involving morality directed toward the self or an identifiable other person, the two moral motives are positively correlated (Janoff-Bulman & Carnes, 2014). People who are high on Not Harming also are more likely to engage in helping, and those who are high in Self-Restraint are also higher on industriousness and hard work. Most important, self-regulatory success is apt to be associated with behavioral flexibility, and thus with reliance on both approach and avoidance, including in the moral realm.

In contrast to the self and interpersonal columns of MMM, the two moral motives in the group column are negatively correlated (Janoff-Bulman & Carnes, 2014). Here the primary level of analysis is not the individual, but the group. And given our concern with politics, it is this column, with the moral motives of Social Justice and Social Order, that is of primary interest and relevance. It is here that we see the approach and avoidance motivations diverging at the level of the individual, but not at the societal level. Just as flexibility at the individual level requires both, flexibility at the societal level requires both as well—but now they can be represented in distinct individuals or populations.

These sets of relationships between the moral motives point to an interesting aspect about functional morality; if different moral motives are solutions to different sorts of threats and challenges of social life, then we might expect a degree of balance both in individuals and society. An individual who relies entirely on one moral value would be poorly equipped for the rich variety of societal contexts of everyday life, and a society that relies entirely on one moral value would be poorly equipped for the many opportunities and challenges that come with living in large social groups. We now have some evidence that is consistent with this proposition. Carnes, Lickel, and Janoff-Bulman (2014) had participants rate how applicable different moral principles were in a variety of real-life social groups, including different exemplars of intimacy groups, loose associations, task groups, and social categories (see Lickel et al., 2000, 2001 on group types). They found a high degree of consensus among raters on the moral principles applied in each social context; critically, people applied a qualitatively distinct profile of moral principles in each social context. This is consistent with the idea that different social contexts may pose relatively unique opportunities and threats, and different profiles of moral principles may apply to these varied situations. Similarly, Janoff-Bulman and Carnes (2014) actually found that the societies that are able to strike a balance in their group-based moral motives may actually be those that are most successful, as reflected in GDP. (We recognize that GDP is a measure of economic success, which may tell us little about the well-being of societal members. GDP nevertheless provides some evidence of general living standards and is currently an available international indicator, whereas comparable well-being measures do not yet exist.) In our research we found a quadratic relationship between the tightness or looseness of a society's social norms (as assessed by Gelfand et al., 2011) and the country's GDP, such that societies right in the middle, not too tight and not too loose, had the highest GDP. This is consistent with the idea that societies that overemphasize either Social Order or Social Justice may actually do worse compared to societies that can strike a balance between these different moral motives.

A fruitful theory about morality should help explain moral diversity, or the many different moral principles people employ in navigating their social worlds. Dean (2012) argues that moral diversity should be selected for by evolutionary forces, either biological or cultural, because there is not one psychological solution that can solve the problems of sociality across highly heterogeneous and variable social and physical environments; instead, evolution should favor a stable polymorphism in the population. Essentially, moral diversity and particularly balance in the societal application of different moral motives may be an evolutionarily stable strategy that maintains different ways of facilitating collaboration in society writ large.

Conclusions

The current state of political polarization in the United States is clearly maladaptive; as the party structure has aligned with ideology, there has been a consequent lack of compromise and an immovable legislative paralysis that has prevented the country from facing many daunting challenges. Some degree of this polarization may result from the tendency of moral values held by members of different social groups to balance and offset one another at the broader superordinate category of society writ large. The strength of our moral convictions may tug and pull on the convictions of others. It may be common for political parties to counterbalance each other, but this becomes problematic when compromise is a dirty word. It is therefore important to remember that although liberals and conservatives support distinct moral orientations, we agree on two-thirds of the moral domain. Furthermore, the moral orientation of the opposing side serves a meaningful social function different from our own, and thus simultaneously balances our own perspective. We suggest that Social Order and Social Justice ultimately serve as counterweights in providing flexibility and balance within societies. When incorporated into social and political life in the context of discussion, respect, and compromise, the outcome may well be a more successful, well-functioning society for all involved.

Note

This research was supported by NSF Grant DGE-0907995 to the first author and NSF Grant BCS-1053139 to the second author.

References

Alexander, R. (1987). *The Biology of Moral Systems*. New York: Aldine de Gruyter.

Altemeyer, B. (1998). The other 'authoritarian personality.' In M. Zanna (Ed.) *Advances in Experimental Social Psychology, 30* (pp. 47–92). San Diego: Academic Press.

Amodio, D. M., Jost, J. T., Master, S. L., & Yee, C. M. (2007). Neurocognitive correlates of liberalism and conservatism. *Nature Neuroscience, 10*(10), 1246–1247.

Ariely, D. (2008). *Predictably Irrational: The Hidden Forces that Shape our Decisions*. New York: HarperCollins.

Ariely, D. (2012). *The (Honest) Truth About Dishonesty: How We Lie to Everyone–Especially Ourselves*. New York: HarperCollins.

Balliet, D., & Van Lange, P. A. (2013). Trust, conflict, and cooperation: A meta-analysis. *Psychological Bulletin, 139*(5), 1090–1112.

Balliet, D., Parks, C., & Joireman, J. (2009). Social value orientation and cooperation in social dilemmas: A meta-analysis. *Group Processes & Intergroup Relations, 12*(4), 533–547.

Baron, J. (2007). *Thinking and Deciding*. 4th edn. Cambridge, UK: Cambridge University Press.

Batson, C. D. (1998). Altruism and prosocial behavior. In D. T. Gilbert, S. T. Fiske and G. Lindzey (Eds.), *The Handbook of Social Psychology*, 4th edn. (pp. 262–316). New York: McGraw-Hill.

Baumeister, R. F., Brataslavsky, E., Finkenauer, C., & Vohs, K. D. (2001). Bad is stronger than good. *Review of General Psychology, 5*, 323–370.

Bersoff, D. (1999). Why good people sometimes do bad things: Motivated reasoning and unethical behavior. *Personality and Social Psychology Bulletin, 25*, 28–39.

Bicchieri, C., Xiao, E., & Muldoon, R. (2011). Trustworthiness is a social norm, but trusting is not. *Politics, Philosophy & Economics, 10*(2), 170–187.

Block, J., & Block, J. H. (2006). Nursery school personality and political orientation two decades later. *Journal of Research in Personality, 40*, 734–749.

Bowles, S. (2006). Group competition, reproductive leveling, and the evolution of human altruism. *Science, 314*, 1569–1572.

Boyd, R. (2006). The puzzle of human sociality. *Science, 314*, 1555–1556.

Brickman, P., Folger, R., Goode, E., & Schul, Y. (1981). Microjustice and macrojustice. In M. J. Lerner & S. C. Lerner (eds.), *The Justice Motive in Social Behavior* (pp. 173–202). New York: Plenum.

Carnes, N. C., & Janoff-Bulman, R. (2012). Harm, help, and the nature of (im)moral (in)action. *Psychological Inquiry, 23*, 137–142.

Carnes, N. C., & Janoff-Bulman, R. (2014). (Dis)Trusting others reveals diverging group moralities. Manuscript submitted for publication.

Carnes, N. C., Lickel, B., & Janoff-Bulman, R. (2014). Shared realities: Morality is embedded in social contexts. Manuscript submitted for publication.

Cartwright, E., Gillett, J., & Van Vugt, M. (2013). Leadership by example in the weak-link game. *Economic Inquiry, 51*(4), 2028–2043.

Carver, C. S. (2006). Approach, avoidance, and the self-regulation of affect and action. *Motivation and Emotion, 30*, 105–110.

Carver, C. S., & Scheier, M. F. (1998). *On the Self-Regulation of Behavior*. New York: Cambridge University Press.

Carver, C. S., & Scheier, M. F. (2008). Feedback processes in the simultaneous regulation of affect and action. In J. Y. Shah and W. L., Gardner (eds.), *Handbook of Motivation Science* (pp. 308–324). NewYork: Guilford Press.

Chirumbolo, A. (2002). The relationship between need for cognitive closure and political orientation: The mediating role of authoritarianism. *Personality and Individual Differences, 32*(4), 603–610.

Crowe, E., & Higgins, E. T. (1997). Regulatory focus and strategic inclinations: Promotion and prevention in decision-making. *Organizational Behavior and Human Decision Processes, 69*(2), 117–132.

Darwin, C. (1998/1871). *The Descent of Man and Selection in Relation to Sex*. Amherst, New York: Prometheus Books.

Dean, T. (2012). Evolution and Moral Diversity. *The Baltic International Yearbook of Cognition, Logic and Communication, 7*.

de Mesquita, B. B., Smith, A., Siverson, R. M., & Morrow, J. D. (2003). *The Logic of Political Survival*. Cambridge, MA: MIT Press.

de Waal, F. B. M. (1996). *Good Natured: The Origins of Right and Wrong in Humans and Other Animals*. Cambridge, MA: Harvard University Press.

de Waal, F. B. M. (2005). *Our Inner Ape: A Leading Primatologist Explains Why We Are Who We Are*. New York: Riverhead Books.

de Waal, F. B. M. (2008). Putting altruism back into altruism: The evolution of empathy. *Annual Review of Psychology, 59*, 279–300.

Dodd, M. D., Balzer, A., Jacobs, C. M., Gruszczynski, M. W., Smith, K. B., & Hibbing, J. R. (2012). The political left rolls with the good and the political right confronts the bad: Connecting physiology and cognition to preferences. *Philosophical Transactions of the Royal Society B: Biological Sciences, 367*(1589), 640–649.

Fehr, E., & Gächter, S. (2000). Fairness and retaliation: The economics of reciprocity. *Journal of Economic Perspectives, 14*, 159–181.

Fehr, E., & Gächter, S. (2002). Altruistic punishment in humans. *Nature, 415*, 137–140.

Fibert, Z., & Ressler, W. H. (1998). Intolerance of ambiguity and political orientation among Israeli university students. *The Journal of Social Psychology, 138*(1), 33–40.

Fiske, S. T. (1993). Controlling other people: The impact of power on stereotyping. *American Psychologist, 48*(6), 621.

Förster, J., Friedman, R. S., Özelsel, A., & Denzler, M. (2006). Enactment of approach and avoidance behavior influences on the scope of perceptual and conceptual attention. *Journal of Experimental Social Psychology, 42*, 133–146.

Fraley, R. C., Griffin, B. N., Belsky, J., & Roisman, G. I. (2012). Developmental antecedents of political ideology: A longitudinal investigation from birth to age 18. *Psychological Science, 23*(11), 1425–1431.

Friedman, R. S., & Förster, J. (2005). The influence of approach and avoidance cues on attentional flexibility. *Motivation and Emotion, 29*, 69–81.

Gable, S. L., Reis, H. T., & Elliot, A. J. (2003). Evidence for bivariate systems: An empirical test of appetition and aversion across domains. *Journal of Research in Personality, 37*, 349–372.

Galinsky, A. D., Gruenfeld, D. H., & Magee, J. C. (2003). From power to action. *Journal of Personality and Social Psychology, 85*(3), 453.

Galinsky, A. D., Magee, J. C., Inesi, M. E., & Gruenfeld, D. H. (2006). Power and perspectives not taken. *Psychological Science, 17*(12), 1068–1074.

Gelfand, M. J. (2012). Culture's constraints: International differences in the strength of social norms. *Current Directions in Psychological Science, 21*(6), 420–424.

Gelfand, M. J., Raver, J. L., Nishii, L., Leslie, L. M., Lun, J., Lim, B. C., et al. (2011). Differences between tight and loose cultures: A 33-nation study. *Science, 332*, 1100–1104.

Graham, J., Haidt, J., & Nosek, B. (2009). Liberals and conservatives use different sets of moral foundations. *Journal of Personality and Social Psychology, 96*, 1029–1046.

Graham, J., Nosek, B. A., Haidt, J., Iyer, R., Koleva, S., & Ditto, P. H. (2011). Mapping the moral domain. *Journal of Personality and Social Psychology, 101*, 366–385.

Gray, J. A. (1982). *The Neuropsychology of Anxiety: An Inquiry into the Functions of the Septo-Hippocampal System*. New York: Oxford University Press.

Gray, J. A. (1990). Brain systems that mediate both emotion and cognition. *Cognition and Emotion, 4*, 269–288.

Gray, K., Young, L., & Waytz, A. (2012). Mind perception is the essence of morality. *Psychological Inquiry, 23*, 101–124.

Greene, J. (2014). *Moral Tribes: Emotion, Reason and the Gap between Us and Them*. London: Atlantic Books Ltd.

Haidt, J. (2007). The new synthesis in moral psychology. *Science, 316*, 998–1002.

Haidt, J. (2012). *The Righteous Mind: Why Good People are Divided by Politics and Religion*. New York: Pantheon Books.

Haidt, J., & Graham, J. (2007). When morality opposes justice: Conservatives have moral intuitions that liberals may not recognize. *Social Justice Research, 20*, 98–116.

Haidt, J., & Joseph, C. (2004). Intuitive ethics: How innately prepared intuitions generate culturally variable virtues. *Daedalus*, Fall, 55–66.

Haidt, J., & Joseph, C. (2007). The moral mind: How 5 sets of innate moral intuitions guide the development of many culture-specific virtues, and perhaps even modules. In P. Carruthers, S. Laurence, and S. Stich (Eds.) *The Innate Mind, Vol. 3*. New York: Oxford, pp. 367–391.

Haidt, J., & Kesebir, S. (2010). Morality. In S. Fiske, & D. Gilbert (Eds.) *Handbook of Social Psychology, 5th Edition*. Hoboken, NJ: Wiley.

Hamilton, W. (1964). The genetical evolution of social behavior I and II. *Journal of Theoretical Biology, 7*, 1–52.

140 Nate C. Carnes and Ronnie Janoff-Bulman

Harbaugh, W. T., Mayr, U., & Burghart, D. R. (2007). Neural responses to taxation and voluntary giving reveal motives for charitable donations. *Science, 316*(5831), 1622–1625.

Henrich, J., Boyd, R., Bowles, S., Camerer, C., Fehr, E., & Gintis, H. (2004). *Foundations of Human Sociality: Economic Experiments and Ethnographic Evidence from Fifteen Small-Scale Societies.* Oxford, UK: Oxford University Press.

Hibbing, J. R., Smith, K. B., & Alford, J. R. (2014). Differences in negativity bias underlie variations in political ideology. *Behavioral and Brain Sciences, 37*(03), 297–307.

Higgins, E. T. (1997). Beyond pleasure and pain. *American Psychologist, 52,* 1280–1300.

Higgins, E. T. (1998). Promotion and prevention: Regulatory focus as a motivational principle. In M. P. Zanna (Ed.), *Advances in Experimental Social Psychology*, Vol. 20 (pp. 1–46). New York: Academic Press.

Inbar, Y., Pizarro, S. A., & Bloom, P. (2009). Conservatives are more easily disgusted than liberals. *Cognition and Emotion, 4,* 714–725.

Inbar, Y., Pizarro, D., Iyer, R., & Haidt, J. (2011). Disgust sensitivity, political conservatism, and voting. *Social Psychological and Personality Science,* 1–8.

Ishii, K., & Kurzban, R. (2008). Public goods games in Japan. *Human Nature, 19*(2), 138–156.

James, W. (1890). *The Principles of Psychology* (Vol. 1). New York: Holt.

Janoff-Bulman, R. (2009). To provide or protect: Motivational bases of political liberalism and conservatism. *Psychological Inquiry, 20*(2–3), 120–128.

Janoff-Bulman, R., & Bharadwaj, P. (2015). Fairness and Social Justice: Two Distinct Moral Principles. In preparation.

Janoff-Bulman, R., & Carnes, N. C. (2013). Surveying the moral landscape: Moral motives and group-based moralities. *Personality and Social Psychology Review, 17,* 219–236.

Janoff-Bulman, R., & Carnes, N. C. (2014). Group morality: Conflicting or complementary moral motives? Manuscript submitted for publication.

Janoff-Bulman, R., & Parker, M. (2012). The moral bases of public distrust: Politics, partisanship, and compromise. In R. Kramer & T. Pittinsky. *Restoring Trust: Challenges and Prospects* (pp. 7–23). New York: Oxford University Press.

Janoff-Bulman, R., Carnes, N. C., & Sheikh, S. (2014). Parenting and politics: Exploring early moral bases of political orientation. *Journal of Social and Political Psychology, 2,* 43–60.

Janoff-Bulman, R., Sheikh, S., & Baldacci, K. G. (2008). Mapping moral motives: Approach avoidance, and political orientation. *Journal of Experimental Social Psychology, 44,* 1091–1099.

Janoff-Bulman, R., Sheikh, S., & Hepp, S. (2009). Proscriptive versus prescriptive morality: Two faces of moral regulation. *Journal of Personality and Social Psychology, 96,* 521–537.

Joe, V. C., Jones, R. N., & Ryder, S. (1977). Conservatism, openness to experience and sample bias. *Journal of Personality Assessment, 41*(5), 527–531.

Jost, J. T., Glaser, J., Kruglanski, A. W., & Sulloway, F. J. (2003). Political conservatism as motivated social cognition. *Psychological Bulletin, 129,* 339–375.

Jost, J. T., Napier, J. L., Thórisdóttir, H., Gosling, S. D., Palfai, T. P., & Ostafin, B. (2007). Are needs to manage uncertainty and threat associated with political conservatism or ideological extremity? *Personality and Social Psychology Bulletin, 33*(7), 989–1007.

Kanai, R., Feilden, T., Firth, C., & Rees, G. (2011). Political orientations are correlated with brain structure in young adults. *Current Biology, 21*(8), 677–680.

Keltner, D. (2009). *Born to be Good: The Science of a Meaningful Life.* New York: Norton.

Keltner, D., Gruenfeld, D. H., & Anderson, C. (2003). Power, approach, and inhibition. *Psychological Review, 110,* 265–284.

Kesebir, S. (2012). The superorganism account of human sociality: How and when human groups are like beehives. *Personality and Social Psychology Review, 16,* 233–261.

Kipnis, D. (1972). Does power corrupt? *Journal of Personality and Social Psychology, 24*(1), 33.

Kipnis, D. (1976). *The Powerholders.* Oxford, UK: University of Chicago Press.

Lavine, H., Burgess, D., Snyder, M., Transue, J., Sullivan, J. L., Haney, B., & Wagner, S. H. (1999). Threat, authoritarianism and voting: An investigation of personality and persuasion. *Personality and Social Psychology Bulletin, 25,* 337–347.

Leary, M. R. (2005). Sociometer theory and the pursuit of relational value: Getting to the root of self-esteem. *European Review of Social Psychology, 16,* 75–111.

Lerner, J. S., Tetlock, P. E., Schneider, S., & Shanteau, J. (2003). Bridging individual, interpersonal, and institutional approaches to judgment and choice: The impact of accountability on cognitive bias. In *Emerging Perspectives on Judgment and Decision Research,* eds. S. L. Schneider and J. Shanteau, 431–457. New York: Cambridge University Press.

Lewis-Beck, M. S., Jacoby, W. G., Norpoth, H., & Weisberg, H. F. (2008). *The American Voter Revisited.* Ann Arbor: University of Michigan Press.

Lickel, B., Hamilton, D. L., & Sherman, S. J. (2001). Elements of a lay theory of groups: Types of groups, relational styles, and the perception of group entitativity. *Personality and Social Psychology Review, 5*(2), 129–140.

Lickel, B., Hamilton, D. L., Wieczorkowska, G., Lewis, A., Sherman, S. J., & Uhles, A. N. (2000). Varieties of groups and the perception of group entitativity. *Journal of Personality and Social Psychology, 78*(2), 223.

McAdams, D. P., Albaugh, M., Farber, E., Daniels, J., Logan, R., and Olson, B. (2008). Family metaphors and moral intuitions: How conservatives and liberals narrate their lives. *Journal of Personality and Social Psychology, 95,* 978–990.

McCrae, R. R. (1996). Social consequences of experiential openness. *Psychological Bulletin, 120,* 323–337.

Messick, D. M., & Kramer, R. M. (2001). Trust as a form of shallow morality. *Trust in Society, 2,* 89–117.

Messick, D. M., & McClintock, C. G. (1968). Motivational bases of choice in experimental games. *Journal of Experimental Social Psychology, 4*(1), 1–25.

Nowak, M., & Highfield, R. (2011). *Super Cooperators: Altruism, Evolution, and Why We Need Each Other to Succeed.* New York: Free Press.

Nowak, M. A., Tarnita, C. E., & Wilson, E. O. (2010). The evolution of eusociality. *Nature, 466,* 1057–1062.

Oxley, D. R., Smith, K. B., Alford, J. R., Hibbing, M. V., Miller, J. L., Scalero, M., Hatemi, P. K., & Hibbing, J. R. (2008). Political attitudes vary with physiological traits. *Science, 321,* 1667–1670.

Parks, C. D., Joireman, J., & Van Lange, P. A. (2013). Cooperation, trust, and antagonism: How public goods are promoted. *Psychological Science in the Public Interest, 14*(3), 119–165.

Pew Research Center (2014). Political Polarization in the American Public. Retrieved from http://www.people-press.org/2014/06/12/political-polarization-in-the-american-public/

Rand, D. G., & Nowak, M. A. (2013). Human cooperation. *Trends in Cognitive Sciences, 17*, 413–425.

Richerson, P. J., & Boyd, R. (2005). *Not by Genes Alone: How Culture Transformed Human Evolution*. Chicago: University of Chicago Press.

Rilling, J., Gutman, D., Zeh, T., Pagnoni, G., Berns, G., & Kilts, C. (2002). A neural basis for social cooperation. *Neuron, 35*, 395–405.

Rock, M., & Janoff-Bulman, R. (2010). Where do we draw our lines? Politics, rigidity, and the role of self-regulation. *Social Psychological and Personality Science, 1*, 26–33.

Rozin, P., & Royzman, E. B. (2001). Negativity bias, negativity dominance, and contagion. *Personality and Social Psychology Review, 5*, 296–320.

Semin, G. R., & Fiedler, K. (1988). The cognitive functions of linguistic categories in describing persons: Social cognition and language. *Journal of Personality and Social Psychology, 54*(4), 558.

Shook, N., & Fazio, R. H. (2009). Political ideology, exploration of novel stimuli, and attitude formation. *Journal of Experimental Social Psychology, 45*, 995–998.

Sober, E., & Wilson, D. S. (1998). *Unto Others: The Evolution and Psychology of Unselfish Behavior*. Cambridge, MA: Harvard University Press.

Thomas, K. A., DeScioli, P., Haque, O. S., & Pinker, S. (2014). The psychology of coordination and common knowledge. *Journal of Personality and Social Psychology, 107*(4), 657–676.

Trivers, R. L. (1971). The evolution of reciprocal altruism. *Quarterly Review of Biology, 46*, 35–57.

Vaish, A., Grossmann, T., & Woodward, A. (2008). Not all emotions are created equal: The negativity bias in social-emotional development. *Psychological Bulletin, 134*, 383–403.

Van Lange, P. A. (1999). The pursuit of joint outcomes and equality in outcomes: An integrative model of social value orientation. *Journal of Personality and Social Psychology, 77*(2), 337.

van der Toorn, J., Napier, J. L., & Dovidio, J. F. (2014). We the people: Intergroup interdependence breeds liberalism. *Social Psychological and Personality Science, 5*, 616–622.

Van Vugt, M., & Kurzban, R. (2007). Cognitive and social adaptations for leadership and followership. *Evolution and the Social Mind: Evolutionary Psychology and Social Cognition, 9*, 229.

Van Vugt, M., Hogan, R., & Kaiser, R. B. (2008). Leadership, followership, and evolution: Some lessons from the past. *American Psychologist, 63*(3), 182.

Warneken, F., & Tomasello, M. (2006). Altruistic helping in human infants and young chimpanzees. *Science, 311*, 1301–1303.

Wilson, E. O. (1975). *Sociobiology: The New Synthesis*. Cambridge, MA: Belknap.

Wilson, E. O. (2012). *The Social Conquest of Earth*. New York: W. W. Norton.

Yamagishi, T., & Yamagishi, M. (1994). Trust and commitment in the United States and Japan. *Motivation and Emotion, 18*(2), 129–166.

7

FROM SILOS TO SYNERGIES

The Effects of Construal Level on Political Polarization

Jaime L. Napier and Jamie B. Luguri

Over the past decade, psychologists have uncovered myriad differences between liberals and conservatives. In their cognitive styles, motivations, and moral judgments (Graham, Haidt, & Nosek, 2009; Jost, Glaser, Kruglanski, & Sulloway, 2003; Jost, Federico, & Napier, 2009), in startle reflexes, brain structure, and neurocognitive functioning (Amodio, Jost, Master, & Yee, 2007; Kanai, Feilden, Firth, & Rees, 2011; Oxley, Smith, Alford, Hibbing, Miller, Scalero, et al., 2008), even in the way they decorate and the kind of beer they drink (Carney, Jost, Gosling, & Potter, 2008; Gosling, 2008; Kahn, Misra, & Singh, 2013), it appears that liberals and conservatives are deeply divided. Social scientists might not have been surprised, then, when the Pew Research Center (2014a) summarized results from recent public opinion surveys by stating: "Republicans and Democrats are more divided along ideological lines—and partisan antipathy is deeper and more extensive—than at any point in the last two decades" (p. 5).

Political polarization is undoubtedly problematic to the health of a society. Can anything be done to reduce partisan conflicts? In this chapter, we summarize emerging research that has demonstrated that relatively subtle changes in people's mindset—or construal level—have the potential to alleviate (or exacerbate) ideological divisions. More specifically, after describing the tenets of construal level theory, we review evidence from an emerging line of work that demonstrates that manipulating people's construal level—that is, inducing people to think *abstractly* as opposed to *concretely*—has proven to successfully reduce ideological divergences in people's moral judgments and attitudes toward "non-normative" groups (e.g., gay men and lesbians). We then discuss research that highlights identity salience as a potentially important moderator of this effect. The summation of this work suggests that abstract (vs. concrete) thinking may serve to bridge (at least some) ideological divides because it brings similar core values

Construal Level Theory

Construal level theory argues that people construe the world on two levels: abstract or concrete. Abstract thinking is gist-based, broad, and decontextualized, whereas concrete thinking is detailed and specific (Trope & Liberman, 2010). The central question driving construal level theory is how and when people are able to transcend the here and now (Liberman & Trope, 2008). In other words, how do people experience the past and the future, understand other people's perspectives, or engage in counterfactual thinking, all of which require one to rise above the current situation? The theory posits that abstract construal is the vehicle that allows us to gain and traverse psychological distance. Put another way, concrete construal is centered in the here and now, whereas abstract thinking is about the then and there (Trope & Liberman, 2010).

People can move from a concrete to abstract mindset (or vice versa) easily and quickly. For instance, people think more abstractly (vs. concretely) when they are thinking about something that will occur in the distant (vs. near) future (Liberman & Trope, 2008; Trope & Liberman, 2010). Construal level is also affected by thinking in general terms (which leads to abstraction) versus thinking in specific terms (which leads to concrete thinking; Freitas, Gollwitzer, & Trope, 2004; Fujita, Trope, Liberman, & Levin-Sagi, 2006). For instance, when thinking about a *specific* wedding, people will likely focus on concrete details—perhaps the color of the flowers or a cringe-worthy speech. Thinking about weddings in general, by contrast, might conjure up thoughts of happiness and felicitations and the anticipation of a celebration. In the first (concrete) case, the focus is on *how* it happened, whereas the emphasis in the latter (abstract) case is on *why* it happened. In other words, abstract (vs. concrete) thinking is about transcending the here and now, and focusing on the bigger picture (Liberman & Trope, 2008).

Construal level has important downstream consequences for how people perceive and interact with the world. Indeed, the effects of abstract (vs. concrete) thinking have been demonstrated across many domains in psychology, including object perception, person perception, self-control, negotiation, power, and affect, among others (Fujita, Trope, Liberman, & Levin-Sagi, 2006; Henderson, Trope, & Carnevale, 2006; Nussbaum, Trope, & Liberman, 2003; Smith & Trope, 2006; Trope & Liberman, 2000).

Most relevant to political polarization, construal level theorists have examined how construal level can influence people's attitudes and values as well as when these attitudes and values will be expressed (Eyal, Liberman, & Trope, 2008; Ledgerwood & Trope, 2010; Ledgerwood, Trope, & Chaiken, 2010). Research has found that people have core ideals that are relatively consistent across time and space, but that the expression of these values is inconsistent and situationally dependent (Eagly & Chaiken, 1998; Darley & Batson, 1973; Krosnick & Petty, 1995). In their model of "evaluative consistency," Ledgerwood, Trope, and Chaiken (2010) propose that construal level can explain when people will be more or less likely to act in ways that are consistent with their core values. Specifically, when people are thinking abstractly (vs. concretely), they are less affected by incidental and situational influences and thus more likely to express their core values and beliefs and to engage in value-consistent behaviors. In other words, concrete construal is associated with evaluative flexibility, whereas abstract construal is associated with evaluative consistency (Ledgerwood & Trope, 2010; Ledgerwood, Trope, & Liberman, 2010).

Construal and Political Polarization

If abstract thinking allows people to rise above situational influences and stay true to their core beliefs, how might it affect political attitudes, in general, and political polarization, in particular? On the one hand, insofar as liberals and conservatives hold different views about a host of issues, an abstract (vs. concrete) construal could exacerbate partisan disagreements because it increases ideological consistency for members of both sides, and thus lessens the likelihood of compromise. Consistent with this, research has shown that when people are thinking concretely, they are more likely to soften their stance on an issue when they anticipate interacting with a person who holds an opposing view; when thinking abstractly, by contrast, participants reported policy attitudes in line with their previously reported ideology, and were unaffected by their partner's attitude (Ledgerwood, Trope, & Liberman, 2010).

On the other hand, it is conceivable that abstraction could reduce political polarization, at least for issues that center on core values shared by liberals and conservatives. This latter proposition has been empirically supported in our research, which has examined how construal level reduces liberal and conservative differences in the domains of group intolerance and moral values. In the remainder of this chapter, we describe the findings from this work, which suggests that abstraction could be a useful tool for promoting ideological consensus, at least in some cases. We then discuss important caveats, including the moderating effects of group identification salience, and areas for future research.

1. Abstraction Reduces Conservatives' Prejudice toward Non-Normative Groups

In his seminal study of American race relations in 1944, Swedish economist Gunner Myrdal concluded that the co-existence of the deplorable situation of Black Americans and American values of justice and equality for all created a "moral dilemma" for White Americans. Specifically, Myrdal wrote:

> The American dilemma... is the ever-raging conflict between, on the one hand, the valuations preserved on the general plane which we shall call the "American Creed," where the American thinks, talks, and acts under the influence of high national and Christian precepts, and, on the other hand, the valuations on the specific planes of the individual and group living, where personal and local interests; economic, social, and sexual jealousies; considerations of community prestige and conformity; group prejudice against particular persons or types of people; and all sorts of miscellaneous wants, impulses, and habits dominate his outlook (p. xliii).

In other words, on the concrete, day-to-day plane, White Americans harbored explicitly discriminatory attitudes toward Black Americans, but this prejudice and oppression was in conflict with the core values of fairness and equality they aspire to adhere to, across time and contexts.

Although prejudicial and exclusionary attitudes toward Blacks are no longer explicitly expressed and tolerated as they were during the time of Myrdal's study, there are many groups in today's society that continue to face overt discrimination, especially from people who are politically conservative. In particular, groups that are perceived to be "non-normative," or deviating from Judo-Christian prescriptions, such as gay men and lesbians, Muslim Americans, and atheists, are the targets of blatantly discriminatory policies promoted primarily by conservative voters and politicians and opposed by liberals (e.g., Pew Research Center, 2013, 2014b). In a series of studies (reported in Luguri, Napier, & Dovidio, 2012), we empirically tested Myrdal's proposition that thinking abstractly (vs. concretely) would reduce conservatives' intolerance toward non-normative groups, and thereby reduce polarized attitudes, because it brings the core value of fairness to the forefront.

In our first study, we took a correlational approach and investigated whether individual differences in abstract (vs. concrete) mindset were related to differences in prejudice toward members of non-normative groups (gay men and lesbians, atheists, and Muslims). Participants (N=66) first responded to a construal measure (Vallacher & Wegner, 1989), in which they made dichotomous choices between concrete and abstract descriptions of ten actions. For instance, the action "ringing a doorbell" could be described as "seeing if someone is home" (abstract) or "pushing a button" (concrete). We used the proportion of abstract (vs. concrete) descriptions chosen as a measure of baseline (or chronic) construal level. Participants then rated the groups on feeling thermometers, ranging from 0 to 100, with higher numbers indicating more positive feelings toward the group.

Results from this study revealed that polarization between liberals and conservatives on attitudes toward non-normative groups only emerged among concrete thinkers (see Figure 7.1). Specifically, among those who were in a concrete mindset, liberals expressed significantly more positive attitudes toward non-normative groups than conservatives. For those in an abstract mindset, by

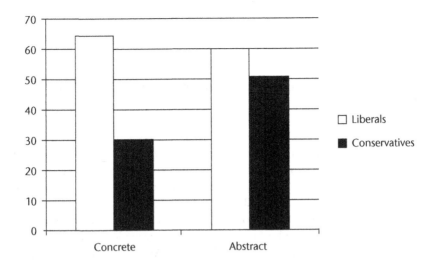

FIGURE 7.1 Feelings of warmth toward "non-normative groups" (gay men, lesbians, Muslims, and atheists) as a function of political ideology and baseline construal level (Luguri, Napier, & Dovidio, 2012; Study 1).

contrast, the difference in attitudes between liberals and conservatives was not statistically significant. Putting it another way, liberals reported relatively positive feelings toward non-normative groups regardless of whether they held an abstract or concrete mindset. For conservatives, abstraction was inversely related to tolerance, such that those with a concrete (vs. abstract) mindset reported the most negative attitudes.

In Study 2, we experimentally manipulated construal to examine whether inducing an abstract (vs. concrete) mindset would reduce polarized attitudes by increasing conservatives' positive attitudes toward non-normative groups. To manipulate construal, participants ($N=64$) filled out one of two versions of a ladder questionnaire about good physical health (Freitas et al., 2004; Fujita et al., 2006). To induce abstract construal, participants generated increasingly superordinate answers about *why* one would maintain good physical health, starting at the bottom of the ladder and working their way up. To induce concrete construal, participants generated increasingly subordinate answers about *how* one would maintain good physical health, starting at the top of the ladder and working their way down. Following this, participants indicated their attitudes (on feeling thermometers) toward the same groups used in Study 1.

Converging with the correlational findings from Study 1, results from this study showed that inducing an abstract (vs. concrete) construal significantly impacted attitudes toward gay men, lesbians, Muslim Americans, and atheists among conservative (but not liberal) participants. As in the first study, liberals and conservatives reported divergent attitudes when thinking concretely, with liberals indicating significantly higher levels of warmth than conservatives; when thinking abstractly, however, this ideological difference was no longer statistically reliable. The reduction in political polarization was due to conservatives' increased warmth when thinking abstractly (vs. concretely; see Figure 7.2).

The results from these two studies were in line with our prediction that thinking abstractly (vs. concretely) would reduce polarization by increasing conservatives' warmth toward members of non-normative groups. We hypothesized that this reduction in polarization was due to increased concerns about fairness. In a third study, we tested this directly by examining whether abstraction increased valuation of fairness, and this, in turn, explained conservatives' reduced prejudice.

In this final study ($N=168$), we manipulated construal level with a categorization task (Fujita et al., 2006). Specifically, participants were presented with 20 words, and asked to generate either a subordinate (concrete condition) or superordinate (abstract condition) exemplar for each word. For example, for the word *dog*, participants in the concrete condition were asked, "An example of a dog is ____," and thus would answer with a subordinate category, such as a type of dog (e.g., "poodle") or even a specific dog (e.g., "Pluto"). Participants in the abstract condition were asked, "A dog is an example of ____," generating superordinate categories such as "animal" or "pet." After this construal induction, participants responded to four items assessing their concerns about fairness (e.g., "Justice is the most important requirement for a society"), and then rated their feelings toward the same groups used in the previous studies.

Once again, we found that putting participants in an abstract (vs. concrete) mindset significantly reduced conservatives' intolerance toward the non-normative

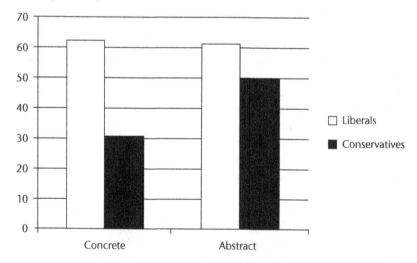

FIGURE 7.2 Feelings of warmth toward "non-normative groups" (gay men, lesbians, Muslims, and atheists) as a function of political ideology and construal condition (Luguri, Napier, & Dovidio, 2012; Study 2).

groups, whereas it had no effect on liberals' (relatively positive) attitudes. In this study, the construal manipulation did not completely eliminate political polarization: conservatives were still more prejudiced toward these groups than liberals in the abstract condition, but this difference was significantly smaller than it was in the concrete condition.

We also found that participants' concerns about fairness were heightened when they were induced to think abstractly (vs. concretely). Results from a bootstrapping procedure confirmed that the increased concerns about fairness significantly accounted for conservatives' lower levels of prejudice toward non-normative groups when thinking abstractly.

Taken together, these three studies provide converging evidence that thinking abstractly, as opposed to concretely, can reduce conservatives' prejudice (and thereby reduce political polarization) because it brings the common, core value of fairness to the forefront. When people are thinking concretely, they are presumably affected by a host of influences from, in Myrdal's (1944) words, "the specific plane of individual and group living"—desires and needs for security, conformity, and status—that give rise to attitudes that are in conflict with their core values. The results from these studies suggest that when people have an abstract, "big picture" mindset, either at baseline (Study 1) or because of a relatively innocuous exercise (Studies 2 and 3), they are able to rise above these situational influences and stay true to their ideals.

It should be noted that, across all three studies, we also measured attitudes toward other groups—specifically, dominant groups (Whites, Christians) and racial/ethnic minorities (Blacks, Latinos). Construal level did not affect attitudes toward these groups, for liberals or conservatives, in any of the studies. Only main effects of ideology emerged for ratings of these groups: conservatives tended to report less positive feelings toward racial/ethnic minorities, and more positive feelings toward dominant groups, as compared to liberals.

We think that this is because people do not experience a conflict between fairness and group attitudes when thinking of these groups because they are not associated with system-sanctioned, overt bias (such as proposals for the explicit denial of civil liberties). For instance, over half of Republicans said they would not vote for a qualified, party-nominated presidential candidate who was atheist or Muslim (52% and 53%, respectively), as compared to just 5% who said similar things about a Black candidate (Gallup, 2012). It seems likely that when bias is less overt, people do not struggle with aligning their group attitudes with their values, presumably because they feel that their negative attitudes are justified.

2. Abstraction Reduces Ideological Differences in Moral Values

One question that arose from this set of studies was whether construal level affects other moral values besides fairness. Specifically, work in the domain of moral foundations theory (Graham, Nosek, Haidt, Iyer, Koleva, & Ditto, 2011;

Graham, Haidt, & Nosek, 2009; Haidt & Graham, 2007) has illuminated differences between liberals and conservatives in the principles that they use when making moral judgments. Liberals' moral sense is guided by "individualizing" values based on concerns for justice and human welfare, whereas conservatives take into account both individualizing and "group-binding" principles— i.e., loyalty to the ingroup, deference to authorities, and purity. In other words, conservatives consider violations to group stability and harmony, such as betrayal of the ingroup or authorities and "impure" or disgusting behaviors, to be not just non-normative or undesirable, but also immoral. According to the theory, these different moral constellations are at the crux of ideological disagreements—liberals do not grasp right-wing stances on many issues because conservatives' morality includes values they do not recognize (Haidt & Graham, 2007).

The proposition that liberals and conservatives consider different sets of concerns when deciding whether something is morally right or wrong has received considerable empirical support. Specifically, numerous studies have shown that liberals prioritize individualizing values (harm and fairness) over binding ones (ingroup loyalty, deference to authority, and purity), whereas conservatives seem to consider both sets of foundations relatively equally (Graham, Haidt, & Nosek, 2009). A question remains, however, about whether binding values are consistent, core values that people apply across time and contexts, or if they are more peripheral (i.e., situation- or target-specific) than individualizing values of fairness and harm.

Some research supports this latter possibility. For instance, Wright and Baril (2011, 2013) found the typical ideological divide in a control condition, such that conservatives reported valuing the five foundations relatively equally, whereas liberals were more likely to endorse the individualizing foundations than the binding foundations. Under cognitive load, however, the morality of conservatives shifted to resemble that of liberals, such that they prioritized individualizing foundations over the binding ones. These researchers argued that conservatives are "cognitively enhancing" their adherence to binding values at baseline because deeming system-challenging acts, such as ingroup betrayal or disobedience to authority, as immoral can satisfy certain epistemic and existential psychological needs for certainty and security. When put under cognitive load, which presumably limits the cognitive resources available to override or enhance justifications, they no longer endorse binding values as much as individualizing ones. Wright and Baril (2011) posited that their findings demonstrate "that considerations of harm and fairness stand (as many have argued) at the core of human morality—for liberals and conservatives alike."

If that is the case, then abstraction, too, should decrease ideological differences in moral judgments, and specifically, should make conservatives value the individualizing foundations of harm and fairness more than the binding foundations. Alternatively, if conservatives (but not liberals) fundamentally and consistently rely on the individualizing and binding values to an equal extent, abstract (vs. concrete) construal should instead *increase* polarization by increasing conservatives' (and decreasing liberals') consideration of the binding values.

To investigate this, we (Napier & Luguri, 2013) randomly assigned participants (N=200) to engage in a categorization exercise (used in Luguri, Napier, & Dovidio, 2012, Study 3, described above) to induce either an abstract or concrete construal priming manipulation and then assessed their moral values with the Moral Foundations Questionnaire (Graham, et al., 2011). This questionnaire assesses people's endorsement of five values (harm, fairness, ingroup loyalty, deference to authority, and purity) in general (e.g., "People should not do things that are disgusting, even if no one is harmed" is an example purity item) and the extent to which each value is relevant in making moral judgments (e.g., "When you decide whether something is right or wrong, to what extent is 'whether or not someone did something disgusting' relevant to your thinking?" for purity).

Results revealed that construal significantly impacted individualizing and binding value endorsement, but in opposite directions: people thinking abstractly (vs. concretely) reported significantly *higher* endorsement of the individualizing values and significantly *lower* endorsement of the binding values. No interaction between ideology and construal emerged, indicating that abstract (vs. concrete) construal affected both liberals and conservatives in the same way. Notably, the pattern of value endorsement in the concrete condition looks similar to the pattern that has emerged in other work, such that liberals significantly prioritize individualizing values over the binding ones whereas conservatives do not differentiate between them. In the abstract condition, however, conservatives significantly favored the individualizing values over the binding ones, rendering their moral profile to resemble that of liberals (Figure 7.3).[1]

This study lends further evidence to the proposition that abstraction could reduce political polarization on issues that include some violation of fairness. Based on the results from this study and evidence from prior research (Wright & Baril, 2011, 2013), it seems as though the binding foundations—while clearly capturing an important ideological divergence in evaluations of behavior and action—might not be as fundamental to people's morality as previously argued. According to construal level theory, the fact that the binding values are reduced when people are thinking abstractly (vs. concretely) suggests that they are not relied on consistently, and could be subject to situational influences. For instance, conservatives' might view noncompliance with an authority as more or less "immoral" depending on whether the authority is a Democrat or Republican. This is good news for scholars concerned about political polarization, insofar as it suggests that, at the core, liberals and conservatives share important, guiding principles.

Of course, endorsing a value and behaving in ways consistent with that value are not the same things. Some work has shown that an abstract (vs. concrete) mindset increases the correlation between how much people care about a value and their (reported) intentions to act in line with that value (Eyal et al., 2008), but

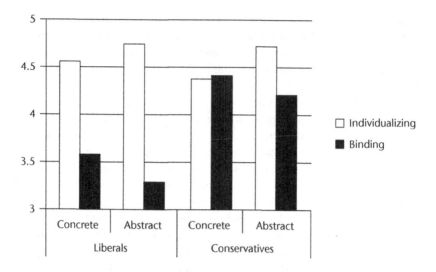

FIGURE 7.3 Endorsement of individualizing and binding values as a function of construal condition and political orientation (conservative or liberal, graphed one standard deviation above and below and mean, respectively; Napier & Luguri, 2013).

more work is needed to know whether changes in attitudes and values, and even changes in intentions to act in value-consistent ways, actually translate to changes in behavior.

Nevertheless, thus far our research appears to point to a relatively simple intervention for reducing bipartisan disagreements: put people in an abstract (vs. concrete) mindset, and conservatives and liberals will be less polarized in their prioritization of fairness, and subsequently, in their attitudes toward non-normative groups. Of course, the simple story is not likely to be the whole story. Will abstraction always tend to reduce partisan differences, or might it even exacerbate them in some cases? While our research has shown abstract (vs. concrete) construal can effectively reduce ideological divides (see also: Yang, Preston, & Hernandez, 2012), other work has shown the opposite to be the case (Ledgerwood, Trope, & Liberman, 2010). In the next section, we describe work that we think sheds light on this paradox—namely, how the type of identity that is salient interacts with abstract (vs. concrete) construal to predict attitudes and values, and how this can determine whether liberals and conservatives will become more or less polarized when thinking abstractly (vs. concretely).

3. Construal and the Moderating Role of Identity Salience

Construal level theory posits that objects and events close to the self will be construed concretely, whereas objects and events distant from the self will be construed abstractly (Trope & Liberman, 2010). Therefore, an important tenet of construal level theory is that the self is the reference point for psychological distance (Trope & Liberman, 2010). Research has demonstrated that when people are thinking abstractly (vs. concretely) they see more self-consistency (i.e., they believe that their personality traits are more consistent across different social roles, e.g., sibling, student, friend; Wakslak et al., 2008). However, little research has considered how the self, with its multi-faceted motivations and identities, might *interact* with construal level.

Abstract (vs. concrete) construal increases the likelihood that people will express attitudes and engage in behaviors that are consistent with their "true" beliefs. However, people have many different identities, some of which might lead to conflicting attitudes. If different identities are associated with different values, it seems plausible that what identity is salient is an important factor in determining how abstract versus concrete thinking will subsequently influence attitudes and values.

In terms of political attitudes, people likely have at least two representations of the self—a superordinate identity, such as nationality, and a political identity, such as Democrat or Republican. In two studies, we (Luguri & Napier, 2013) examined whether making one of these identities salient would influence the effects of construal level on attitude polarization between liberals and conservatives. We predicted that when people's national identity was salient, abstract (vs. concrete) thinking would reduce ideological divergences because it would bring to the forefront the shared values associated with the nationality (e.g., what Myrdal called the "American Creed"). When a partisan identity was salient, however, we predicted that abstraction would intensify polarization between liberals and conservatives (or Democrats and Republicans), presumably because they would be focused on the values and beliefs that are core to their own political beliefs, and that differentiate them from the opposing side.

In Study 1 (N=137), participants were randomly assigned to the abstract or concrete mindset induction (the ladder task used in Luguri, Napier, & Dovidio, 2012, Study 2, described above). Following this, participants were asked to indicate either their political identity (liberal vs. conservative) or their national identity, and then responded to four questions intended to increase the salience of this identity (e.g., "I like to be seen as a member of the ___ population"). Participants then indicated their attitudes toward several policy issues on a scale from 1 ("strong negative feeling") to 9 ("strong positive feeling"), including "increased spending on the military," "universal healthcare," "gay marriage," "tightening U.S. borders," "labor unions," "unemployment benefits," "abortion rights," "allowing prayer in schools," "teaching evolution in schools," and "lowering taxes on corporations."

In line with our predictions, results revealed a significant three-way interaction between the construal (abstract vs. concrete), identity salience (political vs. national), and baseline political orientation, such that abstraction *decreased* polarization between liberals and conservatives on policy attitudes when their national identity was salient, but *increased* polarization when a political identity was salient, albeit marginally significantly (see Figure 7.4). More specifically, when *political identity* was salient, the construal manipulation influenced conservatives' attitudes, such that they reported more conservative stances on the policies when thinking abstractly (vs. concretely); when *national identity* was salient, by contrast, conservatives reported more liberal policy stances when thinking abstractly, as compared to concretely. Unexpectedly, liberals' policy endorsement was unaffected by the construal manipulation in both identity conditions.

We conducted a second study (N=224) to examine whether this pattern of results would replicate in a context more specific to American politics. In Study 2, which used only American participants, after priming construal in the same manner as the first study, participants were randomly assigned to indicate their identity as an "American" (the national condition) or their political party, "Democrat" or "Republican" (the partisan condition). Participants then rated the same ten policy questions used in the first study, as well as three additional policies (raising taxes on the wealthiest 10% of Americans; affirmative action; and legalization of marijuana) that were prominent in American political discourse at the time.

Mirroring the results from the first study, we found a significant three-way interaction between construal, identity, and political orientation. As predicted,

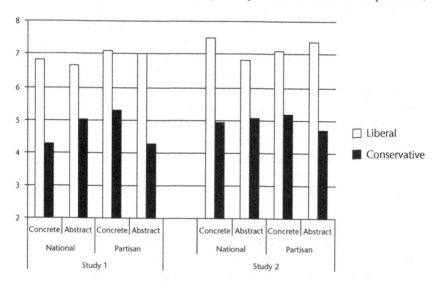

FIGURE 7.4 Mean endorsement of political policies (higher numbers indicate more endorsement of the liberal position) as a function of construal condition (abstract vs. concrete), identity condition (national vs. partisan), and political orientation (conservative or liberal, graphed one standard deviation above and below and mean, respectively; Luguri & Napier, 2013).

results showed that abstract (vs. concrete) thinking significantly *increased* attitude differences when a partisan identity was salient, but (marginally significantly) *decreased* polarization when a national (American) identity was salient (see Figure 7.4). In particular, when reminded of their partisan identity, Republicans reported more conservative stances on the issues in the abstract (vs. concrete) condition, but Democrats' stances were not affected by construal. In the American identity condition, thinking abstractly (vs. concretely) led Democrats to report more conservative stances, but Republicans were unaffected.

In sum, across both studies, we found evidence that abstraction reduces polarization on contemporary political issues, but only when a shared, national identity is salient. When partisan identities are salient, abstract (vs. concrete) mindsets actually increased polarization between the left and right. Although abstraction encourages value-attitude consistency, different identities are presumably associated with different values, and the overall effect of construal on political polarization is seemingly dependent on what identity (and thus what values and ideals) are salient.

Although we did not expect construal to differentially affect liberals and conservatives, the results showed that it did. In the first study, which primed either national or ideological (left/right-wing) identity, we found that the reduction in political polarization from the abstract (vs. concrete) mindset in both identity conditions was due to conservatives moving (becoming more liberal in the national identity condition, and more conservative in the partisan identity condition). In Study 2, which focused on American politics and primed either American or Republican/Democrat identity, results showed that an abstract (vs. concrete) construal affected Republicans' (but not Democrats') attitudes when partisan identities were salient, but affected Democrats' (and not Republicans') attitudes when an American identity was salient.

While we are cautious about reading too much into this unpredicted result, we (Luguri & Napier, 2013) speculated that the different political climates that served as the backdrop for the two studies, conducted roughly eight months apart, could have affected what people perceived as the "national ethos." Given the pattern of results that we observed in these two studies and our past findings, it does seem to be the case that conservatives are more affected by abstract (vs. concrete) thinking as compared to liberals. We submit that this is because some conservative attitudes (e.g., ingroup loyalty) can sometimes be contradictory to the Western ideals of fairness and equality. However, more research is needed to definitively parse out the conditions under which abstraction will affect attitudes, and for whom.

The finding that identity salience moderates the effects of construal has important implications—and qualifications—for using construal manipulations in real-life partisan debates. When proposing a new law, for instance, people are likely to be thinking abstractly, at least insofar as the law should reflect something that is applied consistently across time and contexts. However, most discussions about whether a bill should be adopted as law take place in situations like congressional meetings where the salience of people's partisan identity is likely to be heightened. This work suggests that ideological discordance will be maximized in such environments, but potentially ameliorated if members of both parties can be reminded of their shared national identity.

This work also sheds light on the seemingly contradictory findings on the effects of construal on attitudes. For instance, although some studies have shown that abstract (vs. concrete) thinking makes people more likely to adhere to their previously held beliefs (Ledgerwood, Trope, & Liberman, 2010), other work has shown the opposite to be true (Ledgerwood & Callahan, 2012). In the first case, participants were anticipating an interaction with a person who held an opposing belief, which potentially could have made salient their political identity. In the latter case, participants were told that the majority of students at their university either supported or opposed a new rule; results showed that participants were more likely to conform to the group opinion when thinking abstractly (vs. concretely). It is possible that the information about how the other students of the university felt about the issue invoked the salience of group (in this case, university) identity. In general, our research suggests that different identities— which could be unintentionally made salient based on other attributes of the study—could be systematically influencing the way that construal level affects attitudes.

Summary and Discussion

In this chapter, we reviewed the results from three papers that converge to suggest that construal level—i.e., thinking abstractly versus concretely—can affect political polarization. Abstract (vs. concrete) construal has proven to reduce ideological differences in attitudes toward non-normative groups (e.g., gay men and lesbians, Muslims, and atheists; Luguri, Napier, & Dovidio, 2012) and moral values (Napier & Luguri, 2013). Thinking abstractly (vs. concretely) also reduced polarization between liberals and conservatives on policy issues, but only when people's national identity was salient; when their partisan identity was salient, by contrast, people were more polarized when thinking abstractly, as compared to concretely (Luguri & Napier, 2013).

When examining the effects of construal on prejudice toward non-normative groups, we predicted (and found) that abstraction would reduce polarization by moving conservatives (not liberals). This was based on the rationale that explicit discrimination toward non-normative groups, which is more strongly advocated by conservatives than liberals, conflicts with primary, core values of justice. When thinking abstractly (vs. concretely), we hypothesized that conservatives would be more focused on their core values and less likely to endorse attitudes that conflict with these values, such as prejudice. Results from those three studies supported that prediction.

Concerns about justice, however, might not necessarily always translate into reduced polarization. In particular, conservatives are more likely to see equity-based systems as fair, whereas liberals are more likely to prefer equality-based systems (Skitka & Tetlock, 1993). The groups that we examined—gay men and lesbians, Muslim Americans, and atheists—are discriminated against for reasons that do not have to do with meritocracy. That is, they are not perceived as lazy or "free loaders," but as deviating from society's norms. Thus, differential treatment toward these groups presumably creates a conflict because it violates justice concerns (including both equity- and equality-based principles) more broadly. However, it could be the case that increased concerns about justice lead conservatives to be more consistent with equity-based principles, and liberals to be more consistent with equality-based principles. If that is the case, polarization may be unaffected, or even exacerbated, on issues that violate (or are perceived to violate) equity-based principles for the sake of equality—for instance, policies that aim to redistribute wealth.

Another qualification that we should point out is that, thus far, our research has focused on values. Construal level could affect political and intergroup attitudes through other mechanisms, which might not always lead to increased tolerance. For instance, abstract (vs. concrete) thinking leads people to focus on the causes, as opposed to the consequences, of events (Rim, Hansen, & Trope, 2013). This could potentially increase polarization on attitudes toward disadvantaged outgroups, at least insofar as conservatives see members of disadvantaged groups as personally responsible for their outcomes, while liberals see disadvantage as being caused by system-level inequality (Weiner, Osborne, & Rudolph, 2011).

In addition, research has demonstrated that people are more confident making theory-based predictions when thinking abstractly (vs. concretely; Nussbaum, Liberman, & Trope, 2006). Many lay theories, such as theories of psychological essentialism, are associated with prejudice and stereotyping of outgroups. In a series of studies (Luguri, Napier, Dovidio, & Oltman, 2014), we found that abstract (vs. concrete) construal did indeed increase endorsement of biological essentialist theories, which, in turn, led to more prejudice toward Blacks. Thus, it seems as though the context in which people are thinking abstractly matters. When people are thinking abstractly about values or even the treatment of outgroups, as was the case in our previous studies, abstract (vs. concrete) construal tends to reduce prejudice. If, by contrast, people are thinking abstractly about theories that could serve to justify or promote the acceptance of outgroup derogation, abstract thinking tends to increase people's receptiveness to the theory, and thus facilitate prejudicial attitudes.

Conclusion

Taken together, our research suggests that a relatively innocuous shift in mindset has the potential to meaningfully affect the course of political disagreements. As

158 Jaime L. Napier and Jamie B. Luguri

is the case with any emerging line of research, more work is needed to fully understand how, when, and for whom abstract (vs. concrete) thinking will reduce or amplify political discord. The studies reviewed here provide a promising (and hopeful) start to using construal level as a tool to reduce polarization between liberals and conservatives in the domains of values, attitudes toward non-normative outgroups, and policy attitudes.

Note

1 Prior research using the Moral Foundations Questionnaire has shown that composites of single values tend to have poor reliability, especially ingroup loyalty and deference to authority (Graham, Haidt, & Nosek, 2009; Van Leeuwen & Park, 2009; Wright & Baril, 2011), and this was the case in our study as well (α's<=.58). However, a composite of all the questions assessing bindings values (i.e., purity, ingroup loyalty, and deference to authority) does tend to form a reliable measure (α=.85 in our study), thus we used composites of individualizing and binding values as our dependent measures. In a supplementary analysis, we examined the effect of construal and ideology (and their interaction) on the endorsement of all five foundations with a repeated-measures ANOVA, which showed that abstract (vs. concrete) thinking impacted all five foundations (albeit not always significantly) in the predicted direction, such that in the abstract (vs. concrete) condition, people were higher on fairness (p=.014) and harm (p=.159), and lower on deference to authority (p=.192), ingroup loyalty (p=.489), and purity (p=.012) concerns.

References

Amodio, D. M., Jost, J. T., Master, S. L., & Yee, C. M. (2007). Neurocognitive correlates of liberalism and conservatism. *Nature Neuroscience, 10*, 1246–1247.

Carney, D., Jost, J. T., Gosling, S. D., & Potter, J. (2008). The secret lives of liberals and conservatives: Personality profiles, interaction styles, and the things they leave behind. *Political Psychology, 29*, 807–840.

Darley, J. M, & Batson, C. D. (1973). "From Jerusalem to Jericho": A study of situational and dispositional variables in helping behavior. *Journal of Personality and Social Psychology, 73*, 100–108.

Eagly, A. H., & Chaiken, S. (1998). Attitude structure and function. In G. Lindsey, S. T. Fiske, & D. T. Gilbert (Eds.), *Handbook of Social Psychology* (4th ed., pp. 269–322). New York, NY: Oxford University Press and McGraw–Hill.

Eyal, T., Liberman, N., & Trope, Y. (2008). Judging near and distant virtue and vice. *Journal of Experimental Social Psychology, 44*, 1204–1209.

Freitas, A. L., Gollwitzer, P. M., & Trope, Y. (2004). The influence of abstract and concrete mindsets on anticipating and guiding others' self-regulatory efforts. *Journal of Experimental Social Psychology, 40*, 739–752.

Fujita, K., Trope, Y., Liberman, N., & Levin-Sagi, M. (2006). Construal levels and self-control. *Journal of Personality and Social Psychology, 90*, 351–367.

Gallup (2012, 21 June). Atheists, Muslims see most bias as presidential candidates. Retrieved from: http://www.gallup.com/poll/155285/atheists-muslims-bias-presidential-candidates.aspx

Gosling, S. D. (2008). *Snoopology*. New York: Basic Books.

Graham, J., Haidt, J. & Nosek, B. A. (2009). Liberals and conservatives rely on different sets of moral foundations. *Personality Processes and Individual Differences, 5,* 1029–1046.

Graham, J., Nosek, B. A., Haidt, J., Iyer, R., Koleva, S., & Ditto, P. H. (2011). Mapping the moral domain. *Journal of Personality and Social Psychology, 101,* 366–385.

Haidt, J., & Graham, J. (2007). When morality opposes justice: Conservatives have moral intuitions that liberals may not recognize. *Social Justice Research, 20,* 98–116.

Henderson, M. D., Trope, Y., & Carnevale, P. (2006). Negotiation from a near and distant time perspective. *Journal of Personality and Social Psychology, 91,* 712–729.

Jost, J. T., Federico, C. M., & Napier, J. L. (2009). Political ideology: Its structure, functions, and elective affinities. *Annual Review of Psychology, 60,* 307–337.

Jost, J. T., Glaser, J., Kruglanski, A. W., & Sulloway, F. (2003). Political conservatism as motivated social cognition. *Psychological Bulletin, 129,* 339–375.

Kahn, R., Misra, K., & Singh, V. (2013). Ideology and brand consumption. *Psychological Science, 24,* 326–333.

Kanai, R., Feilden, T., Firth, C., & Rees, G. (2011). Political orientations are correlated with brain structure in young adults. *Current Biology, 21,* 677–680.

Krosnick, J. A., & Petty, R. E. (1995). Attitude strength: An overview. In R. E. Petty & J. A. Krosnick (Eds.), *Attitude Strength: Antecedents and Consequences* (pp. 1–24). Hillsdale, NJ: Erlbaum.

Ledgerwood, A., & Callahan, S. P. (2012). The social side of abstraction: Psychological distance enhances conformity to group norms. *Psychological Science, 23,* 907–913.

Ledgerwood, A., & Trope, Y. (2010). Attitudes as global and local action guides. In J. Forgas, J. Cooper, & W. Crano (Eds.), *The 12th Annual Sydney Symposium of Social Psychology: The Psychology of Attitudes and Attitude Change* (pp. 39–58). New York: Psychology Press.

Ledgerwood, A., Trope, Y., & Chaiken, S. (2010). Flexibility now, consistency later: Psychological distance and construal shape evaluative responding. *Journal of Personality and Social Psychology, 99,* 32–51.

Ledgerwood, A., Trope, Y., & Liberman, N. (2010). Flexibility and consistency in evaluative responding: The function of construal level. In M. P. Zanna, & J. M. Olson (Eds.), *Advances in Experimental Social Psychology* (pp. 257–295). San Diego, CA: Academic Press.

Liberman, N. & Trope, Y. (2008). The psychology of transcending the here and now. *Science, 322,* 1201–1205.

Luguri, J. B. & Napier, J. L. (2013). Of two minds: The interactive effects of construal level and identity on political polarization. *Journal of Experimental Social Psychology, 49,* 972–977.

Luguri, J. B., Napier, J. L., & Dovidio, J. F. (2012). Reconstruing intolerance: Abstract thinking reduces conservatives' prejudice against nonnormative groups. *Psychological Science, 23,* 756–763.

Luguri, J. B., Napier, J. L., Dovidio, J. F., & Oltman, K. (2014). Construing categories: Abstract (vs. concrete) construal leads to greater essentialism. Manuscript under review.

Myrdal, G. (1944). *An American Dilemma: The Negro Problem and Modern Democracy.* New York: Harper.

Napier, J. L., & Luguri, J. B. (2013). Moral mindsets: Abstract thinking increases a preference for 'individualizing' over 'binding' moral foundations. *Social Psychological and Personality Science, 4*, 754–759.

Nussbaum, S., Liberman, N., & Trope, Y. (2006). Predicting the near and distant future. *Journal of Experimental Psychology: General, 135*(2), 152.

Nussbaum, S., Trope, Y., & Liberman, N. (2003). Creeping dispositionism: The temporal dynamics of behavior prediction. *Journal of Personality and Social Psychology, 84*, 485–497.

Oxley, D. R., Smith, K. B., Alford, J. R., Hibbing, M. V., Miller, J. L., Scalora, M., Hatemi, P. K., & Hibbing, J. R. (2008). Political attitudes vary with physiological traits. *Science, 321*, 1667–1670.

Pew Research Center (2013, 6 June). Views of gay men and lesbians, roots of homosexuality, personal contact with gays. Retrieved from: http://www.people-press.org/2013/06/06/section-2-views-of-gay-men-and-lesbians-roots-of-homosexuality-personal-contact-with-gays/

Pew Research Center (2014a, 12 June). Political polarization in the American public: How increasing ideological uniformity and partisan antipathy affects politics, compromise, and everyday life. Retrieved from: http://www.people-press.org/2014/06/12/political-polarization-in-the-american-public/

Pew Research Center (2014b, 16 July). How Americans feel about religious groups. Retrieved from: http://www.pewforum.org/2014/07/16/how-americans-feel-about-religious-groups/

Rim, S., Hansen, J., & Trope, Y. (2013). What happens why? Psychological distance and focusing on causes versus consequences of events. *Journal of Personality and Social Psychology, 104*, 457–472.

Skitka, L. & Tetlock, P. E. (1993). Providing public assistance: Cognitive and motivational processes underlying liberal and conservative policy preferences. *Journal of Personality and Social Psychology, 65*, 1205–1224.

Smith, P. K., & Trope, Y. (2006). You focus on the forest when you're in charge of the trees: Power priming and abstract information processing. *Journal of Personality and Social Psychology, 90*, 578–596.

Trope, Y., & Liberman, N. (2000). Temporal construal and time-dependent changes in preference. *Journal of Personality and Social Psychology, 79*, 876–889.

Trope, Y., & Liberman, N. (2010). Construal level theory of psychological distance. *Psychological Review, 117*, 440–463.

Vallacher, R. R., & Wegner, D. M. (1989). Levels of personal agency: Individual variation in action identification. *Journal of Personality and Social Psychology, 57*, 660–671.

Van Leeuwen, F., & Park, J. H. (2009). Perceptions of social dangers, moral foundations, and political orientation. *Personality and Individual Differences, 47*, 169–173.

Wakslak, C. J., Nussbaum, S., Liberman, N., & Trope, Y. (2008). Representations of the self in the near and distant future. *Journal of Personality and Social Psychology, 95*, 757–773.

Weiner, B., Osborne, D., & Rudolph, U. (2011). An attributional analysis of reactions to poverty: The political ideology of the giver and the perceived morality of the receiver. *Personality and Social Psychology Review, 15*, 199–213.

Wright, J. C., & Baril, G. (2011). The role of cognitive resources in determining our moral intuitions: Are we all liberals at heart? *Journal of Experimental Social Psychology, 47*, 1007–1012.

Wright, J. C., & Baril, G. (2013). The role of dispositional vs. situational threat-sensitivity in our moral judgments. *Journal of Moral Education, 42*, 383–397.

Yang, D. Y.-J., Preston, J. L., & Hernandez, I. (2012). Polarized attitudes toward the Ground Zero mosque are reduced by high-level construal. *Social Psychological and Personality Science, 4*, 244–250.

SECTION III

Ideological Divides in Social Psychology

8

THE POLITICS OF SOCIAL PSYCHOLOGICAL SCIENCE

Distortions in the Social Psychology of Intergroup Relations

Lee Jussim, Jarret T. Crawford, Sean T. Stevens, and Stephanie M. Anglin

"Getting it right" is the *sine qua non* of science (Funder, Levine, Mackie, Morf, Vazire, & West, 2013). Science can tolerate individual mistakes and flawed theories, but only if it has reliable mechanisms for correction. Unfortunately, science is not always self-correcting (e.g., Ioannidis, 2012; MacCoun, 1998; Nickerson, 1998). Although the potential political distortion of psychology has been recognized for some time (MacCoun, 1998; Redding, 2001; Tetlock, 1994), calls for corrective action have gone largely unheeded.

This chapter reviews and critically evaluates evidence suggesting that: 1) Liberals are disproportionately represented in social psychology; 2) Pernicious factors (hostile environment, discrimination) contribute to that disproportion; and 3) Some conclusions in intergroup relations are consistently biased in ways that exaggerate support for narratives of bias and oppression. We also identify possible solutions to the problems of political bias in social psychology.

Some preliminary caveats and qualifications may be necessary in order to put this chapter's claims in context. First, this is not meant to be a balanced or comprehensive review of intergroup relations—it does not focus on everything social psychology gets right, and, instead, focuses quite specifically on erroneous claims and conclusions. Second, it is not even a comprehensive review of the ways in which political biases lead to widely-accepted social psychological conclusions not supported by data. Reviews of how the social cognitive view of intergroup relations sometimes goes wrong can be found in two books published almost 20 years apart (Jussim, 2012a; Oakes, Haslam & Turner, 1994). How similar problems characterize the social psychology of politics can be found in two recent reviews (Duarte, Crawford, Stern, Haidt, Jussim, & Tetlock, 2015; Jussim, Crawford, Anglin, & Stevens, 2015; see also Eagly, 1995, on how politics distorted conclusions about the existence, size, and importance of gender differences). Third, we are not claiming that all or even most of the science of intergroup relations is wrong or problematic. Social psychology has provided important and dramatic insights into stereotypes, prejudice, oppression, and sources of inequality. Nonetheless, this chapter shows that when social psychology does go wrong with respect to intergroup relations, it is often in ways that unjustifiably exaggerate support for liberal narratives of oppression over other potential explanations.

How Much Are Liberals Overrepresented in Scientific Social Psychology? And Why Care?

Domination by researchers with *any* narrow outlook risks creating a social psychology riddled with blind spots and biased interpretations (Haidt, 2012; Jussim, 2012b; Prentice, 2012; Tetlock, 1994). Before reviewing ways in which a narrow ideological perspective could distort social psychology, it is worth considering the following question: How diverse is social psychology's ideological distribution?

Compared to What?

Americans have self-identified as about 35–40% conservative, 34–38% moderate, and 19–23% liberal for 20 years (Gallup, 2014). These percentages, however, suffer from two limitations: 1) There is evidence that many people do not fully understand what it means to be liberal or conservative (Converse, 1964; Feldman & Johnston, 2013; Kinder & Sears, 1985; but see Jost, 2006 for an alternative view); and 2) These data are only for the U.S., whereas social and personality psychologists work all over the world. Over a quarter of the members of the Society for Personality and Social Psychology live outside of the U.S. (Inbar & Lammers, 2012). Nonetheless, the American data provides some basis for comparison to the ideological distribution of a large number of social psychologists.

Results from the Only Survey of the Ideological Leanings of Social Psychologists

It is currently impossible to authoritatively determine the ideological distribution of social psychological scientists because there have been no published reports based on representative samples of research-active social psychologists. The only assessment of social psychology's ideological distribution is a pair of surveys conducted via the listserv of the Society for Personality and Social Psychology (SPSP) (Inbar & Lammers, 2012).

Five hundred and eight of the 1939 participants in the SPSP listserv completed Study 1; 266 completed Study 2. Except for under-representing undergraduates,

The Politics of Social Psychological Science **167**

the gender, nationality, age, and professional positions of those participating closely corresponded to the distribution in the SPSP as a whole. Participants were asked to rate their ideology on a seven point scale (1=very liberal, 2=liberal, 3=somewhat liberal, 4=moderate, 5=somewhat conservative, 6=conservative, 7=very conservative). Responses were then collapsed into liberal (1–3), moderate (4), and conservative (5–7).

Study 1 found that an overwhelming majority of social psychologists self-identified as liberal on social issues (90.6%, with 5.5% identifying as moderates, and 3.9% as conservatives). Results were somewhat less lopsided for economic (63.2% liberal, 18.9% moderate, 17.9% conservative) and foreign policy issues (68.6% liberal, 21.1% moderate, 10.3% conservative).

Results for the ideological distribution were similar for Study 2, but there was one twist. Inbar and Lammers (2012) also asked respondents to rate their ideology "overall." Of these participants, 85.2% self-described as liberal, 8.6% as moderate, and 6.2% as conservative. Furthermore, Study 2 was consistent with the conclusion that the ideological disproportion is increasing: whereas 10% of faculty identified as conservative, only 2% of graduate students and postdocs did so, a difference that was statistically significant, r (234) = .13, p = .044.[1]

These results appear to bolster the conclusion that social psychologists are overwhelmingly liberal, especially with respect to the social issues that bear on much of social psychology. Furthermore, the distribution seems to be becoming more, not less, extreme. Nonetheless, caution in interpreting their results is warranted on several grounds.

Because we are interested in how politics might distort science, it would be optimal to sample from research-active social psychologists. Certainly, SPSP is one of the main organizations for social and personality psychologists, and many research-active social psychologists are members. But being a research-active social psychologist and a participant in the SPSP listserv are not the same thing. Are research-active social psychologists systematically underrepresented in either the listserv or in SPSP more generally? Although a strength of the Inbar and Lammers (2012) studies was that the samples were indeed demographically comparable to the members of the SPSP listserv, we know of no data that can address this issue.

Another limitation to those surveys is that we cannot tell whether nonliberal social psychologists were underrepresented, which could occur in several ways. Perhaps nonliberal social psychologists are less likely to join SPSP, participate in the listserv, or to complete the survey. We are aware of no data that can address these issues. In the absence of fully representative sampling of some target population of research-active social psychologists, it is impossible to know how successful Inbar and Lammers' (2012) studies were at capturing the ideological distribution of social psychologists (see Skitka, 2012, for similar points).

A second limitation stems from the way in which they combined respondents, including "somewhat liberal" and "somewhat conservative" together into the categories "liberal" and "conservative." Although this was, perhaps, reasonable from the standpoint of simplifying their results for presentation, it is unclear what people meant by the "somewhat" modifier. Overall, therefore, the results suggest that social psychology is heavily disproportionately left of center, but the precise extent of that disproportion, and its precise meaning, awaits clarification by additional research.

Studies of Psychology Faculty

One of the earliest surveys of academic psychologists found that 78% identified as Democrats, socialists, or liberals, and 22% identified as Republicans (McClintock, Spaulding, & Turner, 1965). Participants were randomly selected from the APA directory, and were excluded if they were found not to be employed in an academic institution. Secondarily, they also assessed respondents' attitudes, and found self-identified Democrats were far more liberal than self-identified Republicans. These results were consistent with research suggesting that political elites, especially those with the type of higher education necessary to become a psychologist, do indeed understand that Democrats are generally more liberal than Republicans (something consistent with the conclusions of two classic and otherwise conflicting reviews of lay ideology, Converse, 1964; Jost, 2006).

More recent research has suggested that the disproportion of Democrats to Republicans in psychology has been increasing over time. Although the ratio (D:R) was about 3.5 to 1 in the McClintock et al. (1965) study, it has averaged about 10 to 1 in more recent surveys (Gross & Simmons, 2007; Klein & Stern, 2008a; Rothman & Lichter, 2008). Of course, these are surveys of *psychology* faculty, not social psychology faculty. Nonetheless, the evidence of increasing ideological homogeneity among psychologists is consistent with Inbar and Lammers' (2012) results showing greater ideological homogeneity among younger than among older social psychologists.

Conclusions Regarding the Ideological Distribution of Social Psychologists

Data fall short of being definitive about the degree of ideological homogeneity within social psychology because no surveys have been based on representative samples of social psychologists, and because most of the studies that have drawn such samples have focused on psychologists generally. Nonetheless, despite their imperfections, multiple sources of evidence consistently point toward the same conclusion: Social psychologists seem to be disproportionately left-wing in their ideological beliefs, and this disproportion appears to be increasing. What might be the causes and consequences of this disproportion?

The Politics of Social Psychological Science

Pernicious Sources of Ideological Homogeneity in Social Psychology

Many factors can contribute to a disproportion of ideologically left-wing social psychologists. Some may be relatively innocent. For example, people on the left may be more likely to pursue higher education, they may be more attracted than those on the right to careers in scientific research; and they may be particularly attracted to many of the topics central to social psychology (see Duarte et al., 2015, for a review). Less innocent processes, however, also may play a role and are discussed next.

Political Prejudice in General

Prejudice and intolerance have long been considered the province of the political right (e.g., Adorno, Frenkel-Brunswik, Levinson, & Sanford, 1950; Duckitt, 2001; Lindner & Nosek, 2009). Social psychologists have suspected both the existence of a personality type associated with generalized prejudice toward a variety of social groups (Akrami, Ekehammar, & Bergh, 2011), and that this personality type is associated with political conservatism (Roets & van Hiel, 2011). Aspects of right-wing political ideologies (i.e., right-wing authoritarianism and social dominance orientation) correlate with many prejudices (Sibley & Duckitt, 2008). This body of evidence has led to the conclusion that there is a "prejudice gap" (c.f., Chambers, Schlenker, & Collisson, 2013), such that conservatives are more prejudiced than liberals.

More recently, however, theory and new evidence have called this "prejudice gap" into question on several grounds. First, liberals and conservatives both tend to exaggerate their differences, but this tendency is at least sometimes *more* pronounced among liberals (Graham, Nosek, & Haidt, 2013) and among those who care more deeply about the underlying political issues, including liberals (e.g., Chambers, Baron, & Inman, 2006). For example, and probably most relevant to social psychology, Democrats dramatically underestimated (effect size, $d = 1.14$) Republican support for public education and programs designed to reduce inequality. Perceiving more disagreement than actually exists is important because as perceived disagreement increases, unfavorable trait ratings of and anger toward the outgroup increase (Chambers & Melnyk, 2006).

Furthermore, liberals' moral stereotypes (i.e., beliefs about liberals' and conservatives' concerns about purity, authority, ingroup loyalty, harm, and fairness) were least accurate—they *exaggerated* liberal/conservative differences more than moderates or conservatives did (Graham et al., 2013). Exaggerations and excessively unflattering beliefs and attitudes toward one's ideological opponents are rarely recognized by the perceiver (Haidt, 2012; Pronin, 2007).

Consistent with the results of empirical research on laypeople, social psychological conclusions, too, seem to exaggerate differences between liberals and conservatives, typically in ways flattering to liberals and unflattering to conservatives. Such phenomena may go a long way toward explaining why: 1) Recent research provides ample evidence that overall levels of prejudice are fairly similar among liberals and conservatives; even though 2) The bulk of empirical research in social psychology has shown that conservatives are more prejudiced. How can both of these claims be true?

Social psychologists have, until recently, disproportionately investigated prejudice against left-wing target groups (e.g., feminists, ethnic minorities, sexual minorities; see Chambers et al., 2013; Crawford & Pilanski, 2013 for further description of these arguments). Thus, target group has been confounded with ideology. This raises at least three general possibilities: 1) The conclusion that conservatives are more prejudiced than liberals would remain intact when right-wing targets were studied; 2) Liberals would be about as prejudiced against right-wing targets as conservatives are against left-wing targets; 3) Liberals would be even more prejudiced against right-wing targets than conservatives are against left-wing targets.

Three independently-working research groups have demonstrated that the weight of the evidence is most consistent with the second possibility. Summarizing these and other studies with similar results, Brandt, Reyna, Chambers, Crawford, and Wetherell (2014) put forward the *ideological conflict hypothesis* (ICH), which argues very simply that people across the political spectrum are prejudiced against ideologically dissimilar targets. The ICH has been supported on the basis of research designs that include an ideologically diverse array of target groups, and across nationally representative as well as student and community samples. The relationship between conservatism and prejudice is not positive and linear (i.e., more conservatism does not always equal more prejudice). Instead, conservatives *and* liberals are more prejudiced against (Chambers et al., 2013), more politically intolerant toward (Crawford & Pilanski, 2013), and more willing to discriminate against (Wetherell, Brandt, & Reyna, 2013) ideologically dissimilar groups than ideologically similar groups.

This includes social and demographic groups as well as political groups. For example, compared to liberals, conservatives are more intolerant of or prejudiced against Democrats, liberals, and pro-choice activists, but also against atheists and people on welfare. Likewise, compared to conservatives, liberals are more intolerant of or prejudiced against Republicans, conservatives, and pro-life activists, but also against evangelical Christians and rich people (e.g., Chambers et al., 2013; Crawford, Wance, Brandt, Chambers, Inbar, & Motyl, 2014).

Indeed, Chambers et al. (2013) directly compared the ICH and prejudice gap hypotheses by having liberals and conservatives evaluate liberal and conservative Black and White targets. Consistent with the ICH, conservatives liked conservative targets and liberals liked liberal targets, regardless of race. Even more important, conservatives disliked Black liberals as much as liberals disliked Black conservatives, thereby disconfirming the prejudice gap hypothesis. These results suggest that the typical "prejudice gap" finding regarding social groups, such as ethnic minorities, is at least sometimes explained by ideological dissimilarity. Crawford et al. (2014) found a similar pattern: liberal prejudice against evangelical Christians was comparable to that of conservative prejudice against atheists, and both were driven by perceived ideological dissimilarity.

Furthermore, political intolerance and prejudice occur because ideologically dissimilar target groups are experienced as threatening in a variety of ways (Crawford, 2014; Crawford et al., 2014; Crawford & Pilanski, 2013). These results are doubly important with respect to the main ideas of the present chapter. First, they foreshadow our later section on political distortion within social psychology: Why has social psychology labored under the erroneous conclusion that conservatives are inherently more prejudiced than liberals for so long? Although we cannot know for sure, one possibility is that it did not occur to the (most likely, overwhelmingly liberal) researchers examining sources of prejudice that they were primarily studying prejudice against liberal groups (see Haidt, 2012 for a discussion of ideologically-induced blind spots; see Jussim, 2012a for examples applied to intergroup relations). Or, perhaps, most liberal researchers just do not consider prejudice against conservative targets to be an interesting or important phenomenon.

There are, however, two additional reasons such results are important with respect to the present chapter. First, they raise the possibility that the long-standing social psychological claim of greater prejudice among conservatives reflects the ideology of social psychologists (and the concomitant blind spots, to be discussed later) as much as, or more than, it reflected actual liberal/conservative differences. Second, the ICH pattern of results might have important implications for how we understand social psychologists' capacity for political prejudice, and how it might influence their conclusions. The strength and replicability of the ICH findings raises the possibility that social psychologists are not immune to political prejudice.

Political Prejudice in Social Psychology

Although political prejudice typically characterizes both the left and the right (Brandt et al., 2014), the rest of this chapter largely ignores the potential for conservative prejudice because, if there is political prejudice in social psychology, the seemingly heavy disproportion of liberals means that such prejudice is likely to manifest primarily as prejudice against conservatives and, more generally, ideas that contest liberal narratives. Are liberal social psychologists prejudiced against conservative colleagues and ideas? Some certainly are, though the prevalence of such attitudes is unclear. Inbar and Lammers (2012, Study 1) asked their respondents whether they believed there was a hostile climate in social psychology for researchers holding their political beliefs. Essentially, liberals said "No," and conservatives said "Yes" (the correlation between ideology and perceived hostile climate was .50). Furthermore, the more liberal the social psychologist, the less likely were they to believe that conservatives faced a hostile climate ($r=.28$).

Have liberal social psychologists actually created a climate hostile to nonliberal colleagues? To address this question, Inbar and Lammers (2012, Study 2) asked their respondents how reluctant they would be to invite a conservative colleague to participate in a symposium, whether they would be reluctant to accept papers or fund grants taking a conservative perspective, and whether they would be inclined to select a more liberal over more conservative job candidate when choosing between equally qualified candidates.

The results were eye-opening. Any response above 1 (not at all) on the 7-point scale represents *some* stated willingness to discriminate against conservative colleagues. The proportion of liberal social psychology faculty in their survey declaring at least some willingness to discriminate against conservatives in symposia invitations, grant funding, publication acceptance, and hiring were, respectively, 56%, 78%, 75%, and 78%.

Although Inbar and Lammers (2012) did not set out to test the ICH, their results provide evidence that one of its predictions *does* apply to social psychologists. Specifically, there was clear evidence of liberal prejudice against conservative colleagues in social psychology. Whether these results represent the appalling levels of willingness to engage in political discrimination that it seems, however, is unclear. The studies have sufficient limitations to preclude general statements about the levels of bias against conservatives among research-active social psychologists.

The Political Distortion of Social Psychological Science

We next consider whether political prejudice might manifest, in part, by leading to unjustified scientific conclusions. The evidence reviewed thus far raises the possibility that many social psychologists may be hostile not just to conservative individuals, but also to *ideas, studies, and results* that seem to contest liberal narratives or advance conservative ones. If this is the case *even when those ideas, studies, and results are of equal or greater validity* than those supporting liberal narratives, then some of what passes for conventional wisdom or "established science" in social psychology may not be justified.

Theoretical Bases for Predicting that Political Bias Could Distort Social Psychology

Confirmation Bias/Myside Bias/Motivated Reasoning

A family of related terms has grown around a set of similar phenomena, all of which capture the phenomenon of people privileging information that comports well with their pre-existing beliefs, preferences, attitudes, and morals. Confirmation bias refers to seeking information that confirms one's beliefs, hypotheses or

The Politics of Social Psychological Science **173**

expectations (e.g., Nickerson, 1998). Myside bias occurs when people evaluate evidence or test hypotheses in ways biased toward supporting their own attitudes (Stanovich, West, & Toplak, 2013). Motivated reasoning refers to the general phenomena whereby people often seek out, interpret, and evaluate evidence in ways that are partial to their pre-existing views and/or to what they wish to believe (see Kunda, 1990, for a review).

People more easily accept evidence consistent with their existing beliefs than evidence challenging their views (Ditto & Lopez, 1992; Edwards & Smith, 1996; Klaczynski, 2000; Klaczynski & Gordon, 1996; Lord, Ross, & Lepper, 1979). When presented with information challenging their views, people experience negative arousal, which induces effortful processing often aimed at disconfirming the evidence (Munro & Ditto, 1997; Munro, Ditto, Lockhart, Fagerlin, Gready, & Peterson, 2002; Jacks & Devine, 2000; Zuwerink & Devine, 1996). People are largely unaware of the fact that their reasoning is emotionally driven and biased because post hoc rationalization processes provide the illusion of objectivity (Haidt, 2001; Koehler, 1993; Nickerson, 1998).

The Creation of Majoritarian Political/Theoretical Norms

If ideology influences theorizing, then a mere numerical domination by liberals could lead to a scientific zeitgeist disproportionately filled with topics and theoretical explanations interesting and appealing to liberals. These ideas may then become current, easily accessible, default explanations entrenched in the field's "distilled wisdom," and, as such, alternative explanations less flattering to liberals may face considerable resistance gaining access to publication and funding. Thus some scientific conclusions may seem to validate liberal perspectives, not because they provide the best theoretical accounts for data, but because liberal-enhancing theoretical narratives are readily accessible and entrenched, and because few members in the field are able to generate superior alternative explanations. Even if they are able, many may be unwilling to do so, recognizing that they may face a particularly difficult uphill battle (i.e., obtaining funding, persuading reviewers and editors to publish) contesting an entrenched view.

And those are the relatively innocent processes. Prentice (2012, p. 516–517) recently succinctly summarized some of the less innocent implications of decades of research on conformity and social norms for the conduct of social psychological science:

> ideological homogeneity alone is enough to produce strong liberal norms, which in turn give rise to … felt pressures to conform to liberal views (Festinger, Schachter, & Back, 1950); a reluctance to express nonliberal views (Miller & Morrison, 2009); an assumption that liberal views are even more prevalent and extreme than they are (Prentice & Miller, 1996); a tendency to explain the field's liberal bias in terms of the properties of

174 Lee Jussim et al.

conservatives, not liberals, that produce it (Hegarty & Pratto, 2001; Miller, Taylor, & Buck, 1991); and, yes, an inclination to derogate and punish PSPs [personality and social psychologists] who express conservative views. (Schachter, 1951)

Exaggeration, Conflict, and Blind Spots

Given that the conduct of science is not immune to many biases (e.g., Inbar & Lammers, 2012; Ioannidis, 2005; Jussim, 2012a; Redding, 2001; Simmons, Nelson, & Simonsohn, 2011), we see no reason to expect that social psychologists would be *immune* from exaggerating the beliefs of conservatives or from intolerance of beliefs contesting their own. If social psychologists are not immune, then, these findings raise the possibility of a potentially toxic scientific situation in social psychology: 1) Most social psychologists are liberals; 2) Liberals exaggerate the political and moral differences between liberals and conservatives; 3) Doing so is likely to lead to unjustifiably unfavorable views about colleagues believed to be conservatives or whose work contests liberal narratives of conservative deficiencies and of pervasive prejudice; so that 4) It will be far more difficult for research contesting those narratives to see the light of day (publication, funding) than for research supporting those narratives. The potentially problematic consequences of such processes are that: 1) Many widely-accepted conclusions in social psychology that seem to advance liberal narratives may only appear justified because of systematic and possibly pervasive biases in the system that produces social scientific "knowledge"; and 2) It will be far more difficult, and take far longer, to correct flawed scientific conclusions that support liberal narratives than to correct other types of scientific flaws.

Ideologically Biased Reasoning among Scientists?

Even well-intentioned social psychologists may unknowingly contribute to ideological bias through processes that occur outside their awareness. Prominent researchers have recognized the vulnerability of scientists to various forms of confirmation bias, including political ones (e.g., Eagly, 1995; Lilienfeld, 2010). Several lines of research have concluded that most published findings are false, and most published effect sizes are inflated, in large part because of a whole range of confirmation biases (e.g., Fiedler, 2011; Ioannidis, 2005, 2012; Vul, Harris, Winkielman, & Pashler, 2009). We know of only one study to directly examine these processes among social psychology faculty.

Ideological Bias in Social Psychology: An Audit Study

Articles purporting to demonstrate either that anti-war activist college students were psychologically healthier (a liberal-enhancing result) or less healthy (a liberal-contesting one) than their nonactivist peers were submitted to over 300 psychologists for peer review (Abramowitz, Gomes, & Abramowitz, 1975). Except for the result, all aspects of the papers were otherwise identical. The reviewers were designated as more liberal or less liberal based on a known-groups technique. The reviewers assumed to be more liberal were strongly affiliated with the Society for the Psychological Study of Social Issues (SPSSI; as reviewers, editors, contributors or fellows); the reviewers assumed to be less liberal were not associated with SPSSI in any of these ways, but were active in similar ways (reviewer, editor, contributor, fellow) of APA Division 8 (Personality and Social Psychology).

Results confirmed the political bias hypotheses: The more liberal reviewers evaluated the manuscript finding that activists were mentally healthier more positively than the manuscript finding they were less healthy. The pattern was weaker but in the opposite direction for the less liberal reviewers.

The most obvious weakness of this method is its indirect means of identifying researcher ideology. Nonetheless, given SPSSI's commitment to left-wing social activism (e.g., Unger, 2011), it seems likely that there was at least some difference between the strength of liberalism of the two groups. That even a weak ideology predictor produced such an effect could mean that ideological biases might often be considerably more powerful than Abramowitz et al.'s (1975) results suggest. However, the study is about 40 years old, and as far as we know, there have been no attempts at replication. Whether such a pattern would hold today is a matter of speculation until the scientific evidence is produced.

Ideological Bias in Internal Review Boards: Another Audit Study

Ceci, Peters, & Plotkin (1985) found a similar pattern among Internal Review Boards, which, presumably, include researchers from many disciplines. Research proposals hypothesizing either "reverse discrimination" (i.e., against White males) or conventional discrimination (i.e., against ethnic minorities) were submitted to 150 Internal Review Boards. Everything else about the proposals was held constant. The "conventional" discrimination proposals were approved more often than the reverse discrimination proposals.

In this study, there was no assessment of research ideology at all. However, given the evidence that professors in the social sciences are overwhelmingly left-wing (see, e.g., Duarte et al., 2014; Klein & Stern, 2008b), the result is consistent with liberal politics biasing judgments of the value of scholarship. Nonetheless, this study was conducted over 30 years ago, and its replicability is unknown.

Ideological Bias: The (Anecdotal) Story of Urvashi's Grant Proposal

Urvashi was an excellent undergraduate working with Jussim and Anglin. For just such students, Rutgers University has a program that provides small grants to support their research. Urvashi was engaged in a study developing a questionnaire to assess people's willingness to sacrifice advancing science to further their political goals. And so, she submitted a grant proposal. Although 90% or more of the proposals coming out of Jussim's lab have gotten funded in this program, this one was rejected. And the rejection was entirely substantive; the proposal was allegedly unclear, had weak methodology, and did not articulate why the topic was interesting and important.

When Jussim and Anglin re-read the proposal, we concluded that it was excellent except for one fatal flaw. The first page included the following text:

> The field of psychology is dominated by liberals (Redding, 2001), and this political homogeneity can be problematic ... In fact, content analysis of all the articles published in *American Psychologist* during the 1990s revealed that 97% had liberal themes (Redding, 2001). Furthermore, recent research suggests many social psychologists would blatantly discriminate based on politics (Inbar & Lammers, 2012) ...

We decided to resubmit the proposal, and do nothing—that is right, nothing—to address the substantive criticisms in the review. We made no changes, except one—we replaced the fatally flawed text with the following:

> Science has a long and checkered history of periodically being used and exploited as a tool to advance nefarious right-wing political agendas (e.g., social Darwinism; Nazi eliminationist practices; Herrnstein & Murray's (1994) claims about genetic bases of race differences in intelligence).

The proposal was funded. We were pleased to discover that merely lambasting Nazis and racists improved the (perceived) quality of our methods, the clarity of our writing, and successfully communicated why the work was interesting and important.

This is an anecdote (albeit an anecdote informed by experimental methodology—change just one thing and see what happens). It provides no firm basis for causal conclusions. But it is also what some social scientists call "lived experience" (e.g., Jussim, 2012b; Tappan, 1997). It is a case study consistent with the patterns uncovered in Inbar and Lammers' (2012) survey. Research that contests liberal narratives faces obstacles that simply do not exist for, and are therefore invisible to, those whose work does not contest those narratives.

How Ideological Bias Leads Social Psychology Astray: Questionable Interpretive Practices, Examples, and Remedies

The research reviewed thus far suggests that a plausible case can be made that politically biased social psychological research has likely occurred in the past

The Politics of Social Psychological Science **177**

and is probably continuing today. Liberals are openly hostile to conservatives; many liberal social psychologists acknowledge hostility to conservative colleagues (Inbar & Lammers, 2012). Laypeople and psychologists alike are subject to all sorts of motivated biases and distortions, including political ones. All of which raises the following questions: In what ways have political biases led to unjustified claims and conclusions in social psychology? What, specifically, has social psychology gotten wrong? What steps can be taken to mitigate the risks of such distortions?

Questionable Interpretive Practices

Political biases can lead to a variety of *questionable interpretive practices (QIPs)*. Questionable research practices (Simmons et al., 2011) involve undisclosed flexibility in methods and statistical analyses that will often permit researchers to present unreliable and invalid findings as "statistically significant" and thereby reach unjustified conclusions. QIPs also involve reaching unjustified conclusions, but through a very different route. Even if the methods and statistics are conducted with complete integrity, any one of several systematic biases in interpreting research can *still* produce completely invalid conclusions.

QIPs can be viewed as the specific processes by which researcher confirmation biases influence and distort the conclusions reached. There are many types of QIPs, but in this chapter, we focus on double standards, blind spots, and embedded values.

Double Standards

As a QIP in social psychology, double standards refers to reaching contradictory conclusions as long as both support liberal narratives (see also Redding, 2001). Social psychology has an extraordinary record of revealing such biases in lay judgment (e.g., Altemeyer, 1996; Crawford, 2012; Ditto & Lopez, 1992; Rudman, Moss-Racusin, Glick, & Phelan, 2012). They are also fairly common in the conduct and interpretation of social psychological research by social psychologists (see also Duarte et al., 2015; Jussim, 2012a, b; Jussim et al., 2014 for examples beyond those reviewed here).

The Criterion "Problem" in Accuracy but Not Self-Fulfilling Prophecy?

Self-fulfilling prophecies are often discussed in ways consistent with liberal narratives of oppression—as a social process by which stereotypes lead to discrimination and inequality (e.g., Darley & Fazio, 1980; Ross, Lepper, & Ward, 2010; Weinstein, Gregory, & Strambler, 2004). Evidence of accuracy seems to contest those narratives, in part, because self-fulfilling prophecies begin with an erroneous expectation (Merton, 1948), and if the expectation is not erroneous, the phenomenon does not occur. Similarly, accuracy implies that individual or group differences have some objective social reality to them, thereby seeming to undercut liberal narratives blaming oppression and perceiver biases (see Jussim, 2012a for an elaboration of this analysis). Thus, self-fulfilling prophecies seem to support liberal narratives, and accuracy seems to contest those narratives.

If this analysis is true, then one would expect that social psychologists would generally be more critical of accuracy research than of self-fulfilling prophecy research. This is indeed the case. Many researchers have raised the issue of identifying criteria for assessing accuracy as something problematic (e.g., Fiske, 1998; Jones, 1985; Kruglanski, 1989). There is some validity to such a critique because there rarely is a perfect criterion against which to assess the accuracy of lay judgments. Most criteria have advantages and disadvantages, something accuracy researchers have long recognized (for reviews, see Funder, 1987; Judd & Park, 1993; Jussim, 2012a; Ryan, 2002).

A double standard arises when researchers (often the same ones) write enthusiastically and uncritically about the power and pervasiveness of self-fulfilling prophecies (e.g., Fiske & Neuberg, 1990; Jones, 1986; Jost & Kruglanski, 2002) without raising similar issues about criteria. For both self-fulfilling prophecies and accuracy, one must establish correspondence between perceivers' expectation and targets' outcomes. There is a difference in how the correspondence comes about, but there is no difference in the criteria—or in the difficulty in identifying criteria—for establishing whether that correspondence has come about. By routinely raising critical questions about the difficulty in identifying criteria to assess accuracy but not self-fulfilling prophecy, the politically distasteful phenomenon (accuracy) is held to greater critical scrutiny than the politically palatable phenomenon (self-fulfilling prophecy).

The Black Hole at the Bottom of Most Declarations That "Stereotypes Are Inaccurate"

Most scholarly declarations of stereotypes as inaccurate cite either nothing in support of this claim, or cite an article that neither provides nor reviews empirical support for this claim. We next give one example of each, though there are many more (see Jussim, 2012a).

> [S]tereotypes are maladaptive forms of categories because their content does not correspond to what is going on in the environment. (Bargh & Chartrand, 1999, p. 467)

> The term *stereotype* refers to those interpersonal beliefs and expectancies that are both widely shared and generally invalid (Ashmore & Del Boca, 1981). (Miller & Turnbull, 1986, p. 233)

The Politics of Social Psychological Science **179**

These are purportedly statements of scientific facts, which typically require *some sort of scientific evidence*. The far less frequent declarations that stereotypes often have considerable accuracy have *always* provided extensive empirical documentation (e.g., Jussim, 2012a; Jussim, Cain, Crawford, Harber, & Cohen, 2009; Lee, Jussim, & McCauley, 1995; Oakes et al., 1994; Ryan, 2002). That scientists can make the "stereotype inaccuracy" claim without *any* scientific documentation (as in Bargh & Chartrand, 1999, above) reflects a serious dysfunction in social psychology.

Miller and Turnbull (1986), in contrast, did provide a reference—Ashmore and Del Boca (1981). However, Ashmore and Del Boca (1981): 1) Reviewed conceptual issues in the study of stereotypes but did not review the empirical evidence that bore on the accuracy question; 2) Concluded that badness should *not* be a defining component of stereotypes.

It is, of course, understandable why those wishing to declare stereotypes inaccurate do not cite research demonstrating pervasive inaccuracy in stereotypes. That is because such research does not exist (Jussim, 2012a; Jussim et al., 2009; Oakes et al., 1994; Ryan, 2002). The real question is why do so many researchers make this claim either without citing anything in support, or citing articles that do not provide such support? Why do so many reviewers and editors allow them to do so? This reflects a pervasive double standard in social psychology, where it takes no evidence to justify declarations of stereotype inaccuracy and extraordinary amounts to justify declarations of stereotype accuracy.

Such behavior raises the possibility that, to at least some degree, the widespread conclusion in social psychology that stereotypes are inaccurate and irrational distortions is not merely an empirical claim, but, for some, a sacred moral value. Deeply held moral beliefs are often primarily intuitive and non-rational, and held with a conviction that not only does not need proof or evidence, but is impervious to both logic and data (Haidt, 2012; Skitka, Bauman, & Sargis, 2005). Tetlock, Kristel, Elson, Green, & Lerner (2000, p. 854) define a *forbidden base-rate* as "… any statistical generalization that devoted Bayesians would not hesitate to use in their probability calculations but that deeply offends a religious or political community." Imbuing stereotype inaccuracy with such moral beliefs may help explain both the existence of a nearly field-wide blind spot to evidence of stereotype accuracy and why evidence of stereotype accuracy seems to offend some social psychologists (see Jussim, 2012a for a review bearing on both points).

How to Recognize and Avoid Double Standards

There are two simple solutions to avoiding double standards, and one perhaps less simple but probably more constructive for social psychology in the long term. First, if researchers are determined to reach some sort of conclusion in politicized topics, they should: 1) articulate, a priori, their grounds for reaching that conclusion; and then 2) apply those criteria to both their own and others' research

180 Lee Jussim et al.

regardless of whether that research supports or contests liberal narratives. For example, one can declare cognitive ability tests to be invalid because they are supposedly culturally biased. In that case, use of them would invalidate research on stereotype accuracy that uses cognitive ability tests as criteria, just as much as it would invalidate research on self-fulfilling prophecies and stereotype threat that uses cognitive ability tests as criteria.

Second, conduct a turnabout test (Tetlock, 1994), which is, colloquially, putting the shoe on the other foot. If one can declare stereotypes *inaccurate* without citations, then one should be able to declare stereotypes *accurate* without citation. We suspect most scientists would object to this state of affairs, as do we ourselves.

Third, seek out collaborations, or at least input, from colleagues with different political values, or, at least, whose research challenges and contests the values and conclusions inherent in one's own research. In theory, this recommendation should apply equally well to scientists whose work supports or contests liberal narratives. In practice, however, the few social psychologists whose research contests those narratives can safely assume that their colleagues, either informally or formally (e.g., grant or journal reviewers and editors) will likely hold them accountable for unjustifiable claims. Scholarship that advances liberal narratives, however, is far less likely to benefit from this accountability process simply because there are far fewer social psychologists motivated to contest such narratives.

Blind Spots

We use the term "blind spot" to refer to the failure to recognize or acknowledge research that contests one's preferred views. Blind spots may be unintentional, and simply reflect lack of awareness or familiarity with an area of research. Blind spots can also be intentional—and may involve purposely ignoring areas of research inconsistent with one's preferred theoretical or political view. Blind spots are a common lay phenomenon (Haidt, 2012; Pronin, 2007), and a growing literature suggests they exist within the social sciences as well (e.g., Duarte et al., 2015; Ioannidis, 2012; Jussim et al., 2015; Redding, 2001). Ideally, social science works, in part, because Dr. X's blind spots differ from Dr. Y's blind spots, so that eventually valid conclusions emerge. However, a political monoculture risks leading to endemic blind spots, two of which are discussed next.

Overlooking Powerful Effects

To date, over 50 high quality studies of stereotype accuracy have been conducted by multiple independent research laboratories. They have examined stereotypes regarding a wide range of groups (including but not restricted to gender, racial, role, and political stereotypes), and a wide range of attributes (such as personality

The Politics of Social Psychological Science **181**

characteristics, accomplishments, interests, and attitudes—see Jussim, 2012a; Jussim et al., 2009 for reviews; Jussim et al., in press).

Assessing stereotype accuracy is a complex issue beyond the scope of this chapter (see Jussim, 2012a; Jussim et al., 2009). One aspect of stereotype accuracy is correspondence—the correlation of stereotype beliefs with criteria. The average effect size in social psychology is about $r=.20$ (Richard, Bond, & Stokes-Zoota, 2003). Stereotype accuracy correlations for individual perceivers average about .50, and consensual stereotype accuracy correlations (between the mean of a group of perceivers' beliefs and criteria) average about $r=.80$, making stereotype accuracy correlations some of the largest and most replicable effects in all of social psychology.

Stereotypes as discrepancy scores (Judd & Park, 1993) are typically a mix of accurate and inaccurate (Jussim, 2012a). However, discrepancy scores do not readily translate into accuracy effect sizes, so it is not possible at this time to compare the degree of accuracy found in discrepancy scores to typical social psychological effect sizes. Of course, even such mixed findings do not support any general conclusion that stereotypes are inaccurate.

Researchers may have many reasons for not reviewing this evidence. They may be unaware of it or consider it uninteresting. Some prefer to emphasize other aspects of intergroup relations, especially those more obviously related to oppression. Regardless, the continued lack of acknowledgement of what is now an extensive literature demonstrating considerable accuracy in many stereotypes that have been assessed is a glaring and pervasive blind spot in social psychological perspectives on intergroup relations—which one can easily document by reading almost any broad review of intergroup relations published in almost any *Handbook of Social Psychology* or *Annual Review* chapter published in the last 40 years, as well as most other broad reviews.

Overlooking Failed Replications of Classic Bias and Self-Fulfilling Prophecy Studies

Some of the most classic studies in the psychology of intergroup relations and expectancy effects have proven difficult or impossible to replicate. Worse, the existence of failures to replicate has, apparently, gone largely unnoticed, so that both citation counts to the original, possibly irreplicable, studies continue to mount, as do uncritical and enthusiastic acceptance of the original studies' conclusions.

Perhaps the most extreme version of this is how one study of the role of stereotypes in person perception—which has so far proven both irreplicable and inconsistent with almost every other study ever conducted in this area—has captured the imagination of so many social psychologists. Darley and Gross (1983) performed a single study including 70 participants and found no evidence of stereotype bias in the absence of relevant individuating information, but

182 Lee Jussim et al.

evidence of such bias in the presence of relevant individuating information. They interpreted this evidence as demonstrating that "stereotypes lead to their own confirmation"—an interpretation that bolsters liberal narratives of oppression by emphasizing the power of stereotypes to distort judgment. As of this writing, this paper has been cited over 800 times according to Google Scholar.

There are several problems, however, with imbuing this study with particular importance. First, Baron, Albright, and Malloy (1995) obtained the original stimulus materials and performed two exact attempts at replication. Both failed. Since 1996 (i.e., starting a year after the Baron et al. article was published), Darley and Gross (1983) has been cited over 600 times, whereas Baron et al. (1995) about 30 times. Since Baron et al.'s (1995) publication, nearly 600 papers have cited Darley and Gross (1983) without even mentioning Baron et al.'s (1995) failures to replicate.

Before concluding that this reflects a political blind spot, we first consider two alternative explanations. One possibility is that Darley and Gross (1983) was published in a higher impact journal (*Journal of Personality and Social Psychology*) than was Baron et al. (1995), which was published in *Personality and Social Psychology Bulletin*. Another possibility is that perhaps studies published first have an easier time lodging themselves in researchers' understanding of some phenomena. First, we note that, even if one or both of these alternatives have merit, they *explain* the blind spot in nonpolitical ways, *but they do not explain it away*. This is still an almost complete failure to acknowledge the failed replications—a failure which, even if it does not *reflect* political bias, still risks producing overstated narratives of oppression.

Furthermore, both alternative explanations fail because, in fact, a study published before Darley and Gross (1983) found *the exact opposite pattern* and has been cited at only about 30% the rate of Darley and Gross (1983) since 1996. Locksley, Borgida, Brekke, and Hepburn (1980) were the first to investigate the role of stereotypes in person perception in the presence and absence of relevant individuating information. They found that, although stereotypes did influence judgments without relevant individuating information, there was no such effect in the presence of relevant individuating information. Like Darley and Gross (1983), this paper was published in *Journal of Personality and Social Psychology*.

Thus, we can rule out both the "more prestigious journal" and "they have more citations because they got there first" explanations. Locksley et al. (1980) and Baron et al. (1995) essentially found that people engage in approximately rational stereotyping, relying on stereotypes when there is no other useful information, but jettisoning stereotypes in the presence of clear, relevant individuating information. Such a pattern, of course, implicitly contests narratives emphasizing the oppressive nature of stereotypes, whereas the conclusion that "stereotypes lead to their own confirmation" advances such narratives. And this, we suggest, explains the dramatic difference in citations.

The Politics of Social Psychological Science **183**

This state of affairs is summarized in Table 8.1, which also makes clear that the "rational stereotyping" studies are based on combined samples of almost 500 participants, whereas Darley and Gross (1983) is based on a mere 70. By any scientific standard, the major conclusion justified by these studies is that people rely on stereotypes approximately rationally. And if one finds that surprising, that, we suggest, further attests to the power of liberal narratives to lead to an entrenched view that takes on a life of its own, independent of the field's own data.

Second, most other studies of which we are aware that has manipulated the amount of individuating information (e.g., Krueger & Rothbart, 1988; Locksley et al., 1980; Locksley, Hepburn, & Ortiz, 1982; see Jussim, 2012a for a review) has found *the exact opposite pattern* as Darley and Gross (1983)—bias is most likely to occur when individuating information is minimal or absent, and often evaporates completely in the presence of clear and relevant individuating information. Although these studies are not exact replications, they are additional failed tests of the hypothesis that (other) stereotypes in other contexts "lead to their own confirmation" and provided additional support for the rational stereotyping hypothesis. None of these papers are cited at anything near the rate of Darley and Gross (1983).

This citation pattern highlights that the problem here is not Darley and Gross (1983), but the wider field of social psychology. It reveals a truly immense blind spot, especially if one considers the number of social psychologists involved in each post-1995 publication of Darley and Gross (1983)—the

TABLE 8.1 Comparison of three studies of stereotypes and person perception.

	Number of Studies	Number of Participants (Total)	Citations (Total; Since 1996)	Main Conclusion
Locksley et al. (1980)	2	325	415; 237	Individuating information readily eliminates stereotyping
Darley & Gross (1983)	1	70	886; 693	Stereotypes act as hypotheses that are tested in a biased manner and lead to their own false confirmation
Baron et al. (1995)	2	161	36; 34	Individuating information readily eliminates stereotyping; two failed exact replications of Darley & Gross (1983)

184 Lee Jussim et al.

multiple authors involved in each paper, and the reviewers and editors who permitted it. It is, therefore, no overstatement to declare much of the field complicit in the undue elevation of the conclusion that "stereotypes lead to their own confirmation."

Other "classics" of the expectancy-confirmation literature suffer from similar problems. For example, Snyder and Swann (1978) performed a series of studies they interpreted as demonstrating that people seek to confirm their social expectations. Unfortunately, however, Snyder and Swann (1978) gave people no option to ask *diagnostic* questions.

Asking diagnostic questions provides targets with maximal opportunity to *either* confirm or disconfirm the hypothesis, so that asking such questions reflects maximal fairness and rationality on the part of social perceivers and the lowest possible tendency to "seek confirmation." The lack of such questions was, therefore, a major limitation to Snyder and Swann (1978). When people have been given the opportunity to ask diagnostic questions, they have overwhelmingly asked such questions (e.g., Devine, Hirt, & Gehrke, 1990; Trope & Bassok, 1982, 1983; see Jussim, 2012a for a review). Again, revealing a striking blind spot, Snyder and Swann (1978) has been cited more frequently then *all of these other papers combined.*

Although some effects have fared better than those found by Darley and Gross (1983) and Snyder and Swann (1978), many classics of the stereotype- and expectancy-confirmation literature (e.g., Duncan, 1976; Rosenthal & Jacobson, 1968; Snyder, Tanke, & Berscheid, 1977) suffer from replicating difficulties. These replication difficulties should, but rarely do, constrain social psychologists from making strong proclamations about the power of stereotype- and expectancy-confirmation biases, as the following examples illustrate:

> [T]he literature has stressed the power of expectancies to shape perceptions and interpretations in their own image. (E. E. Jones, 1986, p. 42)

> The thrust of dozens of experiments on the self-fulfilling prophecy and expectancy-confirmation processes, for example, is that erroneous impressions tend to be perpetuated rather than supplanted, because of the impressive extent to which people see what they want to see and act as others want them to act ... (Jost & Kruglanski, 2002, pp. 172-173)

> If it is widely believed that the members of some group disproportionately possess some virtue or vice ... one is likely (in the absence of specific legal or social sanctions) to ... deprive or privilege group members in terms of opportunities to ... succeed or fail in accord with the beliefs and expectations that dictated their life chances. (Ross et al., 2010, p. 30)

The Politics of Social Psychological Science   **185**

How to Minimize Blind Spots

Intentional blind spots constitute blatant bias on the part of scholars, and we doubt anything can counter such bias except for a greater diversity of political and theoretical viewpoints in the field. Such diversity increases the chance of scientists being held accountable for such blatant bias during reviews of their papers and grants.

But what about unintentional blind spots? If one is unaware of a literature or failed replication, how can one acknowledge it? Here we offer a simple solution—focus on meta-analyses rather than individual studies, no matter how "classic" or how great a story that individual study makes in the retelling. Meta-analyses involving hundreds of studies and tens of thousands of participants (Kunda & Thagard, 1996; Mazella & Feingold, 1994; Swim, Borgida, Maruyama, & Myers, 1989) demonstrate that the Darley and Gross (1983) pattern of results was quite unusual: 1) Individuating information effects tend to be quite large, averaging about $r=.70$; and 2) Stereotype biases tend to be quite small, averaging about $r=.10$; and the more individuating information there is, the weaker stereotype bias effects.

If the Darley and Gross (1983) pattern of no bias in the absence of individuating information and bias in its presence means that "stereotypes lead to their own confirmation" (as they interpreted it), then doesn't the opposite pattern indicated by meta-analyses mean that, in general, stereotypes *do not* lead to their own confirmation? Although meta-analyses are not beyond criticism, the burden shifts to researchers who wish to maintain the conclusion that "stereotypes lead to their own confirmation" to justify why they consider one study with 70 participants to be more informative, valid, and reliable than the conclusions based on meta-analyses of hundreds of studies and thousands of participants.

Embedded Values

Liberal values and assumptions can and have become embedded into the theories and methods driving certain areas of research in social psychology and other social sciences. Political values can become embedded into research questions, constructs, and measures, in ways that compromise the ability to answer those questions, the interpretation of those constructs, and the validity of those measures (Sniderman & Tetlock, 1986; Tetlock, 1994; Tetlock & Mitchell, 1993). In this article and elsewhere (Duarte et al., 2015; Jussim et al., 2015) we have described some of the ways that liberal values became embedded into social psychological theory and method. In this final section we focus on symbolic racism[2] (Kinder & Sears, 1981; Sears & Henry, 2005).

186 Lee Jussim et al.

Brief Recap of the Symbolic Racism Controversies

Symbolic racism has proven to be a very controversial construct, as have been the questionnaires intended to measure it. We briefly review one of the key aspects of those controversies below (see Huddy & Feldman, 2009 for an excellent and even-handed full review).

Symbolic racism theories began to emerge in the 1970s and early 1980s, which suggested that because blatant racial discrimination had become illegal and blatant expressions of racism had become stigmatized, racism went "underground" (e.g., Kinder & Sears, 1981; McConahay & Hough, 1976). Supposedly, social desirability concerns have caused people to mask their expressions of racism so that it is now expressed in more subtle and covert ways. Specifically, anti-black affect is masked by support for traditional values typically associated with the Protestant Work Ethic: hard work, individualism, personal responsibility, delayed gratification, and sexual repression (Sears & Henry, 2005). Symbolic racism is associated with opposition to busing and affirmative action, beliefs that discrimination is no longer an obstacle for Blacks, that Blacks demand too much from the government, and that Blacks have received more than they deserve from the government (Kinder & Sanders, 1996; Kinder & Sears, 1981; Sears & Henry, 2003; Sears, Hensler, & Speer, 1979; Sears, van Laar, Carrillo, & Kosterman, 1997). It is also associated with negative evaluations of and opposition to Black candidates at the mayoral and presidential levels (Kinder & Sears, 1981; Sears, Lau, Tyler, & Allen Jr., 1980; Sears et al., 1997).

The concept and measurement of symbolic racism, however, have proven controversial (e.g., Sniderman, Piazza, Tetlock, & Kendrick, 1991; Sniderman & Tetlock, 1986). And one of the main bones of contention is that common measures of symbolic racism tap fundamental principles of conservatism. If one is a racist, one will probably oppose affirmative action, busing to achieve integration in schools, and all sorts of social welfare programs. However, one can oppose those programs, not because one is a racist, but because one opposes such government interventions and programs on principle.

The Embedding of Liberal Values in Symbolic Racism Measures?

In short, in addition to partially capturing racism, measures of symbolic racism may have also at least partially captured political ideology. Given that measures of symbolic racism often refer to government policies, they may also partially capture *political prejudice*. Liberals have generally supported government interventions such as affirmative action, busing, and welfare programs. It remains possible that failing to understand or accept conservative principles of individualism, personal responsibility, and meritocracy led to the presumption among (overwhelmingly liberal) social psychologists that opposition to such programs must ipso facto reflect subtle hostility directed toward Blacks.

The Politics of Social Psychological Science **187**

Disliking liberal policies often goes hand in hand with disliking of and intolerance toward liberals (Brandt et al., 2014). Such an analysis raises the possibility that various symbolic racism scales have been embedded with liberal values that indict conservatives for racism, when, at least sometimes, conservative responses reflect, not racism, but opposition to liberal policies and/or dislike of liberals. Feldman and Huddy (2005, p. 170) summarized this critique extremely well:

> Consider the third item in the resentment scale that suggests that if Blacks tried harder they could be just as well off as Whites. A strong individualist would agree with this statement; they would also agree with any other statement that referred to the positive effects of hard work, regardless of the target person's race, gender, or other characteristics. As noted above, Kinder and Sanders (1996) believe that individualism has become entwined with racism so that agreement with the notion that Blacks are unwilling to work hard is a form of racism. But this leaves no room for the expression of general, nonracist individualism.

Symbolic Racism Predicts Generalized Hostility to Social Programs among Conservatives

Consistent with this general perspective, Feldman and Huddy (2005) found that, among conservatives, symbolic racism measures predicted opposition to a scholarship program for both Blacks and Whites. This pattern is clearly inconsistent with the idea that symbolic racism captured racism among conservatives. If it did, it should have predicted greater opposition to the program for Blacks than for Whites. Because it predicted both similarly for conservatives, the scale appeared to capture ideological opposition to social programs more than racism, a result consistent with Chambers et al.'s 2013 findings (described previously) showing that dislike of liberals, rather than racism, explains conservatives' dislikes of African-Americans.

Liberal Symbolic Racism is Racism

Feldman and Huddy (2005) also found that symbolic racism did uniquely predict opposition to the program for Blacks among liberals. That is, liberals high on symbolic racism opposed the program for Blacks more than they opposed the other social programs. Is symbolic racism primarily a phenomenon among liberals? Perhaps. In contrast to conservatives, liberals do not generally hold values that would lead to objections to social programs writ large. Therefore, higher levels of resentment of social programs intended to help Blacks may indeed reflect racism among liberals, even if it does not, or does so more weakly, among conservatives.

188 Lee Jussim et al.

Have Embedded Values Reduced the Predictive Validity of Subtle Measures of Racism?

If modern measures of subtle prejudice, such as symbolic racism, are unintentionally measuring political ideology and political prejudice either instead of or in addition to racism, their predictive validity for discriminatory behavior might be compromised. Indeed, meta-analytic evidence shows that the predictive validity of modern questionnaire measures (post-2000) intending to assess subtle forms of racism correlate only $r=.12$ with anti-Black discrimination (Oswald, Mitchell, Blanton, Jaccard, & Tetlock, 2013). This predictive validity is considerably lower than that found in meta-analyses of research on the prejudice–discrimination link conducted mostly before 1980 ($r=.24$). There are many possible explanations for this difference, most of which are beyond the scope of this chapter. Nonetheless, one possibility is that modern measures poorly predict discrimination because, consistent with our embedded values analysis, they are diluted by ideological content, whereas the earlier research relied on blunter, clearer, and less ideologically confounded measures of racial prejudice.

One alternative possibility is simply that behavioral prediction is generally difficult. This, however, is unlikely to explain the low predictive validity of symbolic racism measures for discrimination. Social psychological effects on other behaviors, such as aggression ($r=.24$), helping ($r=.18$), and nonverbal communication ($r=.22$), are often higher (Richard et al., 2003). Issues of unintentional ideological confounding do not arise as readily when predicting aggression, helping, and nonverbal behavior, thereby providing additional, albeit indirect, evidence that something is amiss with modern explicit measures of prejudice.

One argument against such a conclusion is that racism has gone so far underground that only measures that are outside of conscious awareness, such as the IAT, can successfully capture racial prejudice. Indeed, this seemed to be the conclusion that emerged from a relatively early meta-analysis of the ability of the IAT to predict racial discrimination, which found that effect size to be $r=.24$ (Greenwald, Poehlman, Uhlmann, & Banaji, 2009). However, after uncovering and correcting for some very basic errors (including, among others, one confession of fraudulent data and another that the wrong sign had been attached to an IAT-discrimination correlation), a re-analysis of the same studies yielded an effect size of only $r=.15$ (Oswald et al., 2013; see especially their online supplementary materials, which provide details about the source of errors). Thus, an argument that implicit measures would much more strongly predict discrimination is not supported by these data (explaining why the IAT-discrimination links are so low is also beyond the scope of this chapter, but see Blanton and Jaccard, 2008 for a detailed analysis of limitations to the IAT).

It is also worth noting that the pattern of errors uncovered by Oswald et al. (2013) is consistent with a major theme of the present chapter. Specifically, nearly all of those blatant errors were in the direction of overestimating the size of the IAT-discrimination relationship, thereby overestimating scientific support for conclusions emphasizing the supposed power of implicit and unconscious prejudices to produce discrimination.

How to Recognize and Avoid Embedded Values Biases

Again, a simple, easily applied test is to conduct a turnabout test (Tetlock, 1994). Imagine a counterfactual social psychology field in which conservative political views were treated as "scientific facts" and disagreements with conservative views treated as errors or prejudice. Would a belief that evangelicals have gone too far in their political activities constitute "symbolic religious prejudice"? Embedding ideological values into measures is dangerous to science.

The more difficult solution is to increase the ideological diversity of social psychology. The best solution to scientific blind spots and unintentional distortions are the presence of other scientists who hold *different* blind spots and different values. Furthermore, people are generally much better at spotting biases in *other people* than in themselves (e.g., Haidt, 2012; Pronin, 2008). If there are more social psychologists who do not subscribe to liberal values and worldviews, and who do not suffer liberal blind spots, then blind spots and distortions are more likely to be recognized and rectified earlier, before they unjustifiably become part of the field's entrenched "knowledge."

Conclusion

This chapter has reviewed evidence regarding three primary issues: 1) the seemingly extreme left-wing ideological homogeneity among social psychologists; 2) the role of hostile environment and political prejudice in contributing to that ideological homogeneity; and 3) QIPs that threaten the validity of social psychological science. Space considerations necessarily limited our ability to review QIPs here. Additional examples in the realm of intergroup relations and self-fulfilling prophecies (Duarte et al., 2015; Jussim, 2012a) and political psychology (Jussim et al., 2014) can be found elsewhere.

In our view, the most important threats posed by political homogeneity and discrimination are to creating a robust, valid, and generalizable social psychology. Nonetheless, regardless of researchers' personal ideological beliefs, there are many steps they can take to reduce the effects of political biases and QIPs on their conclusions (see Duarte et al., 2015; Jussim et al., 2015 for additional recommendations). We hope most choose to take those steps.

190 Lee Jussim et al.

Notes

1 We thank Yoel Inbar for providing the raw data on which Inbar and Lammers (2012) was based.
2 The theoretical perspectives of symbolic racism, modern racism (McConahay, 1986), and racial resentment (Kinder & Sanders, 1996) have been operationalized similarly and are not strongly distinguished from each other (Sears & Henry, 2005). In the current chapter we collectively refer to these approaches as the symbolic racism perspective.

References

Abramowitz, S. I., Gomes, B., & Abramowitz, C. V. (1975). Publish or perish: Referee bias in manuscript review. *Journal of Applied Social Psychology, 5*, 187–200.

Adorno, T. W., Frenkel-Brunswik, E., Levinson, D. J., & Sanford, R. N. (1950). *The Authoritarian Personality*. New York: Harper.

Akrami, N., Ekehammar, B., & Bergh, R. (2011). Generalized prejudice: Common and specific components. *Psychological Science, 22*, 57–59.

Altemeyer, B. (1996). *The Authoritarian Specter*. Cambridge, MA: Harvard University Press.

Ashmore, R. D., & Del Boca, F. K. (1981). Conceptual approaches to stereotypes and stereotyping. In D. L. Hamilton (Ed.), *Cognitive Processes in Stereotyping and Intergroup Behavior* (pp. 1–35). Hillsdale: Erlbaum.

Bargh, J. A., & Chartrand, T. L. (1999). The unbearable automaticity of being. *American Psychologist, 54*, 462–479.

Baron, R. M., Albright, L., & Malloy, T. E. (1995). Effects of behavioral and social class information on social judgment. *Personality and Social Psychology Bulletin, 21*, 308–315.

Blanton, H., & Jaccard, J. (2008). Unconscious racism: A concept in pursuit of a measure. *Annual Review of Sociology, 34*, 277–297.

Brandt, M. J., Reyna, C., Chambers, J. R., Crawford, J. T., & Wetherell, G. (2014). The ideological-conflict hypothesis: Intolerance among both liberals and conservatives. *Current Directions in Psychological Science, 23*(1), 27–34.

Ceci, S. J., Peters, D., & Plotkin, J. (1985). Human subjects review, personal values, and the regulation of social science research. *American Psychologist, 40*, 994–1002.

Chambers, J. R., & Melnyk, D. (2006). Why do I hate thee? Conflict misperceptions and intergroup mistrust. *Personality and Social Psychology Bulletin, 32*, 1295–1311.

Chambers, J. R., Baron, R. S., & Inman, M. L. (2006). Misperceptions in intergroup conflict. *Psychological Science, 17*, 38–45.

Chambers, J. R., Schlenker, B. R., Collisson, B. (2013). Ideology and prejudice: The role of value conflicts. *Psychological Science, 24*, 140–149.

Converse, P. E. (1964). The nature of belief systems in mass publics. In D. E. Apter (Ed.), *Ideology and Discontent* (pp. 75–169). New York: Free Press.

Crawford, J. T. (2012). The ideologically objectionable premise model: Predicting biased political judgments on the left and right. *Journal of Experimental Social Psychology, 48*, 138–151.

Crawford, J. T. (2014). Ideological symmetries and asymmetries in political intolerance judgments. Manuscript in preparation.

Crawford, J. T., & Pilanski, J. M. (2013). Political intolerance, right *and* left. *Political Psychology.* doi: 10.1111/j.1467–9221.2012.00926.x

Crawford, J. T., Wance, N. M., Brandt, M. J., Chambers, J. R., Inbar, Y., & Motyl, M. (2014). Differential effects of social and economic ideologies on political prejudice: Further evidence for the ideological conflict hypothesis. Manuscript in preparation.

Darley, J. M., & Fazio, R. H. (1980). Expectancy confirmation processes arising in the social interaction sequence. *American Psychologist, 35,* 867–881.

Darley, J. M., & Gross, P. H. (1983). A hypothesis-confirming bias in labeling effects. *Journal of Personality and Social Psychology, 44,* 20–33.

Devine, P. G., Hirt, E. R., & Gehrke, E. M. (1990). Diagnostic and confirmation strategies in trait hypothesis testing. *Journal of Personality and Social Psychology, 58,* 952–963.

Ditto, P. H., & Lopez, D. F. (1992). Motivated skepticism: Use of differential decision criteria for preferred and nonpreferred conclusions. *Journal of Personality and Social Psychology, 63,* 569–584.

Duarte, J. L., Crawford, J. T., Stern, C., Haidt, J., Jussim, L., & Tetlock, P. (2014). Political diversity will improve social and personality psychological science. Unpublished manuscript.

Duarte, J. L., Crawford, J. T., Stern, C., Haidt, J., Jussim, L., & Tetlock, P. (2015). Political diversity will improve social psychological science. *Behavioral and Brain Sciences, 38,* 1–13. DOI: http://dx.doi.org/10.1017/S0140525X14000430

Duckitt, J. (2001). A dual-process cognitive-motivational theory of ideology and prejudice. *Advances in Experimental Social Psychology, 33,* 41–113.

Duncan, B. L. (1976). Differential social perception and attribution of intergroup violence: Testing the lower limits of stereotyping of blacks. *Journal of Personality and Social Psychology, 34,* 590–598.

Eagly, A. (1995). The science and politics of comparing women and men. *American Psychologist, 50,* 145–158.

Edwards, K., & Smith, E. E. (1996). A disconfirmation bias in the evaluation of arguments. *Journal of Personality and Social Psychology, 71,* 5–24.

Feldman, S., & Huddy, L. (2005). Racial resentment and white opposition to race-conscious programs: principles or prejudice? *American Journal of Political Science, 49,* 168–183.

Feldman, S., & Johnston, C. D. (2013). Understanding the determinants of political ideology: Implications of structural complexity. *Political Psychology.* doi: 10.1111/pops.12055

Festinger, L., Schachter, S., & Back, K. (1950). *Social Pressure in Informal Groups.* New York, NY: Harper & Row.

Fiedler, K. (2011). Voodoo correlations are everywhere—not just neuroscience. *Perspectives on Psychological Science, 6,* 163–171.

Fiske, S. T. (1998). Stereotyping, prejudice, and discrimination. In T. Gilbert & S. T. Fiske (Eds.), *Handbook of Social Psychology* (Vol. 2, pp. 357–411). Boston, MA: McGraw-Hill.

Fiske, S. T., & Neuberg, S. L. (1990). A continuum model of impression formation, from category-based to individuating processes: Influence of information and motivation on attention and interpretation. In M. P. Zanna (Ed.), *Advances in Experimental Social Psychology* (Vol. 23, pp. 1–74). San Diego, CA: Academic Press.

Funder, D. C. (1987). Errors and mistakes: Evaluating the accuracy of social judgment. *Psychological Bulletin, 101,* 75–90.

192 Lee Jussim et al.

Funder, D. C., Levine, J. M., Mackie, D. M., Morf, C. C., Vazire, S., & West, S. G. (2013). Improving the dependability of research in personality and social psychology: Recommendations for research and educational practice. *Personality and Social Psychology Review.* doi: 10.1177/1088868313507536

Gallup (2014). Liberal self-identification edges up to new high in 2013. Retrieved January 23, 2014 from http://www.gallup.com/poll/166787/liberal-self-identification-edges-new-high-2013.aspx

Graham, J., Nosek, B. A., & Haidt, J. (2013). The moral stereotypes of liberals and conservatives: Exaggeration of differences across the political spectrum. *PLoS One, 7*, e50092. doi: 10.1371/journal.pone.0050092

Greenwald, A. G., Poehlman, T. A., Uhlmann, E. L., & Banaji, M. R. (2009). Understanding and using the Implicit Association Test: III. Meta-analysis of predictive validity. *Journal of Personality and Social Psychology, 97*, 17–41.

Gross, N., & Simmons, S. (2007). The social and political views of American professors. Working paper presented at a Harvard University Symposium on Professors and Their Politics, October 6, 2007.

Haidt, J. (2001). The emotional dog and its rational tail: A social intuitionist approach to moral judgment. *Psychological Review, 108*, 814–834.

Haidt, J. (2012). *The Righteous Mind: Why Good People are Divided by Politics and Religion.* New York, NY: Pantheon.

Hegarty, P., & Pratto, F. (2001). The differences that norms make: Empiricism, social constructionism, and the interpretation of group differences. *Sex Roles, 50*, 445–453.

Herrnstein, R. J., & Murray, C. (1994). *The Bell Curve: The Reshaping of American Life by Differences in Intelligence.* New York: Free Press.

Huddy, L., & Feldman, S. (2009). On assessing the political effects of racial prejudice. *Annual Review of Political Science, 12*, 423–447.

Inbar, Y., & Lammers, J. (2012). Political diversity in social and personality psychology. *Perspectives on Psychological Science, 7*, 496–503.

Ioannidis, J. P. A. (2005). Why most published research findings are false. *PLoS Medicine, 2*, e124.

Ioannidis, J. P. A. (2012). Why science is not necessarily self-correcting. *Perspectives on Psychological Science, 7*, 645–654.

Jacks, J. Z., & Devine, P. G. (2000). Attitude importance, forewarning of message content, and resistance to persuasion. *Basic and Applied Social Psychology, 22*, 19–29.

Jones, E. E. (1985). Major developments in social psychology during the past five decades. In G. Lindzey & E. Aronson (Eds.), *The Handbook of Social Psychology* (Third edition, Vol. 1., pp. 47–107). New York: Random House.

Jones, E. E. (1986). Interpreting interpersonal behavior: The effects of expectancies. *Science, 234*, 41–46.

Jost, J. T. (2006). The end of the end of ideology. *American Psychologist, 61*, 651–670.

Jost, J. T., & Kruglanski, A. W. (2002). The estrangement of social constructionism and experimental social psychology: History of the rift and prospects for reconciliation. *Personality and Social Psychology Bulletin, 6*, 168–187.

Judd, C. M., & Park, B. (1993). Definition and assessment of accuracy in social stereotypes. *Psychological Review, 100*, 109–128.

Jussim, L. (2012a). *Social Perception and Social Reality: Why Accuracy Dominates Bias and Self-Fulfilling Prophecy.* New York: Oxford University Press.

Jussim, L. (2012b). Liberal privilege in academic psychology and the social sciences: Commentary on Inbar & Lammers (2012). *Perspectives on Psychological Science, 7*, 504–507.

Jussim, L., Cain, T., Crawford, J., Harber, K., & Cohen, F. (2009). The unbearable accuracy of stereotypes. In T. Nelson (Ed.), *Handbook of Prejudice, Stereotyping, and Discrimination* (pp. 199–227). Hillsdale, NJ: Erlbaum.

Jussim, L., Crawford, J., Anglin, S. M., & Stevens, S. T. (2014). The politics of social psychological science II: Distortions in the social psychology of liberalism and conservatism. To appear in J. Forgas, W. Crano, & K. Fiedler (Eds.), *The Sydney Symposium on Social Psychology and Politics.*

Jussim, L., Crawford, J., Anglin, S. M., & Stevens, S. T. (2015). Ideological bias in social psychological research. In J. Forgas, K. Fiedler, & W. Crano (Eds.), *Social Psychology and Politics*. New York: Psychology Press.

Jussim, L., Crawford, J. T., Anglin, S. M., Chambers, J., Stevens, S. T., & Cohen, F. (in press). Stereotype accuracy: One of the largest relationships in all of social psychology. In T. Nelson (ed.), *Handbook of Prejudice, Stereotyping, and Discrimination* (Second Edition). Hillsdale, NJ: Erlbaum.

Kinder, D. R., & Sears, D. O. (1981). Prejudice and politics: Symbolic racism versus racial threats to the good life. *Journal of Personality and Social Psychology 40*, 414–431.

Kinder, D. R., & Sears, D. O. (1985). Public opinion and political action. In G. Lindzey & E. Aronson (Eds.), *The Handbook of Social Psychology,* (Third Edition, Vol. II). New York: Random House.

Kinder, D. R., & Sanders, L. M. (1996). *Divided by Color: Racial Politics and Democratic Ideals*. Chicago: University of Chicago Press.

Klaczynski, P. A. (2000). Motivated scientific reasoning biases, epistemological beliefs, and theory polarization: A two-process approach to adolescent cognition. *Child Development, 71*, 1347–1366.

Klaczynski, P. A., & Gordon, D. H. (1996). Self-serving influences on adolescents' evaluations of belief-relevant evidence. *Journal of Experimental Child Psychology, 62*, 317–339.

Klein, D. B., & Stern, C. (2008a). Groupthink in academia: Majoritarian departmental politics and the professional pyramid. In R. Maranto, R. E. Redding, & F. M. Hess (Eds.), *The Politically Correct University* (pp. 79–98). Washington, DC: The AEI Press.

Klein, D. B., & Stern, C. (2008b). By the numbers: The ideological profile of professors. In R. Maranto, R. E. Redding, & F. M. Hess (Eds.), *The Politically Correct University* (pp. 79–98). Washington, DC: The AEI Press.

Koehler, J. J. (1993). The influence of prior beliefs on scientific judgments of evidence quality. *Organizational Behavior and Human Decision Processes, 56*, 28–55.

Krueger, J., & Rothbart, M. (1988). Use of categorical and individuating information in making inferences about personality. *Journal of Personality and Social Psychology, 55*, 187–195.

Kruglanski, A. W. (1989). The psychology of being "right": The problem of accuracy in social perception and cognition. *Psychological Bulletin, 106*, 395–409.

Kunda, Z. (1990). The case for motivated reasoning. *Psychological Bulletin, 108*, 480–498.

Kunda, Z., & Thagard, P. (1996). Forming impressions from stereotypes, traits, and behaviors: A parallel-constraint-satisfaction theory. *Psychological Review, 103*, 284–308.

Lee, Y. T., Jussim, L., & McCauley, C. R. (Eds.) (1995). *Stereotype Accuracy: Toward Appreciating Group Differences.* Washington, DC: American Psychological Association.

Lilienfeld, S. O. (2010). Can psychology become a science? *Personality and Individual Differences, 49*, 281–288.

Lindner, N. M., & Nosek, B. A. (2009). Alienable speech: Ideological variations in the application of free-speech principles. *Political Psychology, 30*(1), 67–92.

Locksley, A., Borgida, E., Brekke, N., & Hepburn, C. (1980). Sex stereotypes and social judgment. *Journal of Personality and Social Psychology, 39*, 821–831.

Locksley, A., Hepburn, C., & Ortiz, V. (1982). Social stereotypes and judgments of individuals: An instance of the base-rate fallacy. *Journal of Experimental Social Psychology, 18*, 23–42.

Lord, C. G., Ross, L., & Lepper, M. (1979). Biased assimilation and attitude polarization: The effects of prior theories on subsequently considered evidence. *Journal of Personality and Social Psychology, 37*, 2098–2109.

McClintock, C. G., Spaulding, C. B., & Turner, H. A. (1965). Political orientation of academically affiliated psychologists. *American Psychologist, 20*, 211–221.

McConahay, J. B. (1986). Modern racism, ambivalence, and the modern racism scale. In Dovidio, John F., & Gaertner, Samuel L. (Eds.), *Prejudice, Discrimination, and Racism* (pp. 91–125). San Diego, CA: Academic Press.

McConahay, J. B. & Hough, J. C. (1976). Symbolic racism. *Journal of Social Issues, 32*, 23–45.

MacCoun, R. J. (1998). Biases in the interpretation and use of research results. *Annual Review of Psychology, 49*, 259–287.

Mazella, R., & Feingold, A. (1994). The effects of physical attractiveness, race, socioeconomic status, and gender of defendants and victims on judgments of mock jurors: A meta-analysis. *Journal of Applied Social Psychology, 24*, 1315–1338.

Merton, R. K. (1948). The self-fulfilling prophecy. *Antioch Review, 8*, 193–210.

Miller, D. T., & Turnbull, W. (1986). Expectancies and interpersonal processes. *Annual Review of Psychology, 37*, 233–256.

Miller, D. T., & Morrison, K. R. (2009). Expressing deviant opinions: Believing you are in the majority helps. *Journal of Experimental Social Psychology, 45*, 740–747.

Miller, D. T., Taylor, B., & Buck, M. L. (1991). Gender gaps: Who needs to be explained? *Journal of Personality and Social Psychology, 61*, 5–12.

Munro, G. D., & Ditto, P. H. (1997). Biased assimilation, attitude polarization, and affect in reactions to stereotype-relevant scientific information. *Personality and Social Psychology Bulletin, 23*, 636–653.

Munro, G. D., Ditto, P. H., Lockhart, L. K., Fagerlin, A., Gready, M., & Peterson, E. (2002). Biased assimilation of sociopolitical arguments: Evaluating the 1996 U.S. presidential debate. *Basic and Applied Social Psychology, 24*, 15–26.

Nickerson, R. S. (1998). Confirmation bias: A ubiquitous phenomenon in many guises. *Review of General Psychology, 2*, 175–220.

Oakes, P. J., Haslam, S. A., & Turner, J. C. (1994). *Stereotyping and Social Reality.* Malden, MA: Blackwell Publishing.

Oswald, F. L., Mitchell, G., Blanton, H., Jaccard, J., & Tetlock, P. E. (2013). Predicting ethnic and racial discrimination: A meta-analysis of IAT criterion studies. *Journal of Personality and Social Psychology, 105*, 171–192.

Prentice, D. A. (2012). Liberal norms and their discontents. *Perspectives on Psychological Science, 7*, 516–518.

Prentice, D. A., & Miller, D. T. (1996). Pluralistic ignorance and the perpetuation of social norms by unwitting actors. In M. P. Zanna (Ed.), *Advances in Experimental Social Psychology* (Vol. 28, pp. 161–209). San Diego, CA: Academic Press.

Pronin, E. (2007). Perception and misperception of bias in human judgment. *Trends in Cognitive Sciences, 11*, 37–43.

Pronin, E. (2008). How we see ourselves and how we see others. *Science, 320*, 1177–1180.

Redding, R. E. (2001). Sociopolitical diversity in psychology. *American Psychologist, 56*, 205–215.

Richard, F. D., Bond, C. F., Jr., & Stokes-Zoota, J. J. (2003). One hundred years of social psychology quantitatively described. *Review of General Psychology, 7*, 331–363.

Roets, A., & van Hiel, A. (2011). Allport's prejudiced personality today: Need for closure as the motivated cognitive basis of prejudice. *Current Directions in Psychological Science, 20*, 349–354.

Rosenthal, R., & Jacobson, L. F. (1968). *Pygmalion in the Classroom: Teacher Expectations and Pupils' Intellectual Development*. New York: Holt, Rinehart, & Winston.

Ross, L., Lepper, M., & Ward, A. (2010). History of social psychology: Insights, challenges, and contributions to theory and application. In S. T. Fiske, D. T. Gilbert, & G. Lindzey (Eds.), *Handbook of Social Psychology* (pp. 3–50). New York: McGraw-Hill.

Rothman, S., & Lichter, S. R. (2008). The vanishing conservative—Is there a glass ceiling? In R. Maranto, R. E. Redding, & F. M. Hess (Eds.), *The Politically Correct University* (pp. 60–76). Washington, DC: The AEI Press.

Rudman, L. A., Moss-Racusin, C. A., Glick, P., & Phelan, J. E. (2012). Reactions to vanguards: Advances in backlash theory. In P. Devine & A. Plant (Eds.), *Advances in Experimental Social Psychology* (Vol. 45, pp. 167–227). San Diego, CA: Academic Press.

Ryan, C. S. (2002). Stereotype accuracy. *European Review of Social Psychology, 13*, 75–109.

Schachter, S. (1951). Deviation, rejection, and communication. *The Journal of Abnormal and Social Psychology, 46*, 190–207.

Sears, D. O., & Henry, P. J. (2003). The origins of symbolic racism. *Journal of Personality and Social Psychology, 85*, 259–275.

Sears, D. O., & Henry, P. J. (2005). Over thirty years later: A contemporary look at symbolic racism and its critics. *Advances in Experimental Social Psychology, 37*, 95–150.

Sears, D. O., Hensler, C. P., & Speer, L. K. (1979). Whites' opposition to "busing": Self-interest or symbolic politics? *American Political Science Review, 73*, 369–384.

Sears, D. O., Lau, R. R., Tyler, T. R., & Allen, H. M., Jr. (1980). Self-interest vs. symbolic politics in policy attitudes and presidential voting. *American Political Science Review, 74*, 670–684.

Sears, D. O., van Laar, C., Carrillo, M., & Kosterman, R. (1997). Is it really racism? The origins of white Americans' opposition to race-targeted policies. *Public Opinion Quarterly, 61*, 16–53.

Sibley, C. G., & Duckitt, J. (2008). Personality and prejudice: A meta-analysis and theoretical review. *Personality and Social Psychology Review, 12*, 248–279.

Simmons, J. P., Nelson, L. D., & Simonsohn, U. (2011). False-positive psychology: Undisclosed flexibility in data collection and analysis allows presenting anything as significant. *Psychological Science, 22*, 1359–1366.

Skitka, L. J. (2012). Multifaceted problems: Liberal bias and the need for scientific rigor in self-critical research. *Perspectives on Psychology Science, 7*, 508–511.

Skitka, L. J., Bauman, C. W., & Sargis, E. G. (2005). Moral conviction: Another contributor to attitude strength or something more? *Journal of Personality and Social Psychology, 88,* 895–917.

Sniderman, P. M., & Tetlock, P. E. (1986). Reflections on American racism. *Journal of Social Issues, 42,* 173–187.

Sniderman, P. M., Piazza, T., Tetlock, P. E., & Kendrick, A. (1991). The new racism. *American Journal of Political Science, 35,* 423–447.

Snyder, M., & Swann, W. B., Jr. (1978). Hypothesis-testing processes in social interaction. *Journal of Personality and Social Psychology, 36,* 1202–1212.

Snyder, M., Tanke, E. D., & Berscheid, E. (1977). Social perception and interpersonal behavior: On the self-fulfilling nature of social stereotypes. *Journal of Personality and Social Psychology, 35,* 656–666.

Stanovich, K. E., West, R. F., & Toplak, M. E. (2013). Myside bias, rational thinking, and intelligence. *Current Directions in Psychological Science, 22,* 259–264.

Swim, J., Borgida, E., Maruyama, G., & Myers, D. G. (1989). Joan McKay versus John McKay: Do gender stereotypes bias evaluations? *Psychological Bulletin, 105,* 409–429.

Tappan, M. B. (1997). Interpretive psychology: Stories, circles, and understanding lived experience. *Journal of Social Issues, 53,* 645–656.

Tetlock, P. E. (1994). Political psychology or politicized psychology: Is the road to scientific hell paved with good moral intentions? *Political Psychology,* 509–529.

Tetlock, P. E., & Mitchell, G. (1993). Liberal and conservative approaches to justice: Conflicting psychological portraits. In B. A. Mellers & J. Baron (Eds.), *Psychological Perspectives on Justice: Theory and Applications* (pp. 234–255). New York: Cambridge University Press.

Tetlock, P. E., Kristel, O. V., Elson, S. B., Green, M. C., & Lerner, J. S. (2000). The psychology of the unthinkable: Taboo trade-offs, forbidden base rates, and heretical counterfactuals. *Journal of Personality and Social Psychology, 78*(5), 853.

Trope, Y., & Bassok, M. (1982). Confirmatory and diagnosing strategies in social information gathering. *Journal of Personality and Social Psychology, 43,* 22–34.

Trope, Y., & Bassok, M. (1983). Information-gathering strategies in hypothesis-testing. *Journal of Experimental Social Psychology, 19,* 560–576.

Unger, R. (2011). SPSSI Leaders: Collective biography and the dilemma of value-laden action and value-neutral research. *Journal of Social Issues, 67,* 73–91.

Vul, E., Harris, C., Winkielman, P., & Pashler, H. (2009). Puzzlingly high correlations in fMRI studies of emotion, personality, and social cognition. *Perspectives on Psychological Science, 4,* 274–290.

Weinstein, R. S., Gregory, A., & Strambler, M. J. (2004). Intractable self-fulfilling prophecies: Fifty years after Brown v. Board of Education. *American Psychologist, 59,* 511–520.

Wetherell, G., Brandt, M. J., & Reyna, C. (2013). Discrimination across the ideological divide: The role of perceptions of value violations and abstract values in discrimination by liberals and conservatives. *Social Psychology and Personality Science, 4,* 658–667.

Zuwerink, J. R., & Devine, P. G. (1996). Attitude importance and resistance to persuasion: It's not just the thought that counts. *Journal of Personality and Social Psychology, 70,* 931–944.

9

POLITICAL DIVERSITY IN SOCIAL PSYCHOLOGY

Problems and Solutions

Yoel Inbar and Joris Lammers

Is there a political diversity problem in social psychology? We believe that the answer is "yes." In what follows, we will try to convince you (assuming that you are part of the politically liberal majority of social psychologists) that social[1] psychology has a remarkable lack of political diversity; that this is harmful to individual scientists, to the validity of our research, and to our credibility as a field; and that we can and should do better.

Social Psychology's Political Diversity Problem

If you are a social psychologist, you probably consider yourself politically liberal (i.e., left-wing). You probably voted for Barack Obama, not Mitt Romney, in the last Presidential election (assuming that you are American). You probably believe that your government should spend more on social welfare programs, intervene to promote the interests of women and racial minorities, and tax the wealthy more heavily. We claim that in this respect, you are much like the majority of your colleagues.

We are, of course, not the first to make this claim. For decades, critics have argued that social psychologists are overwhelmingly politically liberal (Duarte et al., in press; Haidt, 2011; Redding, 2001; Tetlock, 1994). A recent example is a provocative talk given by Jonathan Haidt at the 2011 annual meeting of the Society for Personality and Social Psychology (SPSP; APA Division 8). During his talk, Haidt asked any conservatives in the audience to raise their hands. In an audience of more than a thousand, only three hands went up. Haidt also described two other attempts he had made to locate conservatives in social psychology: a web search for "conservative social psychologist," and asking 30 social psychologists to name a conservative colleague. Combined, these latter two methods uncovered one additional conservative social psychologist. Yet although many observers shared the intuition that social psychologists were very likely to be political liberals, we recently noted that there had been no systematic empirical study of the politics of social psychologists. In 2012, we therefore conducted two surveys with the aim of collecting more definitive data on this question. These surveys are described more fully in Inbar and Lammers (2012).

Survey 1

In Survey 1, we asked social psychologists to place themselves on a left–right political spectrum separately for three areas—social issues, economic issues, and foreign policy—using the scale (1) *Very liberal*, (2) *Liberal*, (3) *Somewhat liberal*, (4) *Moderate*, (5) *Somewhat conservative*, (6) *Conservative*, or (7) *Very conservative*. (For non-U.S. respondents, we clarified that "liberal is intended to mean 'left/ progressive' and conservative is intended to mean 'right/traditionalist.'") Alternatively, we could have asked people about their attitudes on specific issues. This would have made the survey much longer, however, and we considered it more important to reach as wide an audience as possible. Also, including more specific items would have made it difficult to design a survey that would be meaningful for all participants, given that many respondents came from outside the United States, where different political issues are controversial. We therefore asked people to simply rate their politics, and relied on research showing that self-rated ideology predicts attitudes on specific issues quite well (see Jost, 2006).

We emailed an invitation to complete our survey to all 1,939 members of the (now-defunct) SPSP e-mail listserv, of whom 508 participated (mean age 36.8 years, 53.6% female). This response rate (26.2% of those contacted) is close to that observed in previous studies where participants were sent surveys to complete via postal mail (e.g., Klein & Stern, 2005). Comparing the demographics of our sample to those of the entire SPSP membership in 2011 (gender, age, and country of residence) showed that our sample matched the SPSP membership reasonably well (full details can be found in the Appendix of Inbar and Lammers, 2012).

Consistent with most people's intuitions, the social psychologists we surveyed were liberal on average for all three areas (social, economic, and foreign policy). However, we only found an overwhelming liberal majority on social issues: Here 90% described themselves as liberal (i.e. left of *Moderate*), and only a handful identified as moderate (6%) or conservative (4%, i.e., right of *Moderate*). But in the two other domains, we found more diversity of opinion. On economic issues, 63% described themselves as liberal, 19% as moderate, and 18% as conservative. Similarly, on foreign policy, 69% described themselves as liberal, 21% as moderate and 10% as conservative. Also consistent with what most people would expect, there was a fair amount of coherence between politics in the three areas, as seen in the correlations between ratings for each domain. Economic conservatism correlated with social conservatism at $r = .53$ and with foreign-policy conservatism at $r = .67$; social and foreign-policy conservatism correlated at $r = .53$.

To sum up, we found that social psychologists were quite liberal for all three areas we asked them about, with the strongest liberal skew for social issues. In a second study, we asked people how they described themselves "overall," and we also asked them how they would act toward conservative colleagues, in order to investigate some consequences of the liberal predominance in social psychology.

Survey 2

Six months after Survey 1, we again contacted all members of the SPSP listserv and asked them to complete another survey. Survey 2 was somewhat longer (requiring about 10 minutes to complete rather than three) and consequently the participation rate was lower. Two hundred and ninety-two people opened the survey (58% female, mean age 38 years), although only 266 answered every question (we used data from all participants that answered a given question). Again, the sample's demographics were very similar to those of the entire SPSP membership. Almost no one completed both surveys (i.e., Survey 2 used almost entirely new participants).

We asked participants about their politics with the same 7-point scale used in Survey 1, but now also added a fourth, "overall" item. Again, an overwhelming majority (93%) described themselves as liberal on social issues (3% described themselves as moderate and 4% as conservative). Also, as in Survey 1, there was a larger non-liberal minority on economics (70% liberal, 12% moderate, 18% conservative) and foreign policy (74% liberal, 16% moderate, 10% conservative). Finally, overall most respondents described themselves as liberal (85%) with small moderate (9%) and conservative (6%) minorities. It should be noted, though, that the liberal majority on the "overall" item was not quite as overwhelming as the liberal majority for social issues.

Summary

In two surveys we found that social psychologists are largely politically liberal. The liberal skew was most pronounced for social issues, but even where politics were more diverse, liberals were still a large majority. The topic with the smallest liberal majority—63%—was "economic issues" in Survey 1. In both surveys, respondents were overwhelmingly liberal on social issues (90% in Survey 1; 93% in Survey 2). This is broadly consistent with other research findings that academics—and especially in the social sciences and liberal arts— tend to be politically left-wing (Cardiff & Klein, 2005). However, social psychologists tend to be especially liberal even by the standards of academics. Cardiff and Klein, for example, found a 5:1 Democrat:Republican ratio among all professors at 11 California universities, whereas the liberal:conservative ratio in Survey 2 (on the "overall" item) was around 14:1. Of course, liberal/conservative do not map perfectly to Democrat/Republican, but it nonetheless seems safe to conclude that social psychologists are quite a bit more left-wing than academics in general.

Consequences of the Lack of Political Diversity in Social Psychology

If there were no negative consequences to the predominance of political liberals in social psychology, it would be questionable to call it a problem. We do not demand perfect ideological balance in every field—if it happens that plumbers and accountants are largely right-wing, and car mechanics and insurance brokers largely left-wing, this is not necessarily a problem. However, we believe that there are substantial costs that result directly from the ideological imbalance in social psychology. These are of three types: costs to (non-liberal) individual researchers, costs to the scientific integrity of our research, and costs to the credibility of social psychology.

Costs to Individuals

Part of our aim in Survey 2 was to explore the consequences of being in the ideological minority for individual researchers. We had two main questions: 1) Do non-liberals experience a hostile climate, or even outright discrimination, as a consequence of their political views; 2) Do at least some liberal researchers say they would discriminate against conservative colleagues?

Hostile Climate

As part of Survey 2, we asked participants how much they felt a hostile climate toward their political beliefs in their field, whether they were reluctant to express their political beliefs to their colleagues for fear of negative consequences, and whether they thought colleagues would actively discriminate against them on the basis of their political beliefs. Scores on a composite of these three questions ($\alpha = .93$) correlated significantly with political orientation, $r(289) = .50$, $p < .0001$: The more conservative respondents were, the more they had personally experienced a hostile climate. Treating ideology as a categorical variable, conservatives experienced a significantly more hostile climate ($M = 4.7$) than did liberals ($M = 1.9$; $t[17.61] = 5.97$, $p < .0001$) or moderates ($M = 3.7$; $t[30.43] = 2.06$, $p = .05$). Moderates also experienced a more hostile climate compared to liberals, $t(26.10) = 5.40$, $p < .0001$.

Political Diversity in Social Psychology   **201**

Discrimination against Conservative Social Psychologists

We also asked all our participants whether they thought *they themselves* would discriminate against conservative colleagues. The first two questions asked if, when doing peer review, a feeling that a grant application (Question 1) or paper (Question 2) took a "politically conservative perspective" would negatively influence their decision. The third question asked whether they would be reluctant to invite "a colleague who is generally known to be politically quite conservative" to participate in a symposium (on an unspecified topic). The fourth question asked whether, in choosing between two equally-qualified job candidates for one job opening, they would be inclined to vote for the more liberal candidate over the conservative (i.e., whether they would use politics as a "tie-breaker" in hiring). All responses were on 7-point scales (1 = *Not at all*, 4 = *Somewhat*, 7 = *Very much*). For each question, fewer than half of respondents said they were "Not at all" likely to discriminate (grant review, 24%; paper review, 28%; symposium invitation, 47%; hiring, 26%). A substantial proportion of respondents chose the scale midpoint of 4 (*Somewhat*) or above (grant review, 24%; paper review, 19%; symposium invitation, 14%; hiring, 38%). The more liberal respondents were, the more they said they were willing to discriminate against conservatives on each question: paper reviews, $r(279) = -.32$, $p < .0001$; grant reviews, $r(280) = -.34$, $p < .0001$; symposium invitations, $r(277) = -.20$, $p = .001$; hiring decisions, $r(279) = -.44$, $p < .0001$. These responses suggest that conservatives are not wrong to think that there is hostility toward them among at least some of their colleagues. Substantial percentages of social psychologists say that they would discriminate against conservatives, and the more liberal they are the more likely they are to say so.

Do the liberal majority realize this? In order to investigate this question, we asked all respondents (again, in Survey 2) whether they felt that there was a hostile climate toward the political beliefs of social/personality psychologists "who would rate themselves as 'somewhat conservative', 'conservative', or 'very conservative' overall." We used the same three hostile climate questions described above, but with "conservative social/personality psychologists" as the target. The more liberal respondents were, the less they believed that conservatives faced a hostile climate, $r(263) = -.28$, $p < .0001$ (for a composite of the three hostile climate questions). This correlation was driven entirely by more conservative respondents' greater *personal* experience of a hostile climate: controlling for personal experience, the relationship disappeared ($r = .01$), suggesting that the hostile climate reported by conservatives is invisible to those who do not experience it themselves. This is especially remarkable given that a significant proportion of liberal respondents had just told us that they themselves would discriminate against conservative colleagues!

Costs to Scientific Validity

In a recent paper, Duarte et al. (2014) outlined three threats to the validity of social psychological science resulting from a lack of political diversity: the embedding of left-wing values into psychological constructs and measures; a focus on topics and conclusions congenial to the left (and avoidance of those uncongenial to it); and the mischaracterization of conservatives.

Embedding of Left-Wing Values into Constructs and Measures

It is easier to notice the problematic embedding of political and moral values into research when one disagrees with them—values that one agrees with are often seen as self-evidently true. Conservatives are more able to spot the problematic inclusion of liberal values in research questions (and vice versa, of course), and their absence makes it more likely that social psychological research will incorporate left-wing values in a way that undermines scientific integrity. For example, consider the construct "denial of environmental realities" from Feygina, Jost, and Goldsmith (2010). This construct refers to the incorrect belief (according to the authors) that there are no limits to the human ability to control the natural environment. This "denial" is assessed using questions such as "Humans will eventually learn enough about how nature works to be able to control it," and "The Earth has plenty of natural resources if we just learn how to develop them." Clearly, these are factual questions whose answers are open to debate. It is a logical possibility that people will indeed some day learn enough about how nature works to be able to control it. People may learn to develop enough of Earth's natural resources to have plenty of them. The only way that one can call disagreement with these (debatable) factual statements denial is to *assume* that the answers favored by political liberals (i.e., that we will not learn enough about how nature works to control it, and that natural resources are dwindling dangerously) are correct by definition. Calling legitimate disagreement about factual questions "denial" is a symptom of embedding value judgments into allegedly value-free measures.

Topic Selection

Of the threats to research validity, the embedding of left-wing values is in some ways the easiest to notice—once one is aware of the possibility, liberal values in social psychology are quite noticeable. Selective attention to certain topics—and neglect of others—is often more difficult to spot, because it is just as much about what is *absent* as what is present. Here is one example: much research has documented the pernicious consequences of stereotypes—i.e., expectations about group members based on implicit or explicit impressions of the group as a whole. In some cases stereotypes can have extremely harmful consequences—and the study of these consequences is clearly worthwhile. However, a separate question

Political Diversity in Social Psychology **203**

is the extent to which stereotypes are accurate, that is, based on reality. This is an eminently testable question: As Duarte et al. (2014) argue, many stereotypes are "subjective estimates of population characteristics (e.g. the proportion of people who drop out of high school, are victims of crime, or endorse policies that support women at work)." However, there is very little research on the extent to which these subjective estimates are accurate or not (Jussim, 2012, is one notable exception). One reason is probably that the very idea that some stereotypes might be accurate makes many liberals very uncomfortable; the notion of testing such a question empirically seems almost morally offensive—in part because bigots may justify and defend their beliefs with such research. Such moral reactions may motivate the widespread practice in social psychology of simply asserting, without evidence, that most stereotypes are inaccurate (see Jussim, Crawford, Stevens, & Anglin, Chapter 8, this volume). It is worthwhile to take a moment to introspect about one's reactions to other topics that seem equally morally uncomfortable. Is it possible that there are a substantial number of questions that are not being studied because they evoke this sort of discomfort? It seems at least plausible to think that there are—and it also seems plausible that more diversity in political ideology would make certain topics less "untouchable."

Mischaracterizing Conservatives (and Liberals)

It is extremely difficult to portray one's political opponents fairly—the constant temptation is to see them as stupid, deluded, dishonest, or all three. And, in fact, social science research going back to Adorno et al. and *The Authoritarian Personality* (1950) has tended to cast those on the political right in an unflattering light. It is unlikely that a more ideologically balanced field would have painted quite such a negative portrait of conservatives, and indeed recent research has found much more symmetry in bias between liberals and conservatives than researchers had assumed. For example, a great deal of past research has focused on the bias and hypocrisy of conservatives (e.g., Altemeyer, 1996, 1998). However, more recent research has shown that under many circumstances liberals can be just as biased and hypocritical (Brandt et al., 2014; Crawford, 2012; Crawford, Modri, & Motyl, 2013). Past research simply focused on situations in which conservatives showed bias and neglected situations in which liberals did so. Likely, one reason that this was not noticed for so long is that it is comfortable for liberals to see conservatives (i.e., the "other side") as biased and hypocritical. In a more ideologically balanced field, conservative researchers would surely have disputed this characterization more quickly.

Costs to the Credibility of Social Psychology

In June 2014, the U.S. House of Representatives Committee on Science, Space, and Technology approved a bill that would cut National Science Foundation

(NSF) funding for the social sciences by roughly 40%, redirecting that money to the physical sciences (Jan, 2014). This bill is the latest in a long history of attempts by Republican legislators to reduce or eliminate funding for the social sciences. In 2013, an amendment introduced by Republican Senator Tom Coburn eliminated NSF funding for nearly all political science research (Barlow, 2013), and in 2006 Republican Senator Kay Bailey Hutchison proposed eliminating NSF social science funding entirely (Mervis, 2006).

Politicians on the right might want to de-fund social science research regardless of the ideological make-up of social science researchers. It may be that politicians do not like that social scientists discover uncomfortable truths, or, alternatively, that their research is seen as too trivial or theoretical to justify the investment of scarce funds. However, it is at least worth considering the possibility that part of the motivation results from conservatives seeing social scientists as political ideologues seeking to denigrate conservative beliefs. Elected officials have generally not said this explicitly, but others on the right have. For example, in a biting attack on the social psychology of liberal–conservative differences, Ferguson (2012) writes that "[S]ocial science has lately become a tool of Democrats who want to reassure themselves that Republicans are heartless and stupid." Ferguson argues that social scientists—and journalists who popularize their work—are using the authority of science in a dishonest attempt to win political and moral arguments: "In embracing Science, the psychopundit believes he is moving from the spongy world of mere opinion to the firmer footing of fact. It is pleasing to him to discover that the two— his opinion and scientific fact—are identical." The merits of this claim aside, if many conservatives really do regard social scientists as partisan flacks rather than as disinterested truth-seekers, it should not be surprising that conservative lawmakers repeatedly attempt to reduce or eliminate government funding for the social sciences.

A turnabout test (Tetlock, 1994) may be helpful here. If you are politically liberal, imagine the U.S. government funding a nearly exclusively conservative group of researchers who use government funds to conduct and publish "research" that is, in your eyes, nothing more than right-wing propaganda dressed up in pseudo-scientific clothing. This specious research is amplified and promoted by conservative pundits, journalists, and bloggers who use it to buttress their claims that liberals are naïve, foolish, and vacillating; whereas conservatives are clear-headed, sensible, and resolute. Finally, imagine that much of the research in question assumes that conservative positions on controversial political issues are factually correct by definition, and attempts to explain why liberals are unwilling or unable to acknowledge the obvious truth of these facts. Does it not seem likely that your reaction would be scorn, derision, and a firm conviction that these shameless hacks should not get another dime of the taxpayers' money?

Of course, many social psychologists do research that has nothing or very little to do with their politics. And even when it does, many are scrupulous to separate

Political Diversity in Social Psychology **205**

their personal beliefs from their professional activities. However, as we have described above, the predominance of liberals in social psychology has led to predictable biases in social psychological research.

What Can Be Done?

Having (hopefully) convinced the reader that there is remarkably little political diversity in social psychology, and that this is a problem for a number of reasons, a natural question is what we can do to make things better. We believe that the answer depends partly on why there is such a preponderance of liberals in social psychology.

One possibility is self-selection—it may be that liberals, due to some combination of interests and ability, are simply more attracted to academia, to the social sciences, or to social psychology. As Gilbert (2011) put it, liberals may be "more interested in new ideas, more willing to work for peanuts, or just more intelligent." There is indeed research showing that self-selection partly explains liberals' over-representation in academia (Gross & Fosse, 2012)—although the idea that liberals are more intelligent seems to be a myth (Kemmelmeier, 2008). Even if self-selection *entirely* explained the liberal over-representation in social psychology, there is a version of it that is not so benign. If we are communicating to non-liberal undergraduate students that they are not welcome in social psychology—perhaps by telling them about research that portrays conservatives as stupid and heartless, or by communicating the field's liberal norms in other, more subtle ways—they may decide that pursuing a career as a social psychologist would be an unwise choice or at least may make them unhappy. This would still be self-selection (in the sense that conservative students are deciding that another career would be a better fit for them) but it would be intellectually dishonest to say that non-liberals are simply "opting out" if they are doing so due to the impression that they would be unwelcome in social psychology.

At any rate, self-selection clearly is not the whole story. In our survey, conservatives (and moderates) told us that they felt inhibited from discussing their politics openly for fear of negative consequences. And a substantial minority of liberal respondents said that they would indeed discriminate against conservatives. This suggests that although some conservatives may opt out of psychology, others are being pushed out the door. This is also reflected in the comments that some moderate and conservative social psychologists wrote as part of our surveys (both surveys included free-text fields where respondents could enter comments if they wished). One respondent described how a colleague was denied tenure because of his political beliefs. Another wrote that if the department "could figure out who was a conservative they would be sure not to hire them." Various people described how colleagues silenced them during political discussions simply because they had voted Republican. One respondent wrote "it causes me great stress to not be able to have an environment where open dialogue is acceptable.

Although most colleagues talk about tolerance, and some are, there are a few vociferous voices that make for a closed environment."

Most of the people reading this would (hopefully) not discriminate so blatantly against people with whom they disagree politically. However, there are also a number of more subtle norms and behaviors that communicate to non-liberals that they are not welcome in social psychology. Luckily, these can be changed. If you are part of the liberal majority in social psychology, here are four things that you can easily do:

Avoid Signaling That Non-Liberals Are Not Welcome in Social Psychology

As our surveys show, although liberals are the majority in social psychology, there is also more political diversity than people think. For example, over 30% of Survey 1's respondents described themselves as moderate or conservative on economic and foreign-policy issues. Nonetheless, in papers, conference presentations, and casual conversations, many social psychologists assume that their audience consists entirely of political liberals. Professional talks and conference presentations sometimes contain jokes at the expense of Republican politicians (and Republicans only), and speakers sometimes openly disparage conservative beliefs. Obviously, this is alienating to colleagues who do not share your politics. As Bloom (2011) put it, "Nobody wants to be part of a community where their identity is the target of ridicule and malice." This may sound obvious—and it *is* obvious—but as blatantly exclusionary (and unprofessional) as this behavior is, it still happens with some regularity (although our subjective impression is that it happens less than it used to as recently as a few years ago). When you give a talk, write a paper, or even just chat with colleagues, keep in mind that the politics of your audience might be more diverse than you think, and avoid sending signals that only one political point of view is correct or acceptable. This obviously does not mean not expressing your political beliefs, but it does mean treating others' political beliefs with respect, not derision.

Be Especially Careful Around Students

There is an obvious power imbalance between students and faculty. Faculty must be careful not to take advantage of this imbalance to push their political beliefs on their students, even if only unintentionally. In fact, many of the respondents to our survey who described behavior that they thought created a hostile climate were students or post-docs who encountered bias from more senior colleagues. For example, one post-doc who took our survey described being insulted publicly by a senior colleague for having voted Republican. Duarte (2014) described being pressed by a faculty member to clarify his views on Jimmy Carter during a graduate school admissions interview (the admissions committee had discovered a blog post of Duarte's where he criticized Carter's views on the Middle East). Most of us realize that this is not acceptable, but we may not be as aware of the more subtle ways in which we are communicating what the "correct" political beliefs are. When talking to students, faculty should be mindful that students' political beliefs may differ from their own, and should work to avoid creating an environment where students feel excluded or intimidated because of their politics.

Take Conservative Beliefs Seriously

Simply dismissing conservative beliefs as the product of ignorance, religious fanaticism, or stupidity is itself lazy and ignorant. Of course, liberal social psychologists need not be less critical of political ideas they disagree with, but they should criticize respectfully and remain open to the possibility that they are wrong—or at least not entirely right. People develop political beliefs at least partially in response to the personal challenges that they face in their life. Different challenges can lead to different beliefs. People can reach a deeper understanding of politics by engaging in a meaningful dialogue and discussion with their opponents, rather than by surrounding themselves exclusively with like-minded people. An easy way to start doing this would be to use social media. For example, a number of thoughtful moderate and conservative writers are active Twitter users. If, like many of us, you have not spent much time engaging seriously with the arguments of your ideological opposites, following some conservatives on Twitter can be very educational. Certainly, it will disabuse you of the notion that all conservatives are stupid, ignorant, or religious fanatics.

Practice Tolerance

You may be thinking that this is easier said than done. But we often need to interact with people with whom we disagree politically (most of us can probably think of at least one family member who meets this description). Generally, we manage to do this: if we disagree, we can disagree respectfully; if we find we are unable to disagree respectfully, we can avoid certain hot-button topics. Most working people manage to do this in their professional lives, as most professions are nowhere near as ideologically homogenous as psychology is. If so many people manage to tolerate those who disagree with them—if we ourselves are able to do so in many areas of life—is it too much to ask that we do it in our professional lives as well?

Are Conservatives Unscientific?

One common response to our work pointing out the lack of ideological diversity in social psychology has been that the exclusion of conservatives is justified, because conservative ideology is fundamentally incompatible with science. It is indisputable that some socially conservative beliefs, especially those that are religiously based, conflict with what most mainstream scientists believe to be true. Contrary to what some (although by no means all) religious fundamentalists believe, nearly all geologists agree that Earth is more than 10,000 years old, and nearly all biologists agree that humans and modern apes evolved from a common non-human ancestor. However, as we have pointed out elsewhere (Inbar & Lammers, 2012), there are also many conservative beliefs that are not—indeed, that cannot be—true or false. Take, for example, the belief that abortion is morally wrong, or that economic inequality is not in and of itself objectionable. These are ethical/moral beliefs, not factual ones. They cannot be factually mistaken.

The pertinent question, then, is whether conservative would-be social psychologists are committed to factually mistaken beliefs that make them unqualified to be scientists. Intuitively, this seems implausible: are there really a great many young-Earth creationists or evolution deniers lining up to be social psychologists? Our surveys back up this intuition. Conservative social psychologists are conservatives largely in the areas of fiscal and foreign policy, with only a small number of social conservatives. Of course, even among social conservatives, there is a huge amount of variation in what individuals believe, and many socially conservative beliefs are in no way unscientific. More generally, the notion that all conservatives are unscientific religious fundamentalists seems to us to be an example of the hostile environment that our more conservative respondents describe. Consistent with what research on intergroup social perception would lead us to expect (e.g., Park & Rothbart, 1982), conservatives are seen as a stereotyped and homogenous outgroup, instead of as individuals holding a varied and nuanced set of political and moral beliefs.

Furthermore, in Survey 2 (described above) even those who described themselves as politically *moderate* encountered a more hostile climate compared to liberals. In two further analyses, we checked whether more conservative economic and foreign-policy ideology predicted experiencing a more hostile climate, *even controlling for social conservatism*. In both cases the relationships were positive and highly significant ($p < .001$). Thus, it is not just social conservatives who encounter a hostile climate in social–personality psychology (and in fact, very few of our respondents described themselves as socially conservative at all). Political moderates and those who hold more conservative economic and foreign-policy views encounter a hostile climate as well.

Conclusion: Benefits of Greater Ideological Inclusivity

We believe that greater inclusivity will yield substantial long-term benefits for social psychology. First and most important, we believe ideological diversity will lead to better science: it will highlight new research questions that we are

Political Diversity in Social Psychology **209**

currently overlooking and make it less difficult to publish work that contradicts values important to political liberals (e.g., McCauley, Jussim, & Lee, 1995). Second, our scientific credibility depends on not being seen as ideological warriors by the public (see Tetlock, 1994). It is worrisome that the reaction to our research among many conservatives was "well, obviously." If we are seen as ideologues instead of scientists, we will only convince those who already agree with us.

Finally, greater ideological inclusivity may also have personal benefits. Political discussion can be informative and educational, but only if it is more than an echo chamber of the like-minded—research shows that this is a recipe for ever-greater extremism and polarization (Myers & Lamm, 1975). As scientists, we also know that intellectual openness, freedom to dissent, and vigorous but respectful debate are our best weapons against complacency and error. Let us make use of them now.

Note

1 We here use "social psychology" broadly to include personality psychology, cross-cultural psychology, etc.

References

Adorno, T., Frenkel-Brunswik, E., Levinson, D. J., & Sanford, R.N. (1950). *The Authoritarian Personality*. New York: Harper.

Altemeyer, B. (1996). *The Authoritarian Specter*. Cambridge, MA: Harvard University Press.

Altemeyer, B. (1998). The other "authoritarian personality." *Advances in Experimental Social Psychology, 30*, 47–92.

Barlow, R. (2013, April 9). Congress cuts political science research grants. *BU Today*. Retrieved from www.bu.edu/today

Bloom, P. (2011). *Comment on "The Bright Future of Post-Partisan Social Psychology."* Retrieved from http://www.edge.org/3rd_culture/haidt11/haidt11_index.html#bloom

Brandt, M. J., Reyna, C., Chambers, J. R., Crawford, J. T., & Wetherell, G. (2014). The ideological-conflict hypothesis: Intolerance among both liberals and conservatives. *Current Directions in Psychological Science, 23*, 27–34.

Cardiff, C., & Klein, D. (2005). Faculty partisan affiliations in all disciplines: A voter-registration study. *Critical Review, 17*, 237–255. doi: 10.1016/S0065-2601(01)80004-6

Crawford, J. T. (2012). The ideologically objectionable premise model: Predicting biased political judgments on the left and right. *Journal of Experimental Social Psychology, 48*, 138–151.

Crawford, J. T., Modri, S. A., & Motyl, M. (2013). Bleeding-heart liberals and hard-hearted conservatives: Subtle political dehumanization through differential attributions of human nature and human uniqueness traits. *Journal of Social and Political Psychology, 1*, 86–104.

Duarte, J. L. (2014). I was denied admission to a social psychology program because of my political views [web log post]. Retrieved from http://www.joseduarte.com/

blog/i-was-denied-admission-to-a-social-psychology-program-because-of-my-political-views.

Duarte, J. L., Crawford, J. T., Stern, C., Haidt, J., Jussim, L., & Tetlock, P. E. (2014). Political diversity will improve social psychological science. *Behavioral and Brain Sciences, 18*, 1–54.

Ferguson, A. (May 21, 2012). The new phrenology. *The Weekly Standard, 17*, (34). Retrieved from http://www.weeklystandard.com/articles/new-phrenology_644420.html.

Feygina, I., Jost, J. T., & Goldsmith, R. E. (2010). System justification, the denial of global warming, and the possibility of "system-sanctioned change." *Personality and Social Psychology Bulletin, 36*, 326–338.

Gilbert, D. (2011). *Comment on "The Bright Future of Post-Partisan Social Psychology."* Retrieved from http://www.edge.org/3rd_culture/haidt11/haidt11_index.html#gilbert

Gross, N., & Fosse, E. (2012). Why are professors liberal? *Theory and Society, 41*, 127–168.

Haidt, J. (2011, January). *The Bright Future of Post-Partisan Social Psychology.* Talk given at the annual meeting of the Society for Personality and Social Psychology, San Antonio, TX. Retrieved from http://people.virginia.edu/~jdh6n/postpartisan.html

Inbar, Y., & Lammers, J. (2012). Political diversity in social and personality psychology. *Perspectives on Psychological Science, 7*, 496–503.

Jan, T. (2014, April 14). GOP pushes funding cuts for social science work. *The Boston Globe.* Retrieved from http://www.bostonglobe.com.

Jost, J. (2006). The end of the end of ideology. *American Psychologist, 61*, 651–670. doi: 10.1037/0003-066X.61.7.651

Jussim, L. (2012). *Social Perception and Social Reality: Why Accuracy Dominates Bias and Self-Fulfilling Prophecy.* New York: Oxford University Press.

Kemmelmeier, M. (2008). Is there a relationship between political orientation and cognitive ability? A test of three hypotheses in two studies. *Personality and Individual Differences, 45*, 767–772.

Klein, D. B., & Stern, C. (2005). Professors and their politics: The policy views of social scientists. *Critical Review, 17*, 257–303. doi: 10.1080/08913810508443640

McCauley, C. R., Jussim, L., & Lee, Y. T. (1995). Stereotype accuracy: Toward appreciating group differences. Concluding chapter in Lee, Y.T., Jussim, L., McCauley, C. R. (eds.), *Stereotype Accuracy: Toward Appreciating Group Differences* (pp. 293–312). Washington, DC: American Psychological Association.

Mervis, J. (2006). Senate panel chair asks why NSF funds social sciences. *Science, 312*, 829.

Myers, D. G., & Lamm, H. (1975). The polarizing effect of group discussion. *American Scientist, 63*, 297–303.

Park, B., & Rothbart, M. (1982). Perception of out-group homogeneity and levels of social categorization: Memory for the subordinate attributes of in-group and out-group members. *Journal of Personality and Social Psychology, 42*, 1051–1068.

Redding, R. (2001). Sociopolitical diversity in psychology: The case for pluralism. *American Psychologist, 56*, 205–215. doi: 10.1037/0003-066X.56.3.205

Tetlock, P. (1994). Political psychology or politicized psychology: Is the road to scientific hell paved with good moral intentions? *Political Psychology, 15*, 509–529.

INDEX

Abramowitz, A. I. 42–4
Abrams, S. J. 44
abstract thought 143–56
accuracy, ideological bias 177–8
African-Americans: abstract thought
145–9; enclavement 9, 12–13;
moral coherence 108–9,
see also racism
agricultural imports 50–2, 54
AIDS 88–9
Albright, L. 182
allocation tasks, moral 70–1
altruism 123–42
ambient belonging cues 10–13
American National Election Study
(ANES) 87–8
Anderson, C. A. 82
anecdotal evidence 107–8
anecdotal narrative, ideological bias
175–6
ANES *see* American National Election
Study
animals 69–70
anthropomorphism 69–70
anti-death penalty essays 115–16
approach motivation 129
Ashmore, R. D. 179
assimilation 112–13
attitude attribution paradigm 86
audit studies on ideological bias
174–5
authority 66–7, 128–31, 134–5

avoidance motivation 127–31

"bad apples" 90
Badger, E. 11–12
Bafumi, J. 13–14
balanced morality 135–6
Balliet, D. 134
Baril, G. 150
Baron, R. M. 182, 183
Barry, D. 15
baseline conditions of empathy 68
behavioral polarization 50
belonging cues 10–13
betrayal 66–7
bias: altruism/self-interest 129–30;
intergroup despising 20–1; moral
coherence 112–13, 117–18; negativity
bias 129–30; social psychology 166–8,
172–89, 206
Bicchieri, C. 133
bivariate correlation of left–right politics
45–6
blacks *see* African-Americans
"bleeding heart liberals" 62
blind spots 174, 180–5
Bloom, P. 206
Borgida, E. 182
Brekke, N. 182
Bush, G. W. 107

capital area 50–2, 53
care/harm 66–7

212 Index

Carnes, N. C. 124–7, 133–6
Caucasians: enclavement 9; moral coherence 108–11
Ceci, S. J. 175
Chambers, J. R. 170–1
cheating 66–7
Cheney, D. 102–6
Chip–Tyrone studies 108–9
Christian religion 63
Church of Latter Day Saints 9
classic bias 181–4
cognitive enhancement 150
cognitive load study 88–9
cognitive misers 80
cognitive-motivational psychology 64
coherence-based models 102–22; culture war 116–18; effectiveness 112–16; factualization 104–6; problem with principle 106–12; top down politics 103–4, 107–8, 114–15
collaboration 132–4, 180
collateral damage 110
collective morality 126–31
College Bowl Study 84–6
colorblind ideology 12–13
compassion 68–9
competitors 134
concrete thought 143–56
confirmation bias 172–3, 181–4
conflict: moral coherence 102–22; social psychology 170–1, 174
consequentialist morality 105–6
conservatives: altruism/self-interest 123–42; construal level effects 143–61; discrimination 201; duality with liberals 78–101; embedded symbolic racism 187; empathy 61–77; geographical division 7–37; intergroup distortions 165–96; Mars 78–101; mischaracterizing 203; seriousness of belief 207; tolerance 207; unscientific 207–8
Constitution 106–7
construal level effects 143–61
cooperation 133–5
coordination 132–3
correction attributional patterns 87–8
cougar study 84, 91–2
credibility of social psychology 203–5
cross-group contact 27–8
cues: ambient belonging 10–13; ideology 13–16
culture wars 14, 116–18

Darley, J. M. 181–5
Dean, T. 136
death penalty 115–16
degradation 66–7
Del Boca, F. K. 179
democracy 38–58
deontological morality 105–6
despising 20–3, 25–8
Devine, P. O. 81–2
discrimination 201, see also prejudice
dispositional hypothesis 79–80
distrust 133–4
Ditto, P. H. 114–16
diversity 197–210
divisive politics see ideological divides
double standards 177–80
Duarte, J. L. 202–3, 206–7

economic success 136
Elson, S. B. 179
embedded values 185–9, 202
emotional preference 106
empathy 61–77; cognitive-motivational psychology 64; empirical research 67–71; enclavement 23; future directions 71–3; ideology 62–4; implications 71–3; moral foundations 66–7; motivational orientations 65–6; personality traits 64–5; summary 67
enclavement: bias 20–1; comparing and contrasting theories 23–4; cross-group contact 27–8; extremist attitudes 22–3; extremitization 21–2; future directions 24–8; homophily 9; implicit misunderstanding 23; intergroup despising 20–3; intra/interpersonal and intragroup thriving 19–20; intuitions 16–19; moral values 10–16; naïve realism 22
environmental issues 50–2
equality 145–6
essay attribution studies 84, 86–7
ethnic homophily 9
EU application 50–2, 54
evidence 107–8
exaggeration 174
expanse of empathy see empathy
expectancy-confirmation see confirmation bias
explanation process model 82
extremist attitudes 22–3, 186–9
extremitization of enclavement 21–2

factualization, moral coherence 104–6
faculty studies in social psychology 168, 206–7
failed replications of classic bias and self-fulfilling prophecy 181–4
fairness 66–7, 126–31
family-oriented conditions of empathy 68
Feldman, S. 187
Fiorina, M. P. 44
First Amendment 106–7
Fiske, S. T. 131
"fog of war" 90
forbidden base-rates 179
friendships, enclavement 27–8
friends-oriented conditions of empathy 68
functional morality 131–5

GDP as measure of economic success 136
gender equality 50–2, 53
General Social Survey (GSS) 62–3
geographical division 7–37
Gilbert, D. 205
Glaser, J. 64
Goffman, E. 12–13
Gore, A. 107
Gosling, S. D. 12
Graham, J. 46
grant schemes 175–6
Green, M. C. 179
Green Movement see Left–Green Movement
Gross, P. H. 181–5
group morality 126–31
GSS see General Social Survey
gun control 113

Haditha study 84, 90–1
Haidt, J. 46
Halliburton workers 90–1
harm 66–7, 126–7
Harris, V. A. 86–7
Hawkins, C. B. 13–14
helping/fairness 126–31
Hepburn, C. 182
Herrnstein, R. J. 85
high-prejudiced people 81–2
homogeneity, social psychology 169–72
homophily 9
hostility: lack of diversity 200; symbolic racism 187
Huddy, L. 187

Icelandic National Election Study (ICENES) 38–58
ICENES see Icelandic National Election Study
ICH see ideological conflict hypothesis
IDAQ see Individual Differences in Anthropomorphism Questionnaire
ideal moral allocation 70–1
Identification with All Humanity Scale (IWAHS) 69
identity: construal level effects 152–6; enclavement 12–13, 26
ideo-attribution effect 79–84, 88–92
ideological conflict hypothesis (ICH) 170–1
ideological divides 5–58; altruism/self-interest 123–42; duality 78–101; geographical division 7–37; left-right landscape over time 38–58; moral coherence and conflict 102–22; psychological mechanisms 59–161; silos 143–61; social psychology 163–210; synergies 143–61
Ideological Enclavement Theory 8–37
ideological script hypothesis 80–1
ideology: ambient cues 13–16; migration hypothesis 17–19, see also ideological divides
implicit misunderstanding 23
imports 50–2, 54
Inbar, Y. 166–7, 171–2
Independence Party 39, 44–5, 47–50
Individual Differences in Anthropomorphism Questionnaire (IDAQ) 70
individualists 134
industriousness 126–31
ingroup/loyalty 128–31
inherited intelligence 85–6
intergroup despising 20–3
intergroup distortions in social psychology 165–96
internal review boards, ideological bias 175
interpersonal morality 126–7
Interpersonal Reactivity Index (IRI) 68
intra/interpersonal and intragroup thriving 19–20
intuitions: migration and enclavement 16–19; moral coherence 107–8
Iraq War 80, 109–11
IRI see Interpersonal Reactivity Index
Ishii, K. 133–4

issue position polarization 50
IWAHS *see* Identification with All Humanity Scale
Iyer, R. 15–16

James, W. 131
Janoff-Bulman, R. 124–7, 129, 133–6
Jews 9
Joireman, J. 134
Jones, E. E. 86–7
Jost, J. T. 64
justice, abstract thought 145–6

Keltmer, D. 46
Kluegel, J. R. 81
Kristel, O. V. 179
Kruglanski, A. W. 64
Krull, D. S. 82
Kurzban, R. 133–4

Lammers, J. 166–7, 171–2
leadership 134–5
"leaning" views 13–14
left-right landscape over time 38–58
left-wing embedded values 202
Left–Green Movement 39, 44–5, 47–50
Lepper, M. R. 12–13
Lerner, J. S. 179
lesbian, gay, bisexual and transgender (LGBT) individuals 7–8, *see also* non-normative groups
liberals: altruism/self-interest 123–42; "bleeding heart" 62; construal level effects 143–61; discrimination 201; duality with conservatives 78–101; embedded symbolic racism 186–7; empathy 61–77; geographical division 7–37; intergroup distortions 165–96; mischaracterizing 203; Venus 78–101
Lickel, B. 135–6
Liu, B. S. 114–16
Locksley, A. 182, 183
loose societies 132–3
Lord, C. G. 12–13
love of humanity scale 68–9
low-prejudiced people 81–2
loyalty 66–7, 128–31

majoritarian political and theoretical norms 173–4
Malloy, T. E. 182
Marines 90–1
Mars, conservatives 78–101

media silos 112–13
migration: enclavement 16–19; ideology 17–19; mobility 16–17
military 109–11, *see also* war
Miller, D. T. 179
mind-blindness, enclavement 23
minorities, ambient belonging cues 12–13
mischaracterizing 203
misunderstanding 23
MMM *see* Model of Moral Motives
mobility, migration 16–17
Model of Moral Motives (MMM) 125–36
Moral Foundations Theory (MFT) 66–7, 128–31
morality: abstraction 149–52; allocation tasks 70–1; altruism/self-interest 123–42; ambient belonging cues 12–13; balanced morality 135–6; coherence 102–22; concern for nonhumans 69–70; duo-regulatory system 124–7; enclavement 10–16, 23; functional morality 131–5
Morgan, G. S. 90–1
motivated reasoning hypothesis 22–3, 81–4, 172–3
"motivated skepticism" 117–18
motivational morality 127–31
motivational orientations 65–6
Motyl, M. 15–16
Muldoon, R. 133
Mullen, E. 90
multi-party democracy 38–58
Murray, C. 85
Muslims 9
mutualistic collaboration 132–3
Myrdal, G. 145–6, 149, 153
myside bias 172–3

naïve realism, enclavement 22
National Election Study (NES) 13–14
nationality 153–5
National Public Radio (NPR) 15
National Science Foundation (NSF) 203–4
nature, anthropomorphism 69–70
negativity bias 129–30
NES *see* National Election Study
Noël, A. 40–2
non-attributions 87–8
nonhumans, moral concern 69–70
non-normative groups 143–56
norms, majoritarian 173–4
Nosek, B. A. 13–14, 46

not harming 126–31
NPR *see* National Public Radio
NSF *see* National Science Foundation

Obama, B. 62
Oswald, F. L. 188–9
overrepresentation of liberal social psychology 166–8

Parks, C. 134
partisan behavior 13–14, 153–5
People's Alliance 39, 44–5, 47–50
personal attributional patterns 84, 87–8, 90–2
personal inference 90
personality traits 64–5
personal morality 70–1, 126–7
Peters, D. 175
Plotkin, J. 175
power 134–5, 206–7
powerful effects, overlooking of 180–1
prejudice 81–2, 145–9, 169–72, 186–9, 206
Prentice, D. A. 173–4
presidency 107
problem with principle 106–12
pro-EU Democratic Alliance 39, 44–5, 47–50
Progressive Party 39, 44–5, 47–50
proscriptive/prescriptive morality 126–31
prosocials 134
public opinion and volatility 13–14
purity/degradation 66–7
purity/sanctity 128–31

questionable interpretive practices (QIPs) 176, 177
questionnaires, IDAQ 70

racial homophily 9
racism 186–9
realism 22
reasoning: enclavement 22–3; motivated reasoning 22–3, 81–4, 172–3; social psychology 172–6
reciprocity 126–31
religion 9, 12–13, 63
repeated prompt study 84, 87–8
respect 128–31
reverse-correction attributional patterns 87–8
right wing politics *see* left-right landscape over time

Robber's Cave National Park, Oklahoma 20–1
Robinson, R. 46
Rock, M. 129
Roscoe Village neighborhood of Chicago 91–2
Ross, L. 12–13, 46
rural areas 50–2, 53

safe spaces 12–13
salience, identity 152–6
sanctity 128–31
Saunders, K. L. 42–4
Schwartz Values Inventory 68–9
SDA *see* Social Democratic Alliance
SDO *see* social dominance orientation
second World War 80
selective migration 16–19
self-fulfilling prophecy 177–8, 181–4
self-interest 123–42
self-placement 40–54
self-restraint 126–31
sexual orientation 7–8, 88–9, 143–4
Shapiro, R. Y. 13–14
shared humanity and values, enclavement 25–6
Shi'a Muslims 9
silos 112–13, 143–61
situational attributional patterns 84, 87–8, 90–2
situational inference 90
skepticism 112–13, 117–18
Skitka, L. J. 87, 90
Smith, E. R. 81
Snyder, M. 184
social cooperation 133–4
social coordination 132–3
Social Democratic Alliance (SDA) 39, 44–5, 47–50
Social Democratic Party 39, 44–5, 47–50
social dominance orientation (SDO) 63
social order and justice 126–35
Social Value Orientation (SVO) 134
Society for Personality and Social Psychology (SPSP) 166–7, 197–9
stereotypes 178–9, 181–2
student diversity 206–7
subversion 66–7
suicide rates 17–18
Sulloway, F. J. 64
Sunni Muslims 9
superordinate identities 26
Supreme Court 106–7

216 Index

Swann, W. B. 184
symbolic racism 186–9
synergies 143–61

taxes 50–2
technology, anthropomorphism 69–70
television shows 107–8
Tetlock, P. E. 179, 180, 204
The Bell Curve (Herrnstein and Murray) 85
Thérien, J. P. 40–2
threats, enclavement 26
thriving, enclavement 19–20, 25–8
tight societies 132–3
tolerance 207
top down moral coherence 103–4, 107–8, 114–15
true attitude 86–7
trust 133–4
turnabout tests 180, 204
Turnbull, W. 179

Uhlmann, E. L. 109–11

Van Lange, P. A. 134
Venus, liberals 78–101
Vietnam War 80

war 80, 90–1, 109–11, *see also* culture wars
Ward, A. 46
Weiner, B. 82
Western European multi-party democracy 38–58
Wetherell, G. 170
White Americans, abstract thought 145–6
whites *see* Caucasians
Women's Alliance 47–50
World Value Survey (WVS) 40–2
World War II 80
Wright, J. C. 150

Xiao, E. 133

YourMorals.org 114

Zaller, J. R. 80